India: A National Culture?

India: A National Culture?

Edited by

Geeti Sen

Sage Publications
New Delhi ◆ Thousand Oaks ◆ London

India International Centre
New Delhi

First published in 2003 by

India International Centre
New Delhi

and

Sage Publications India Pvt Ltd
B-42, Panchsheel Enclave
New Delhi 110 017

Sage Publications Inc
2455 Teller Road
Thousand Oaks, California 91320

Sage Publications Ltd
6 Bonhill Street
London EC2A 4PU

Published by K.N. Venugopal for India International Centre and by Tejeshwar Singh for Sage Publications India Pvt Ltd, phototypeset by Print Services, B-17, Lajpat Nagar 2, New Delhi, and printed at Chaman Enterprises, New Delhi.

Library of Congress Cataloging-in-Publication Data available.

India-HB ISBN available.

US-HB ISBN: 0–7619–9831–4

CONTENTS

National Culture and Cultural Nationalism

The last two decades of the 20th century are witness to a spectacular return of national consciousness, and not only in India! We thought it a good idea to focus on one essential ingredient—an aspect indispensable to the making of *Indian* nationalism, and one that has now resurfaced in everyday experience. Surprisingly, this idea was greeted with enthused response from all our authors, who include among them eminent historians of politics and culture, art historians and film critics, a sociologist, a psychologist, professors in language, literature and education, four editors, a professional dancer and two photographers. Their essays here contribute incisive analytical comment, and very different readings on the fabric that constitutes Indian 'culture'.

The ideology of a *national* culture is after all, not new to this country. It's history returns us to the early stirrings of national fervour in the second half of the 19th century—to songs and plays invoking the motherland in the Hindu *melas* in Bengal; to vows pledged by terrorists from 1905 to sacrifice their lives for the Mother of the nation. Later V.D. Savarkar's conceptualisation of Hindutva marked out the revised cultural parameters of what it meant to be 'Indian'; and in the construction of Independent India, the ideology of a secular culture was written into the Constitution to suit the needs of a pluralist society.

Culture as used in this framework refers to the formulation of national identity: to the way in which we perceive ourselves in relation to the country. Culture here is not that *inner* refinement, the grooming of a deep enriching sensibility with which the concept of *sanskriti* is associated, and which was indeed practised as recently as at Rukmini Devi's school at Kalakshetra. Increasingly culture has come to be associated with the theatre of politics and rhetoric—as we are affected profoundly by *outer* influences which shape the way we speak, educate our young, and profess allegiance to 'national' icons. In his essay in this volume Krishna Kumar puts this admirably, though in a different way:

> In this ethos, it may feel strange to be reminded of the ordinary fact that cultures thrive on tacit knowledge, and therefore, the need to indulge in explicit glorification betokens death.

It may be recalled, this link between culture and ideology grew with all good intentions. As perceived by Balaram, Gandhi was foremost in understanding how cultural values could become a means of effecting national identity. He conceived very simple strategies to accomplish this—firstly by retrieving what was indigenous and innately Indian, such as the *charka* which became both a household symbol and a means to active engagement in becoming self-reliant; secondly, by making the spinning of *khadi* into a *habit* accessible to all people. Once it is a habit, a way of life, "it becomes a culture and then it is indestructible—at least not by physical force." The salt march to Dandi was again symbolic gesture; but it mobilised millions of people into action, to participate and resist colonial dominance. Gandhi created a culture, a way of thinking which was intangible. "A culture transcends time; it is more pervasive, and lasts."

Rabindranath Tagore also believed in integrating culture with life, but he thought differently from Gandhi. After initially espousing the *swadeshi* cause, from 1908 he became concerned by growing incidents of terrorism. His experiments supported the nationalist emphasis on self-respect, but he rejected it's unreasoned patriotism. Abandoning politics, he conceived an alternate culture of education at Santiniketan—looking both east and west beyond the frontiers of India, to build "upon the spiritual unity of all races". His objective as stated was of nurturing young minds to expand into "a higher freedom, a freedom from all racial and national prejudice".

Another ideology was to emerge in Independent India. Assessing the politics of linguistic and regional nationalism, Alok Rai argues that "the inherent and exhilarating (and sometimes infuriating) diversity of India lends itself to being configured...to yield...different and competing ideas of India." In their vision of the nation's future, the founding fathers had foreseen these cultures in conflict, and they had recommended tolerance. Sri Aurobindo noted: "the ancient diversities of the country carried in them great advantages as well as drawbacks.." Mahatma Gandhi emphasised the point, "No culture can live, if it attempts to be exclusive". Dr. Radhakrishnan recommended, "we want a world order which preserves regional cultures". Dr. Maulana Azad asserted, "our languages, our poetry, our literature, our culture, our art, our dress, our manners and customs ... bears the stamp of our joint endeavour."

Hence in the Nehruvian era of the '50s secularism held out its reasoned appeal, endorsing policies for a multicultural society. Were these new government policies effective? Kapila Vatsyayan's essay interrogates this question in its complex issues, moving from land to society to *adivasi* communities who have excelled in crafts and oral traditions, who contribute to this country's rich and diversified culture and yet continue to be marginalised under categories of SC/STC.

Inherent paradoxes are many in the reconstruction of this new India. We take one instance: the construction of a new national museum which became "an act of symbolic importance"—to retrieve and reconstruct the past and assign values to our own heritage. Kavita Singh analyses how these galleries follow inevitably old patterns, differentiating between 'mainstream' sculpture and the hybridity of regional achievements and many histories. The Museum has not changed over five decades. It becomes the "unintended victim" of colonial epistemologies and tacit approval of 'fine arts' and 'crafts'—where the stated objective of plural identities is lost.

We may concede in retrospect that by resisting the influence of both culture and religion in India, secular thinking has not widened in appeal nor grown in its constituency. On the other hand, Savarkar had taunted the Congress in their obsessive concerns with territorial sanctity and integrity; he had proposed then an alternative vision: that of *cultural nationalism*. By introducing the generic concept of Hindutva he defined the cultural boundaries of this country thus:

> The Hindus possess a common Holyland. The Vedic rishis are their common pride, their grammarians Panani and Patanjali, their poets Bhavabhuti and Kalidas, their heroes Sri Ram and Sri Krishna, Shivaji and Pratap, Guru Gobind and Banda are a common source of inspiration. Their prophets Buddha and Mahaveer, Kannad and Shankar, are held in common esteem...

From the 1980s this program has grown significantly, with dramatic televised megaserials, ritual performances and spectacles, and popular public response. The Indian propensity to create, resurrect and revere icons infuses a sense of *cultural* identity. As argued in my paper, if in the 1880s a religious icon had once been the means to introduce *national unity*, from the 1980s cultural nationalism became the strategy to induce *religious unity*—using cultural allegiance to legitimise the divide between those born of the soil and 'the other' minorities.

This phenomenon of refashioning culture to political purpose extends beyond India—creating *militant nationalism*. Edward Said sums up superbly this modern predicament, and I am indebted to his perceptions (Said, 1995:xiii):

> In time, culture comes to be associated, often aggressively, with the nation or state; this differentiates "us" from "them", almost always with some degree of xenophobia. Culture in this sense is a source of identity, and a rather combative one at that, as we see in recent "returns" to culture and tradition. These "returns" accompany rigorous codes of intellectual and moral behaviour that are opposed to the permissiveness associated with such relatively liberal philosophies as multiculturalism and hybridity.

This cultural identity (as also resistance) is now both pervasive and persuasive. As suggested in Ram Rahman's photo essay, it confronts us everywhere: at shrines on street corners, in shops and market places and *maidans*; in the form of wall graffiti, giant cutouts and hoardings; in calendar art, cinema, sports, media and entertainment. This is no longer a matter of national culture as *practised* but as it is *perceived,* or referring to Benedict Anderson's useful term, as it is "imagined". Popular taste is an index of the vitality of culture as it changes to reflect new values—in the print media, television, cinema and what is now referred to as 'electronic capitalism'—reflecting the effects of consumerism and global outreach which are discussed in section V.

> The modern state in this view, grows less out of natural facts— such as language, blood, soil and race—but is a quintessential cultural product, *a product of cultural imagination.* (Appadurai: 1993, 414)

We conclude, culture is not a static entity. It is dynamic and alive, at least in this country, and not to be taken for granted. Visibility is all-important—popular icons register change, moving from religious to national leaders to movie-political giants (Jayalalitha's cutouts dominating over temple *gopurams*) and now to cricket megastars. And cricket is no longer innocent sport but even more vehemently than in *Lagaan*, a game of fierce patriotism (not to mention consumerism)—as witnessed in the frenzied response to the Cricket World Cup currently being played out as we go to press. And this 'sport' alone unites all communities in a common goal....

Indian cinema reaches out to millions all over the world, to become a significant marker of cultural trends. If feminine allure is now replaced by the male muscular body finding potent expression (exemplified in Rithwick Roshan's 'tandav' dance in *Fiza:* 2000), this phenomenon is coupled with violent aggression informing recent films on war and terrorism like *Roja, Border, Pukar, Maa Tujhe Salaam*. In this context, as the essays by Deshpande and Doraiswamy suggest, the film project of *Lagaan* is outstanding, and almost unique in revisiting earlier positions and formulations of national identity.

We have traversed a long distance from the visions of our founding fathers...Culture can be refashioned, reinvented, co-opted and subverted to suit political purpose. In this reinvention of patriotism we have come a long way from the growth of national culture—we have arrived at a militant cultural nationalism. In this new fantasy a macho India preens and flexes its muscles, ready to go to war, creating rationales for a monolithic culture. It is time to reinvent an Indian popular culture that is 'intangible'—that gets under the skin to resist the vicissitudes of political agendas.

GEETI SEN
27 February 2003

I
VISIONS: SCRIPTING THE NATION

VISIONS: *scripting the nation*

Sri Aurobindo

India's Rebirth

India, shut into a separate existence by the Himalayas and the ocean, has always been the home of a peculiar people with characteristics of its own recognisably distinct from all others, with its own distinct civilisation, way of life, way of the spirit, a separate culture, arts, building of society. It has absorbed all that has entered into it, put upon all the Indian stamp, welded the most diverse elements into its fundamental unity. But it has also been throughout a congeries of diverse peoples, lands, kingdoms and, in earlier times, republics also, diverse races, sub-nations with a marked character of their own, developing different brands or forms of civilisation and culture, many schools of art and architecture which yet succeeded in fitting into the general Indian type of civilisation and culture. India's history throughout has been marked by a tendency, a constant effort to unite all this diversity of elements into a single political whole under a central imperial rule so that India might be politically as well as culturally one. Even after a rift had been created by the irruption of the Mohammedan peoples with their very different religion and social structure, there continued a constant effort of political unification and there was a tendency towards a mingling of cultures and their mutual influence on each other; even some heroic attempts were made to discover or create a common religion built out of these two apparently irreconcilable faiths and here too there were mutual influences.

The ancient diversities of the country carried in them great advantages as well as drawbacks. By these differences the country was made the home of many living and pulsating centres of life, art, culture, a richly and brilliantly coloured diversity in unity;

all was not drawn up into a few provincial capitals or an imperial metropolis, other towns and regions remaining subordinated and indistinctive or even culturally asleep; the whole nation lived with a full life in its many parts and this increased enormously the creative energy of the whole. There is no possibility any longer that this diversity will endanger or diminish the unity of India. Those vast spaces which kept her people from closeness and a full interplay have been abolished in their separating effect by the march of Science and the swiftness of the means of communication. The idea of federation and a complete machinery for its perfect working have been discovered and will be at full work. Above all, the spirit of patriotic unity has been too firmly established in the people to be easily effaced or diminished, and it would be more endangered by refusing to allow the natural play of life of the sub-nations than by satisfying their legitimate aspirations. The Congress itself in the days before liberation came had pledged itself to the formation of linguistic provinces, and to follow it out, if not immediately, yet as early as may conveniently be, might well be considered the wisest course.*

India's national life will then be founded on her natural strengths and the principle of unity in diversity which has always been normal to her and its fulfillme..t the fundamental course of her being and its very nature, the Many in the One, would place her on the sure foundation of her Swabhava and Swadharma.

December, 1948

Extracts from a message to the Andhra University, which on December 11, conferred on Sri Aurobindo the Sir Cattamanchi Ramalinga Reddy National Prize.

Mohandas Karamchand Gandhi

The Indian culture of our times is in the making. Many of us are striving to produce a blend of all the cultures which seem today to be in clash with one another. No culture can live, if it attempts to be exclusive. There is no such thing as pure Aryan culture in existence today in India. Whether the Aryans were indigenous to India or were unwelcome intruders, does not interest me much. What does interest me is the fact that my remote ancestors blended with one another with the utmost freedom and we of the present generation are a result of that blend. Whether we are doing any good to the country of our birth and the tiny globe which sustains us or whether we are a burden, the future alone will show.

All Men are Brothers, Life and Thoughts of Mahatma Gandhi as told in his own words, UNESCO/Orient Longman: Paris and Calcutta, 1959, p. 156

Hinduism

I am a reformer through and through. But my zeal never takes me to the rejection of any of the essential things of Hinduism. I have said I do not disbelieve in idol worship. An idol does not excite any feeling of veneration in me. But I think that idol worship is part of human nature. We hanker after symbolism. Why should one be more composed in a church than elsewhere? Images are an aid to worship. No Hindu considers an image to be God. I do not consider idol worship a sin.

It is clear from the foregoing that Hinduism is not an exclusive religion. In it there is room for the worship of all the prophets of the world. It is not a missionary religion in the ordinary sense of the term. It has no doubt absorbed many tribes in its fold, but this absorption has been of an evolutionary, imperceptible character. Hinduism tells every one to worship God according to his own faith or dharma, and so it lives at peace with all the religions.

That being my conception of Hinduism, I have never been able to reconcile myself to untouchability. I have always regarded it as an excrescence. It is true that it has been handed down to us from generations, but so are many evil practices even to this day. I should be ashamed to think that dedication of girls to virtual prostitution was a part of Hinduism. Yet it is practised by Hindus in many parts of India. I consider it positive irreligion to sacrifice goats to Kali and do not consider it a part of Hinduism. Hinduism is a growth of ages. The very name, Hinduism, was given to the religion of the people of Hindustan by foreigners. There was no doubt at one time sacrifice of animals offered in the name of religion. But it is not religion, much less is it Hindu religion. And so also, it seems to me that when cow protection became an article of faith with our ancestors, those who persisted in eating beef were excommunicated. The civil strife must have been fierce. Social boycott was applied not only to the recalcitrants, but their sins were visited upon their children also. The practice which had probably its origin in good intentions hardened into usage, and even verses crept into our sacred books giving the practice a permanence wholly undeserved and still less justified. Whether my theory is correct or not, untouchability is repugnant to reason and to the instinct of mercy, pity or love. A religion that establishes the worship of the cow cannot possibly countenance or warrant a cruel and inhuman boycott of human beings. And I should be content to be torn to pieces rather than disown the suppressed classes. Hindus will certainly never deserve freedom, nor get it if they allow their noble religion to be disgraced by the retention of the taint of untouchability. And as I love Hinduism dearer than life itself, the taint has become for me an intolerable burden. Let us not deny God by denying to a fifth of our race the right of association on an equal footing.

The Writings of Gandhi: **A selection edited and with an introduction by Ronald Duncan, Rupa & Co., New Delhi, 1971, pp. 182–183**

Jawaharlal Nehru

The Discovery of India

What is my inheritance? To what am I an heir? To all that humanity has achieved during tens of thousands of years, to all that it has thought and felt and suffered and taken pleasure in, to its cries of triumph and its bitter agony of defeat, to that astonishing adventure of man which began so long ago and yet continues and beckons to us. To all this and more, in common with all men. But there is a special heritage for those of us of India, not an exclusive one, for none is exclusive and all are common to the race of man, one more especially applicable to us, something that is in our flesh and blood and bones, that has gone to make us what we are and what we are likely to be.

It is the thought of this particular heritage and its application to the present that has long filled my mind and it is about this that I should like to write, though the difficulty and complexity of the subject appeal to me and I can only touch the surface of it. I cannot do justice to it, but in attempting it I might be able to do some justice to myself by clearing my own mind and preparing it for the next stages of thought and action.

Inevitably, my approach will often be a personal one; how the idea grew in my mind, what shapes it took, how it influenced me and affected my action. There will also be some entirely personal experiences which have nothing to do with the subject in its wider aspects, but which coloured my mind and influenced my approach to the whole problem. Our judgements of countries and peoples are based on many factors; among them our personal contacts, if there have been any, have a marked influence. If we do not personally know the people of a country we are apt to misjudge them even more than otherwise, and to consider them entirely alien and different.

In the case of our own country our personal contacts are innumerable, and through such contacts many pictures or some kind of composite picture of our countrymen form in our mind. So I have filled the picture gallery of my mind. There are some portraits, vivid, life-like, looking down upon me and reminding me of some of life's high points—and yet it all seems so long ago and like some story I have read. There are many other pictures round which are wrapped memories of old comradeship and the friendship that sweetens life. And there are innumerable pictures of the mass—Indian men and women and children, all crowded together, looking up at me, and I trying to fathom what lies behind those thousands of eyes of theirs. ...

It is curious how one cannot resist the tendency to give an anthropomorphic form to a country. Such is the force of habit and early associations. India becomes Bharat Mata, Mother India, a beautiful lady, very old but ever youthful in appearance, sad-eyed and forlorn, cruelly treated by aliens and outsiders, and calling upon her children to protect her. Some such picture rouses the emotions of hundreds of thousands and drives them to action and sacrifice. And yet India is in the main the peasant and the worker, not beautiful to look at, for poverty is not beautiful. Does the beautiful lady of our imaginations represent the bare-bodied and bent workers in the fields and factories? Or the small group of those who have from ages past crushed the masses and exploited them, imposed cruel customs on them and made many of them even untouchable? We seek to cover truth by the creatures of our imaginations and endeavour to escape from reality to a world of dreams.

Jawaharlal Nehru, *The Discovery of India*, 1946: published by Jawaharlal Nehru Memorial Fund and Oxford University Press, 1989, pp.36–38 and The John Day Company, New York, p.184.

Sarvepalli Radhakrishnan

The Sanskrit classics tell us the way to the hidden country to which our real selves belong. The brief span of life given to us is to be used to reveal the enduring, the universal, the spiritual in us. "He is not a sage who observes silence, nor he who lives in the woods, but he who knows his own nature is the best of sages."

Our classics have been translated into Indian and foreign languages. Great works are national in one sense, but they are also universal in character. Any literature, if it is to fulfil its aim as literature, should go beyond the restricted limits of its peculiarities and endeavour to portray the feelings and sentiments common to humanity, and demonstrate the essential universality of man. Only thus can a national literature maintain its special character and yet fulfil its role as a part of world literature.

Sanskrit is the main language of the Hindu scriptures which have inspired a distinctive way of life. They tell us that Hindu religion is more than a creed, dogma, rite, or ceremony. It is an outlook which calls upon us to organise the life of the individual as well as that of society. The work of this institution has received the blessings of the acaryas of the different religious persuasions—Advaita, Visistadvaita and Dvaita. Respect for other religious views is an expression of ahimsa or love. "Like a bee collected honey from flowers the intelligent should glean truths from all scriptures, small and great."

Too much blood has been unnecessarily and unjustly shed in the name of dogmatic obsessions. We want a world order which preserves regional cultures and not a world where everyone wears the same clothes, speaks the same words and cherishes the same beliefs. The conception of a great family of nations living together in peace, practising their own beliefs and regulated by justice within the law remains our common objective.

It is our duty to be loyal to the spirit of our ancient seers and make changes in the letter of their directions. Simply because we repeat an old question, it does not follow that the question is the same. Questions are framed in relation to their context. The intellectual presuppositions of one age are not those of another. The conditions of our lives have been basically altered in the last fifty years more than in the last two or three thousand years. Civilization is not a static condition. It is a perpetual movement. We have inherited not only elements which make for greatness but also forces of reaction, narrow-mindedness, disunion. We keep a tradition alive not by repeating what has been said but by meeting our problems in the same spirit in which the old seers met theirs. Our respect for tradition should not harden into an abandonment of independent thought and an unquestioning submission to authority. It is our duty to cast off whatever hampers our sense of justice even though it may be venerable with the history of ages or consecrated by familiarity.

February 1957

Sanskrit College, Mylapore, Madras, Golden Jubilee celebrations, 27 January, 1957, *Occasional Speeches And Writings (Second Series),* **by S. Radhakrishnan, The Publications Division, Ministry of Information & Broadcasting, Government of India, Delhi, 1957, pp. 190–192.**

Maulana Abul Kalam Azad

The Musalmans and a United Nation

It was India's historic destiny that many human races and cultures and religions should flow to her, finding a home in her hospitable soil, and that many a caravan should find rest here. Even before the dawn of history, these caravans trekked into India and wave after wave of newcomers followed. This vast and fertile land gave welcome to all and took them to her bosom. One of the last of these caravans, following the footsteps of its predecessors, was that of the followers of Islam. This came here and settled here for good. This led to a meeting of the culture-currents of two different races. Like Ganga and Jumna, they flowed for a while through separate courses, but nature's immutable law brought them together and joined them in a sangam. This fusion was a notable event in history. Since then, destiny, in her own hidden way, began to fashion a new India in place of the old. We brought our treasures with us, and India too was full of the riches of her own precious heritage. We gave our wealth to her and she unlocked the doors of her own treasures to us. We gave her, what she needed most, the most precious of gifts from Islam's treasury, the message of democracy and human equality.

Full eleven centuries have passed by since then. Islam has now as great a claim on the soil of India as Hinduism. If Hinduism has been the religion of the people here for several thousands of years, Islam also has been their religion for a thousand years. Just as a Hindu can say with pride that he is an Indian and follows Hinduism, so also we can say with equal pride that we are Indians and follow Islam. I shall enlarge this orbit still further. The Indian Christian is equally entitled to say with pride that he is an Indian and is following a religion of India, namely Christianity.

Eleven hundred years of common history have enriched India with our common achievements. Our languages, our poetry, our literature, our culture, our art, our dress, our manners and customs, the innumerable happenings of our daily life, everything bears the stamp of our joint endeavour. There is indeed no aspect of our life which has escaped this stamp. Our languages were different, but we grew to use a common language; our manners and customs were dissimilar, but they acted and reacted on each other and thus produced a new synthesis. Our old dress may be seen only in ancient pictures of bygone days; not one wears it today. This joint wealth is the heritage of our common nationality and we do not want to leave it and go back to the times when this joint life had not begun. If there are any Hindus amongst us who desire to bring back the Hindu life of a thousand years ago and more, they dream, and such dreams are vain fantasies. So also if there are any Muslims who wish to revive their past civilization and culture, which they brought a thousand years ago from Iran and Central Asia, they dream also and the sooner they wake up the better. These are unnatural fancies which cannot take root in the soil of reality. I am one of those who believe that revival may be a necessity in a religion but in social matters it is a denial of progress.

These thousand years of our joint life have moulded us into a common nationality. This cannot be done artificially. Nature does her fashioning through her hidden processes in the course of centuries. The cast has now been moulded and destiny has set her seal upon it. Whether we like it or not, we have now become an Indian nation, united and indivisible. No fantasy or artificial scheming to separate and divide can break this unity. We must accept the logic of fact and history and engage ourselves in the fashioning of our future destiny.

March 1940

Presidential Address delivered by Maulana Abul Kalam Azad at the Fifty-third session of the Indian National Congress, held at Ramgarh, March 19–20, 1940. See P.N. Chopra, *Maulana Abul Kalam Azad. Unfulfilled Dreams*, Appendix III, 'The Musalmans and a United Nation', pp.149–50.

II
MEMORIES ARE MADE OF THIS...

BAPUJI
12.4.1930

Dandi March - A woodcut by Nandlal Bose

Singanapalli Balaram

Gandhi's Retrieval of Indigenous Culture

"Why didn't Gandhi wear a shirt?"
"Because he believed in Freedom of movement. If you ask me he was a big hindrance to our Independence"

This reply, given by a youth in Delhi in a magazine survey reflects the cultural mindset of the *present* generation in this country. It also reflects the role of Gandhian symbols in that mindset.

Intentional or not, the point made by the pun in the youth's reply is significant. 'Freedom of movement' is a fashion statement. Freedom movement on the other hand is not a statement. It is an action; a great political struggle which required immense sacrifices of millions of people and their lives. The former is an opulence based on a commercial phenomenon, while the latter is based on a crying need of the poor masses. They both reflect cultural values at different times of Indian history—of the pre-independent and the post-independent era.

While investigating the roots of culture, it is necessary for one to seek clarity of the term itself. The term culture, like all magnificent terms, is obscured due to over use. One of the obscurities is that it is often misunderstood as religion, and at other times as tradition. While culture has connections with religious practices and traditional processes, it is too limiting to consider these as culture itself. Culture, simply put, is an accepted way of life; a habit of a people, in any group, community or a country; its boundaries extending and contracting depending on the acceptance and commonality.

Mahatma Gandhi is remarkable in his understanding of the indigenous roots of our culture, its power and influence on people. Like a true scientist, he, after understanding the roots of the culture, tried to change them and use them towards a greater cause. He spent his life on these trials and thus rightly titles the autobiography of his life as *My experiments with truth*.

The Intangible Over the Tangible

Gandhi is not unique in recognising the immense significance of cultural forces. There are millions before and after him who knew it and articulated it. But Gandhi is unique in applying these forces which are intangible against tangible forces such as military force or violence. Interestingly, this is what Lord Krishna did in the great Indian epic of the *Mahabharata**.

There are three essential reasons for this power of the intangible over the tangible, and here lies the cause of Gandhi's difference with Netaji Subhash Chandra Bose, who wanted to fight the colonial power with military force in a conventional war.

Firstly, behind every physical action, there is a thought. The root is therefore in the thought and not at the tip of the barrel of a gun which is no more than mere materialisation. Secondly, a material can be destroyed because it is a physical entity, while an idea or thought is a non-physical entity, and indestructible. Thirdly, material is possessed by the fortunate few and it could be seized transacted, amassed etc, and controlled. It is not accessible to all—while a thought or idea is available to every human being. Its access is unlimited and easiest.

However thought is located in a human being who is physical; and he can be destroyed. This is where the role of culture becomes vital. An individual can be destroyed. But his thought, once expressed, is held by a group in practice and made into a habit; it becomes a culture and then it is undestructable—at least not by physical force.

During the emergency in India, while traveling in a crowded train, I heard a revolutionary song against the Emergency—from a beggar. I was shocked because during those days any author or speaker against the Emergency was jailed. On enquiry, the beggar told me—"No one knows who wrote this sir, we take from each other. People like this song. How can it be stopped?" An idea cannot be arrested and if arrested, it would only be further strengthened. Thus an idea gets its

SINGANAPALLI BALARAM / 17

sustenance and strength from the number of people holding it. Gandhi realised this and deliberately searched for ideas so simple that even the most ignorant person can hold to them and the poorest person can afford to express them.

Death of Materials

I t is a fact that Gandhi's insistence on travelling in third class compartments cost the nation so much more because of the security involved; his insistence on staying only in a mud-hut cost Rabindranath Tagore more because he had to build a mud-hut specially for his visit to Shantiniketan; and his stubborn refusal not to use dentures cost more in terms of his food care. Those who criticise Gandhi on these factors have missed the core idea behind his insistence. He knew that in fact his idiosyncrasies cost more; but he was not as bothered about the material costs as he was about the intangible image. The image and its preservation and promotion is worth many times the physical cost.

Quite interestingly, death of the material seems to be the emerging world order of the future. The technological revolution caused it and industrialised nations are already experiencing it. In America, if one pays $ 100 for a Levis trousers he is paying $10 for the trouser and $90 for the Levis label: the intangible image. It is called the brand and even people who knew these facts don't complain.

The Power of Culture over Power and Politics

T hough Gandhi spent his life and death in politics, he never acknowledged himself as a mere politician. In one court case he declared his profession as "Farmer and Weaver". His aspiration had been to reach beyond politics, to the level of culture. It is not difficult to reason out this attitude. Power and politics are limited in their time and space. A culture transcends time; is more pervasive, and lasts. Gandhi firmly believed in integrated approaches. He vehemently argued that a one sided progress is not a progress and it could even be dangerous. Before Independence, inspite of struggling so hard and sacrificing so much for freedom, he once declared that he was not in a hurry to get freedom to his people. He felt that his people should be educated first so that they could handle freedom properly.

Freedom is such a boon; in the hands of un-educated people it is not only worthless but could be misused and made destructive.

Reflecting over more than half a century of our freedom, one cannot agree more with Gandhi: A recent 'Times of India' poll of young students in elite institutions across the country has put Adolf Hitler in the third place, as the kind of leader India ought to have. Such thinking of India's future citizens is the result of the value-starved education—wherever it is given—and no education to the majority of the people. Democratic freedom in the hands of uneducated masses is a sword in the hands of a child. India can only claim to have obtained political freedom in 1947; but without education, without economic development and without cultural transformation, there is no real freedom.

The main aspect of culture is that it is democratic, while politics and power by their very nature are hierarchical and control-oriented. Culture as a way of living can only be influenced and accepted. Gandhi emphasised cultural transformation for these reasons. Culture also lasts long. Though Gandhi was assassinated more than half a century ago, the ideas and symbols developed by Gandhi continue even today. Of course their meanings have changed with the changes in social, cultural and political contexts; but they very much exist and communicate to the old and the young.

Everyday Objects as Symbols

Gandhi is intensely aware that 'functional' communications such as speeches and writings have limited application in India, where people are mostly illiterate. He therefore deliberately chose to communicate with people through symbols—the symbols which the masses can identify easily and clearly. He also had to make sure that these symbols are indigenous. It is obvious that these very symbols may not work in another culture, with another group of people.

Another great facility with a symbol or symbolic action is that it does not demand unaffordable sacrifices. For instance, if one is donating for the struggle he can give only a little as a symbolic gesture. The power of gesture is more important to Gandhi than the size of donation. Among the prominent symbols used by Gandhi was the 'charkha' as the object symbol and 'spinning' as the action symbol. A bit of cotton is available to even the poorest Indian and the charkha is also common in households. If the charkha is not available, one can use the simple *Takli* to spin. What will become of the cotton yarn thus produced? It has lead to the creation of another strong symbol—khadi.

By asking all people to spin irrespective of their caste, creed, sex, religion or geographical location, Gandhi instilled in them a feeling of unity; a solidarity which the colonial ruler had no way to break. People need not come to Gandhi's meetings. By being where they are, but doing the same action—spinning; they could feel oneness.

Khadi both in terms of functionality and life may be inferior to mill-made cloth; but as a symbol it is superior. During the freedom struggle it sent out the strong message that the wearer is a freedom fighter and the colonial rulers must give him his freedom. Gandhi who was interested in integrated development added many other messages with it such as truth, sacrifice, self-reliance and non-discrimination.

He complimented the above with other easily practicable actions such as prayers and fasts. He knew that his message of change will be more accepted if constructed around the prevailing socio-cultural milieu. He was perhaps intuitively aware that the Indian mind is religious no matter, Hindu, Muslim, Sikh or Christian. His meetings always had prayers; speaking in the local language (even a few local words as a token) and his speech would make use of metaphors from the Indian epics and God.

Values in a Product or Action

Every product, communication or action can be said to have four values in the following order. Their emphasis however varies according to the way the product or action is designed and promoted.

- Functional Value
- Aesthetic Value
- Symbolic Value
- Spiritual Value

Take the every day example of a watch. Its apparent value is functional: to indicate time. But it has an aesthetic or decorative value of adding beauty to the wearer. These two values are physical. The next two values are non-physical and Gandhi is unique in realising the power of these values, and focusing on them in his culture promotion. A watch also expresses symbolically the wearer's personality, depending on the brand of the watch; the material used for the strap—gold, stainless steel, leather or simple cloth. It also speaks of the wearer's taste; his special status; his modern or conservative attitude and even his age and sex. It is a huge multiplicity of expressions, which Gandhi rightly realised and consciously applied, effectively. The last and the highest value in a watch is spiritual—whether it has nobility or benevolence in its making, or in operating or in its disposal. If the watch is made by orphans, or it is a memento or gift of your late mother, or it is made of recyclable or biodegradable material, then it has more spiritual value.

It is particularly interesting to note that Gandhi was conscious that these values apply to actions as much as to products and communications. Take a daily task such as eating. Eating to nourish the body is at the functional level, and taste is the aesthetic level. The symbolic level is the brand of food or the restaurant, the way we eat, the plates and cutlery we use, the variety, opulence or lack of it and so on.

Gandhi, in his food habits, strongly identified with the poor who had very little to eat. He followed this principle so staunchly that even in London when the Queen arranged a banquet in his honor, he ate none of the royal food and stuck to his bowl of curd and peanuts. For Gandhi, simplicity like sharpness was a virtue in communicating with the Indian masses. If simplicity of the object symbolised was his first principle, spotless, undiluted maintenance of it was his second principle. When he fasted or advised fasting to people, he was aiming at the spiritual value involved in the act. He wanted to stir the souls of the British rulers as well as world humanity through such actions.

Power of the Transparent Image

A goal set in terms of a transparent image has enormous effect in strengthening the individual's resolve. Indian history sets the example of Chanakya who vowed not to tie his hair till he overthrew the Nanda Dynasty. Gandhi used this method frequently; and the most notable one is his vow of wearing only the loin cloth until he attained *swaraj* for India. None of his followers except Vinoba had the courage to wear only the loin cloth, considered indecent in society. Gandhi chose to wear it also as an act of identification with the poorest of the poor among Indians, who could only afford that. He knew the risk of upsetting the sentiments of people, particularly women, who visited him; so he explained at great length the symbolic significance of his act. He also made sure that his cloths were spotless, emphasising the importance of cleanliness. He communicated not only through symbols but also through the *absence* of certain symbols. He gave up wearing the sacred thread, which he saw as a symbol of inequality which set him apart from his people.

Turning the Mundane into Mega Power

The best known example of Gandhi's action is the Dandi March, which proves his third principle: that a well understood, undented symbol will have better acceptance and thus will have enormous power. Gandhi saw great opportunity in a symbolic defiance of the British imposed Salt Tax. Salt is very mundane and its importance understood by the most ordinary people. Thus it has immense symbolic strength. The misery caused by the tax was not of consequence. It was a simple act designed around an issue, which every India could understand and identify with, regardless of caste, class or religion. It unified the entire country.

The method he selected was a march so that he could reach out to people and mobilise them. It was participatory, giving time for the symbol to grow. He gave the march worldwide publicity because he believed in the power of world sympathy. At the age of 61, with few colleagues, Gandhi conducted the 241-mile march as a symbolic action to culminate at the Dandi seashore—culminating with the simple act of picking up a handful of salt. As the walk progressed, the crowds and world opinion gathered more and more momentum, the British Empire started to shake because they did not know how to fight this new symbolic battle. How many people could they put in jail? People can be put in jail but a symbol cannot be. Gandhi also asked his people to observe non-violence. So, when a non-defending, unarmed, ordinary man was being beaten and put in jail, Gandhi was symbolically sending the message to the world that this is 'might against right' . He was appealing to the inner humanity in all human beings, and the power of that appeal, is irresistible. As mentioned earlier, every action is rooted in a thought; and if that thought influences others, the action is bound to change too.

Gandhian Symbols Today

Symbols need constant reinforcement because they are affected by atrophy. Symbols also need contextual re-shaping so that they remain relevant to the changing socio-cultural contexts.. Many thinkers believe that Gandhian symbols started loosing their power even before Gandhi's death. One of the reasons is that with the attainment of Independence, the greatness of that cause, the prime force of motivation, had ceased. The symbols thus lost their potency. They could have been reshaped to become tools in the great nation building that followed; but the overwhelming complexities of problems of partition and power politics of democracy obscured the Gandhian ideology. More out of sentiment and gratitude than respect to his ideas, the nation in general attempted to perpetrate some of the symbols, particularly the charkha and khadi. Both these objects conveyed a totally different meaning before the Indian Independence. Before Gandhi, the charkha was a symbol of violence and compulsion because in the past, throughout Indian history, the kings and sultans down to the East India Company took forced labour from women and depressed classes through the use of the charkha. Gandhi attempted to *reverse* the meaning of this symbol of the masses by making the charkha a tool of voluntary spinning—to convey to the oppressor that people want to be self-reliant through the non-violent route.

Gandhi maintained that "just as arms symbolize violence the charkha symbolizes non-violence. In the sense that we can most directly realize non-violence through it". Gandhi was instrumental in the several designs of the charkha: to make it compact, portable and eight fold more efficient. These physical improvements immensely increased the charka use by people, and thereby the role of the symbol.

Gandhi introduced khadi cloth as an extension of the charkha. Khadi was the most popular symbol of the freedom movement perhaps because of its ease of use and very high visibility, requiring very little sacrifice from the user. It was the most eloquent of Gandhian symbols. But when khadi started being sold in Khadi Bhandars in the cities and being looked upon as an occupation to earn a livelihood, Gandhi realised its shift of focus and he was much concerned. In 1944, in his talks with the trustees at Sevagram, Gandhi stated, "What I am quite clear about is that Khadi should not be for sale but for self-consumption."

> I first introduced Khadi and only later studied its implications and experimented with it. I find that I have been deceiving myself. What I gave to the people was money but not the real substance-self-reliance. I gave them money in the form of wages and assured them that it contained Swaraj. People took me at my word and believed me, and continue to believe me. But I have now my own misgivings as to how far such Khadi can lead to Swaraj. I am afraid that Khadi has no future if we continue it as today.
>
> At least this much should be clear to all that Khadi is not an occupation or craft merely to earn a livelihood. None of us should harbour this idea. For if Khadi is an industry it would have to be run purely on business lines.

After India's winning of *swaraj*, the significance of charkha and khadi as symbols of *swaraj* has been lost. *The nation however tried to retain them for sentiment—without promoting them for the values they stood for. The result has been the inevitable corruption of the symbol.*

Corruption of Symbols

After Independence, economic and industrial developments gave way to the freedom struggle and social reform. In the changed milieu, people started using khadi either for its superficial material qualities or for reasons of government subsidised cheapness. Politicians started using them to convey their status of belonging to a party—as an extension of the past reputation rather than their belief in Gandhian principles and Ahimsa. As a result the symbols got corrupted and the reverse of what Gandhi intended has happened. Since most khadi wearing politicians are corrupt, people now perceive khadi as a symbol of corruption. Films and plays started showing the khadi-clad person as a standard icon of a corrupt man.

The charkha in pre-independence India was a symbol of self-reliance and freedom. In the new economy, which is no longer based on cottage industry, the concept of self reliance has changed. Since the context changed, the charkha is now seen merely as "nostalgic mnemonic of the days gone by". From a symbol of non-violence and the poor, it has now become an exotic show piece for the rich elite—symbolising their taste and as quoted in a 1987 advertisement, " a fine conversation piece that will add a touch of class to any décor".

Idolatry Replacing Ideals

The assassination of Gandhi, the apostle of non-violence, with heartless violence is an irony. But perhaps the more saddening irony is that after Independence we as a nation are too busy building monuments to Gandhi to listen to his voice once more—to understand the true spirit of his ideas communicated through actions and symbols. We run the crippled Khadi Bhandars with subsidy crutches. The symbol is lost for the object. There are efforts more recently to promote khadi as a fashion fabric, so it can be sold to the elite Indian and foreign buyers. This is also the opposite of what khadi stood for in the hands of Gandhi. This is nothing but 'branding' Gandhi to cash in on the old associations of patriotism and sacrifice. One wonders whether it is respect or disrespect to the great man? There is vested interest. The same vested interest which prevents, us the "free Indians", from empowering people by making the country fully literate even after fifty five years. It is easy and convenient to kill a man, make a statue of him and worship him ritualistically, rather than keeping the man alive or the principles alive. How can the young generation of India be blamed then for their misinformed disrespect to the father of the nation?

Relevance is more important than respect. Early this year, there were unprecedented communal riots in Gujarat in which thousands died. And every moment Gandhi's principles of non- violence were remembered by the conscientious world. At this year's the World Summit on sustainable development at Johannesburg, Gandhi's words on world greed and need set the tone. The 2001 Global Summit on water and sanitation remembered Gandhi's exemplary habit when living at Sabarmati Ashram. He would take only a tumbler of water out of the overflowing Sabarmati river to do his morning ablutions.

Gandhi's principles of truth and non-violence are relevant in this strife torn, violent, digitally divided and eco-struggling world. Practising his principles properly, adapted to the changed context, would be the paying of real respect.

References and Notes
1. S. Balaram *Thinking Design* National Institute of Design, Ahmedabad, 1998.
2. *The Collected Works of Mahatma Gandhi*, volume 24, Publications Division Govt. of India, 1967.
3. *Outlook*, 9 August 2002, Akash, Arora, 17, Delhi.
4. Gandhi M.K. "Reorientation of Khadi" Sarvodaya Prachuralaya, Tanjavur, 1964; p.53.

Uma Das Gupta

In Pursuit of a Different Freedom: Tagore's world university at Santiniketan

The first question you may well ask is: what urged me to take up education. I had spent most of my time in literary pursuits till I was forty or more. I had never any desire to take my part in practical work, because I had a rooted conviction in my mind that I had not the gift...When I was thirteen I had finished going to school. I do not want to boast about it, I merely give it to you as a historical fact...I afterwards realised that what then weighed on my mind was the unnatural pressure of the system of education which prevailed everywhere...[1]

Rabindranath Tagore, 1925.

From the commencement of our work we have encouraged our children to be of service to our neighbours from which has grown up a village reconstruction work in our neighbourhood, unique in the whole of India. Round our educational work the villages have grouped themselves in which the sympathy for nature and service for man have become one. In such extension of sympathy and service our mind realises its true freedom...

Along with this has grown an aspiration for even a higher freedom, a freedom from all racial and national prejudice...We are building up our institution upon the spiritual unity of all races. I hope it is going to be a meeting place for individuals from all countries who believe in the divine humanity, and who wish to make atonement for the cruel disloyalty displayed against her by men. Such idealists I have often met in my travels in the West, unknown persons of no special reputation who suffer and struggle for a cause most often ignored by the clever and the powerful...[2]

Rabindranath Tagore, 1931.

Rabindranath Tagore (1861-1941) was primarily a poet, a writer of essays, plays, novels, and a dedicated educationist. For a short time, he was among the leaders of the *swadeshi* movement (1903-1907) which he had joined to protest against the British Government's decision to partition Bengal. But he withdrew from the movement, unable to take its sectarian and coercive ways. He turned instead to educational work, retreating to the countryside in 1901 where he established a school for children at a place called Santiniketan. He described it as 'an indigenous attempt in adapting modern methods of education in a truly Indian cultural environment'.[3] Twenty years later he added a 'world university' to this school, and called it Visva-Bharati.[4] Santiniketan in his own words was to grow into Visva-Bharati, 'a widely-branching tree'.[5]

Visva-Bharati was conceived to be a meeting place of the like-minded from all over the post-war world. Tagore felt that the war had brought a new age into being. "The task of my last years is to free the world from the coils of national chauvinism", he wrote.[6] Visva-Bharati's motto, *Yatra visvam bhavati ekanidam*, meaning 'where the world finds its nest', was taken from an ancient Sanskrit verse. What was the poet's idea for a brotherhood of the 'world' and why was it so crucial to him? How and to what extent could he implement this idea at his Santiniketan institution?

In many ways the Santiniketan institution was a representation of Rabindranath's personal history. It was for him a response to the troubled questions of his changing times. He grew up when India was a British colony. Government schools imparted education in English. They taught subjects of which Indian children had no natural knowledge. Rabindranath later wrote of them as 'machine-made lessons'.[7] Personally, he sought escape from them at the youthful age of thirteen.[8]

But even if he found freedom from the pressures of the prevailing school system when he was thirteen, thanks to his unusual family, his grown-up ideas and actions brought other pressures all through his life. He found his ideas to be no less alien among his countrymen than was the presence of the British.[9] His concept of an Indian nation, freed from the conflict of communities, was not in line with the prevailing political movement. He wrote,

> In Indian education we have to collect together treasures of Vedic, Puranic, Buddhist, Jaina and Islamic minds. We shall have to find out how the Indian mind has flown along these different chan-

nels. By some such means India will feel her identity in her diversity. We must understand ourselves in this extended and interlinked way or else the education we will receive will be like that of the beggar. No nation can be rich on begging.[10]

He left the political movement, and sought freedom by acting on his own ideas. But his actions drew a mere handful of his countrymen to his cause.

Rabindranath's ideas have received attention in recent scholarship on nationalism[11]. His experiments with education at Santiniketan worked out his 'dual' approach to nationalism, by supporting its emphasis on self-respect but rejecting its unreasoned patriotism. Rabindranath's thought focused on the importance of the freedom of the mind and intellectual force, by which one could accept ideas from the whole world even in conditions of alien rule, and have commitment towards people who are distant as well as near. He launched his world university project when the nationalists were mobilising support for the Non-cooperation Movement under Mahatma Gandhi. When the news of the movement reached Tagore in Europe, he wistfully wrote, "What irony of fate is this that I should be preaching cooperation of cultures on this side of the sea just at the moment when the doctrine of non-cooperation is preached on the other side"?[12] He went ahead with establishing Visva-Bharati of which he wrote in 1921, "I have taken courage to invite Europe to our institution. There will be a meeting of truths here".[13]

Family, Culture, Religion and Contemporary Bengali Society

> Looked at from the outside, our family appears to have accepted many foreign customs, but at its heart flames a national pride that has never flickered. The genuine regard my father had for his country he never forsook through all the vicissitudes of his life, and in his descendents it took shape as a strong patriotic feeling. Such, however, was by no means characteristic of the times of which I am writing. Our educated men were then keeping at arms' length both the language and thought of their native land. My elder brothers had nevertheless always cultivated Bengali literature.[14]

> Rabindranath Tagore, 1890.

> It is regrettable of course that we had lost the power of appreciating our own culture, and therefore did not know how to assign western culture its right place.[15]

> Rabindranath Tagore, 1913.

L iving in the palatial Jorasanko House built by Prince Dwarkanath Tagore, the Tagore family were a world unto themselves. The family had lived through varied fortunes and different phases of history. Grandfather Dwarkanath(1794-1846) was a very rich man, being a leading merchant of his times.[16] A cosmopolitan by conviction, he went to England and gained the confidence of Queen Victoria. In contrast his son Debendranath(1817-1905) was a man of the high Hindu tradition of the Upanishads and austere.[17] For this, his countrymen called him Maharshi, 'the great sage', just as his father was called the 'Prince' for his large-hearted charities and lavish ways. The flow continued as the third generation of Tagores grew up: Rabindranath and his siblings. Among them were Satyendranath, the first Indian to join the Indian Civil Service; philosopher Dwijendranath whom Gandhi revered and who was a staunch supporter of the Non-cooperation Movement; and Jyotirindranath who was an artist, a capable composer of songs and an innovator of *swadeshi* (home-made) enterprise. The brothers were also dedicated to the development of modernism in Bengali language and literature.[18] In religion, the family was profoundly influenced by the monotheism of Rammohun Roy(1772-1883), and became the leaders of a Hindu reform movement which took Rammohun's work further towards establishing the Brahmo Samaj.[19]

Among Rabindranath's important contributions to contemporary culture in 20th century Bengal, and India, was the restoration of the Upanishadic perception of the notion of one world—as a dominant ideology in the new system of knowledge. Rammohun Roy began the process, despite the conflicting tendencies of the times when he died in 1833. The 'renaissance' in 19th and 20th century Bengal, and some other parts of India, was a complex phenomenon. It was partly the outcome of the new ideas from the West arising out of the colonial connection, and partly a revival of traditional Indian thinking. There were many revivalists at the time who were determined to counter the changes brought about by the West's impact. In contrast, there were also those like the members of the Young Bengal Movement who were out to damn their past, and embrace only what the West had brought. Initially, Rabindranath was inclined to a Hindu view of the past. But he matured and moved on to build a strong secular and liberal-democratic interpretation of Indian history.

Patriotism, the Swadeshi Movement, and the Elite Nationalist Leadership

> *I remember the day during the Swadeshi Movement in Bengal when a crowd of young students came to see me, and said that if I would order them to leave their schools and colleges, they would instantly obey. I was emphatic in my refusal to do so, and they went away angry, doubting the sincerity of my love for my motherland.[20]*
>
> Rabindranath Tagore, 1908

> *Our students are bringing their offering of sacrifices to what? Not to a fuller education but to a non-education.[21]*
>
> Rabindranath Tagore, 1921

> *Then when the Bangadarshan magazine came into my hands, Bengal was beside herself at the sound of the sharpening of the knife for her partition. The boycott of Manchester, which was the outcome of her distress, had raised the profits of the Bombay mill-owners to a super foreign degree. And I had then to say: "This will not do, either; for it is also of the outside. Your main motive is hatred of the foreigner, not love of country.[22]*
>
> Rabindranath Tagore, 1921

Rabindranath learnt his political lessons well from the Swadeshi Movement, having actually participated in it during the years 1903-1907. In 1905 he outlined his original vision of a self-governing and self-reliant nation in an important essay called 'Swadeshi Samaj', meaning National Society.[23] It was addressed to all those young people's associations from the urban middle class which supplied the Swadeshi Movement with its most ardent activists. There he hoped for a revival of traditional society or samaj for the good of all concerned, irrespective of caste or creed. The bond of unity was sought through the Hindu religion and *samaj* as Rabindranath believed that Hinduism had helped to unite the diverse elements in India's history. But this hope was shattered with the rise of political extremism, group manoeuvring, and the outbreak of communal rioting. He withdrew from the movement in protest. He realised that the politics of the day was not for him. During the emergence of the Non-cooperation Movement he felt the same inner resistance. He respected Gandhi's real worth for the country, but found his strategy of non-cooperation unacceptable. So he wrote,

> What I heard on every side was that reason and culture, as well, must be censured. It was only necessary to cling to an

unquestioning obedience. Obedience to whom? To some mantra, some unreasoned creed![24]

Whatever their disagreement Gandhi understood Rabindranath's concern and called him a 'sentinel', a soldier for a larger cause.[25]

Despite withdrawing from the movement, Rabindranath's responses to politics was close to Gandhi's thoughts and actions. Rabindranath held that Gandhi was the one leader in Indian politics who was committed wholly to truth and love. In his essay 'The Call of Truth' he wrote,

> The movement, which has now succeeded the swadeshi agitation, is ever so much greater and has moreover extended its influence all over India. Previously, the vision of our political classes had never reached beyond the English knowing classes, because the country meant for them only that bookish aspect of it which is to be found in the pages of the Englishman's history. Such a country was merely a mirage born of vapourings in the English language, in which flitted about thin shades of Burke and Gladstone, Mazzini and Garibaldi. Nothing resembling self-sacrifice or true feeling for their countrymen was visible. At this juncture Mahatma Gandhi came and stood at the cottage door of the destitute millions, clad himself as one of them, talked to them in their own language. Here was the truth at last, not a mere quotation out of a book ... Who else has felt so many men of India to be his own flesh and blood?[26]

Rabindranath's withdrawal from the political movements made him unpopular with the nationalist leadership; but not with Gandhi and Nehru, who found his ideas for a liberal and secular democracy crucial in shaping India's future, particularly in the inter-War years. Rabindranath continued to protest single-handedly against the Raj on a number of occasions. He was unequivocal about the brutal nature of alien rule in his letter of 20 May 1919 to the Viceroy, when renouncing his knighthood over the Amritsar massacre.[27] But even there he explained his action by writing, "There is such a thing as a moral standard of judgement. When India suffers injustice, it is right that we should stand against it; and the responsibility is ours to right the wrong, not as Indians but as human beings".[28] In a message to his own countrymen over Amritsar he declared, "Let us forget the Punjab affairs—but never forget that we shall go on deserving such humiliation over and over again until we set our house in order. Do not mind the waves of the sea, but mind the leaks in your own vessel".[29] That was Rabindranath's theory of education for you: that of training the people in self-examination and self-reliance as an essential need in the struggle for Indian independence to which he remained firmly rooted.

City and Village: Science, Education and Rural Life

A deep despair now pervades rural life all over the country, so much so that the high sounding phrases like home rule, autonomy, etc., appear to me almost ridiculous and I feel ashamed even to utter them.[30]

Rabindranath Tagore, 1908.

Outside the bhadralok class pathetic in its struggle to affix university labels to the names of its members, there is a vast obscure multitude who cannot even dream of such a costly ambition. With them we have our best opportunity if we know how to use it there, and there only can we be free to offer to our country the best kind of all-round culture not mutilated by the official dictators. I have generally noticed that when the charitably minded city-bred politicians talk of education for the village folk they mean a little left-over in the bottom of their cup after diluting it copiously...Our people need more than anything else a real scientific training that could instill in them the courage to experiment and initiative of mind that we lack as a nation.[31]

Rabindranath Tagore, 1937.

Tagore grew up in the city till he was sent to manage his family estates in rural Bengal when he was twenty-nine years old. He did this from 1890 to 1920. There he saw for the first time the great natural beauty in the East Bengal landscape, lined by mighty rivers and wrote ecstatically about it. But he also learnt with great sadness what poverty meant seeing the lives of the villagers. "I, the town-bred, had been received into the lap of rural loveliness and I began joyfully to satisfy my curiosity. Gradually the sorrow and poverty of the villages became clear to me, and I began to grow restless to do something about it."[32]

The idea of doing something constructive for his country's poor arose from that experience. The situation in 19th and 20th century Indian society was such that while the peasant still adhered to his traditions with no exposure to anything else, the English-educated Indian intelligentsia felt superior to their village brethren out of their newly-found university education. Both Gandhi and Rabindranath were convinced that if India were to become free and independent, and recover self-respect, work must begin to overcome the weaknesses of poverty and division from within society.

While Gandhi chose the political path, Rabindranath chose education. To him, it was a catastrophe that the educated elite regarded a large part of their own countrymen as *chhotolok*, literally small people. Rabindranath developed his most trenchant critique of English education on the following grounds: first, that it was there to create only an army of job-seekers to feed the colonial administration and their businesses; second, that it divided fathers and sons socially and emotionally; third, that such an education was a waste for society as there was no understanding nor love between the teacher and the taught; fourth, that it was totally dissociated from Indian life.[33]

He felt that the only way to overcome such a demeaning state was by uniting each one of us, and feeling compassion for one another through a new education for all. In modern times, the town had become the repository of knowledge, wealth and power. It was necessary that the village should benefit from this by cooperation with the town. A new education would have to bridge the gap between the city and the village, and would introduce a variety of knowledge from the cultures of other lands.

As a first step in that direction he chose to establish his school in the heart of rural Bengal, not far from the big city of Calcutta. Such a location gave him the ability to draw upon both raw materials and cultural products indigenously. Teaching was given in the mother tongue. Those who joined the school as pupils were from urban backgrounds. The school was made strictly residential with students and teachers and families of teachers all living closely, in an educational colony that became a community. Rabindranath insisted on the urban children's need to live and learn in a different atmosphere away from their city homes; and that their education would be incomplete without knowledge of rural living. For him and Gandhi there was no forgetting that the majority of Indians lived in the villages and lived in poverty.

Santiniketan and Visva-Bharati as Training Ground for Freedom of Mind: Success or Failure?

> *I have said repeatedly and must repeat once more that we cannot afford to lose our mind for the sake of any external gain ...we must refuse to accept as our ally the illusion-haunted magic-ridden slave mentality that is at the root of all poverty and insult under which our country groans.*[34]
>
> *Rabindranath Tagore, 1921.*

For Rabindranath, the Santiniketan institution became a lifelong engagement to establish an environment of reasoned thinking and living by breaking down the forces of bigotry and separatism. For this, he advocated neither the boycott of government, nor cooperation with government. He did not seek the government's favour for education, sanitation, peace, order and justice. He was embarrassed to find that even the movement for an Indian 'renaissance' sought the British government's intervention to remedy the imperfections of Indian society. Thus freeing himself of the 'renaissance' he turned to work away from the limelight of all movements. His goal was unity among people. The Santiniketan education was an experiment to bring about cultural understanding and unity at two levels: first, between the urban and the rural through education in the mother-tongue, and learning about each other's skills; second, between India and the West through exchange of knowledge, and a recognition of each other's contribution to civil society. Visva-Bharati was the home to both a Centre for Advanced Study in Cultures and a Centre for Rural Reconstruction, within a radius of two miles. Rabindranath's hope was to make the Santiniketan-Sriniketan experiment show the rest of the country that a broader education and wider exposure to the life of man and his wide-ranging creativity would eliminate cultural domination, ultimately even political domination, of any one group over the other.

Given those beginnings, Santiniketan was clearly able to establish a way of life which attracted men and women from other parts of India, and indeed from the world. Some twenty years ago, in the 1980s, I travelled in many parts of India searching for the institution's pupils from the twenties and thirties. They came from Madras, Kerala, Andhra Pradesh and Gujarat to Santiniketan. Most were looking for cultural education, and some of them came from a nationalist milieu. "I had taken part in *satyagraha*", V.Balgangadhar Menon (b.1916) told me.

> After that I could continue my education only in a nationalist in-
> stitution. Santiniketan and Sabarmati were the only two
> institutions which came to our mind in this connection. I had heard
> of many students who had boycotted government colleges at
> Gandhiji's call and gone to Sabarmati and made good. I too had a
> recommendation for Sabarmati from Kellapan, the father of the
> nationalist movement in Kerala. But I hankered for a more cul-
> tural and philosophical education. So I wrote off myself for ad-
> mission to Santiniketan supported by my eldest brother.[35]

Sriniketan

Santiniketan
Tagore Museum and Archives,
Viva Bharati University Santiniketan

V. Gopala Reddy was also from a nationalist background. He spent the years 1924-27 at the Santiniketan College. In 1982 he told me,

> I was thirteen and half when I boycotted government school at Gandhiji's call for non-cooperation. My brother and I were immediately sent off to the Andhra Jatiya Kalachalam at Masulipatam, where I stayed for four years. By then I had read Tagore and felt greatly attracted towards him. I was determined to leave Masulipatam for Santiniketan. My nationalist commitment was not at all hampered there. On the contrary there were other things there that interested me. There was music, art; I loved that in Santiniketan. There I began to learn other Indian languages in Santiniketan, Tamil from my Tamil friends, Gujarati from my Gujarati friends.[36]

Mrinalini Sarabhai (b.1923) came to Santiniketan in 1939-1940. When speaking about her experience she said, "It was as though I had been touched by Santiniketan. I was lucky. So many of us live through life without being touched".[37] Indira Gandhi spent a year studying in the Santiniketan College in 1933. She said,

> Santiniketan revived in me certain traditions which I used to know in my childhood. These traditions, which were an essential part of my grandfather's household at the time of my childhood became a little inconsequential after his death. But they were revived in me in Santiniketan—traditions like observing Vasant Sri Panchami. I have observed them in my own life ever since.[38]

One can add to these examples from the testimony of people who were touched by the Santiniketan way of life. What was clear from their experience is that they had individually and together learned to appreciate and identify an Indian culture. Some also came from the West, either invited by the poet himself as were the Indologists Sylvain Levi from the Sorbonne or Guiseppe Tucci from Rome, also the young English graduate in agriculture from Cornell who was asked to start Visva-Bharati's centre for rural reconstruction. Some came of their own explorations such as Alex Arenson who had escaped Nazi Germany and come to study in England. He came to Santiniketan in 1937 and stayed there till 1944 teaching English. There were other westerners like W.W.Pearson and C.F. Andrews who chose to dedicate themselves to the ideals of the Santiniketan institution in preference to their missionary work. When Andrews died in 1940, Gandhi wrote about Andrews to Rabindranath, "Santiniketan was his as much as it is yours".[39] It is through them all that Rabindranath felt that `the true India is an idea and not a mere geographical fact'.[40]

Indians and foreigners came together, with the fusion of studies combining courses on Indian traditions, Western culture, China, Japan and the Middle East. The poet once wrote happily to Andrews in 1920: "Now I know more clearly than ever before that Santiniketan belongs to all the world and we shall have to be worthy of that fact."[41] But he did not take long to add that "[he] did not have the courage to go all the way...to come completely out of the net in which the system of education has enmeshed our country".[42] That he could not do all he wanted to with his experiments at Santiniketan and Sriniketan was becoming evident in his own lifetime. Voicing disappointment over Santiniketan he called it `a borrowed cage' as the students were demanding a more prosaic curriculum to help them get degrees and jobs.[43]

What must have also hurt is that Santiniketan and Sriniketan remained apart. While the Santiniketan institution contributed to the cultural enrichment of the elite, its surrounding villages hardly changed. The founder's idea of integrating the city and the village was clearly not realised even within that small radius of space. Did Santiniketan and Visva-Bharati then prove what Tagore's nationalist critics were saying about his idea? They said from the start that the poet was 'dissociated from reality', that his world university was merely an 'abstract' idea, even "opposed to human history".[44]

Rabindranath did not agree. To him the value of education at Santiniketan was that those who came were given freedom to know themselves.[45] He wrote "What I wanted to do was to free the student's minds through education ... that is why I could not bring our school under the discipline of any university". Therefore, calling Santiniketan a successful or a failed institution does not help. Its relevance was as a greatly encompassing idea, an unprecedented one in the range it offered. Rabindranath put his faith in a united world in more ways than one. His school and university were witness to that effort against every odd.

References and Notes

1. Rabindranath Tagore, 'My School'(1925) in *Santiniketan Vidyalaya 1901-2000*, Calcutta: 2000, p. 9.
2. Rabindranath Tagore, 'My Educational Mission'(1931) in op.cit., p.30.
3. Rabindranath Tagore, *Visva-Bharati,* pamphlet, Santiniketan: 1929.

4. For papers on a history of Santiniketan and Sriniketan, see Uma Das Gupta, 'Santiniketan: The school of a poet' in Mushirul Hasan ed., *Knowledge, Power and Politics: Educational Institutions in India*, New Delhi: 1998, pp.258-303; also 'Tagore's educational experiments at Santiniketan and Sriniketan 1910-41' in Sabyasachi Bhattacharya ed., *The Contested Terrain: Perspectives on Education in India*, New Delhi: 1998, pp. 265-74; also 'Rabindranath Tagore on Rural Reconstruction: The Sriniketan Programme 1921-41' in *The Indian Historical Review*, IV, 2, pp.354-78 and 'Santiniketan and Sriniketan: A Historical Introduction' in *Visva-Bharati Quarterly*, IV: 1-4, 1975-6, pp.1-56.

5. Rabindranath to Suhrid Kumar Mukhopadhyaya, 11 December 1920, Bengali Letters, Rabindra Bhavana Archives [Henceforth, R.B.A.], Santiniketan. Mukhopadhyaya was a student at the Santiniketan school from 1910-18, teacher from 1922-4.

6. Rabindranath to Rathindranath Tagore, 11 October 1916: Bengali Letters, R.B.A. Rathindranath was the poet's eldest son; a trained horticulturist he dedicated his life's work to the Santiniketan-Sriniketan endeavour.

7. Rabindranath to Ajit Kumar Chakrabarty, 30 January 1913, Bengali Letters, R.B.A. Chakrabarty was a teacher at the Santiniketan School 1904-18.

8. Rabindranath Tagore, *My Reminiscences*, Papermac edition, London: 1991, p.116-34.

9. For biographies of Rabindranath, see Krishna Dutta and Andrew Robinson's *Rabindranath Tagore The Myriad Minded Man*, London: 1994, and Krishna Kripalani, *Rabindranath Tagore A Biography*, Calcutta: 1984.

10. Rabindranath Tagore, *Visva-Bharati* [collected writings in Bengali] Calcutta: 1963, p.8, also *The Twentieth Anniversary Celebration of the Santiniketan Asram*, Bolpur: 1918, p.4.

11. To cite some examples. Ranajit Guha's *History at the Limit of World History* (NewYork:2002), Dipesh Chakravarty's *Provincializing Europe: Postcolonial Thought and Historical Difference* (Chicago:2000), Isaiah Berlin's "Rabindranath Tagore and the consciousness of nationality" in *The Sense of Reality: Studies in Ideas and their History*(Henry Hardy ed.;London:1996), Partha Chatterjee's *Nationalist Thought and the Colonial World*(Delhi:1996) and Ashis Nandy's *The Illegitimacy of Indian Nationalism:Rabindranath Tagore and the Politics of Self* (Delhi:1994).

12. Rabindranath to C.F.Andrews, 13 July 1921, English Letters, R.B.A.

13. Rabindranath Tagore, *Visva-Bharati*, [collected writings], pp.13-15.

14. Rabindranath Tagore, *My Reminiscences*, p. 104.

15. Rabindranath to Ajit Kumar Chakrabarty, 18 March 1913, Bengali Letters, R.B.A.

16. Krishna Kripalani, *Dwarkanath Tagore, A Forgotten Pioneer: A Life*, New Delhi: 1980.

17. *The Autobiography of Maharshi Devendranath Tagore*, London: 1914, Introduction by Satyendranath Tagore, pp.1-33.

18. Rabindranath Tagore, *My Reminiscences*, op.cit., pp.90-101.

19. David Kopf, *The Brahmo Samaj and the Shaping of the Modern Indian Mind*, Princeton: 1979.

20. Rabindranath Tagore, 'Reflections on Non-cooperation' in *The Mahatma and the Poet*, ed. Sabyasachi Bhattacharya, New Delhi: 1997, p.58. [Henceforth, *Mahatma and the Poet*].

21. Ibid., p.57.

22. Rabindranath Tagore, 'The Call of Truth', in ibid., p.70.

23. Rabindranath Tagore, 'Swadeshi Samaj'(1904), *Rabindra- Rachanabali (Collected Works)*, vol.2, Visva-Bharati edition: 1986, pp.625-58.
24. Rabindranath Tagore, 'The Call of Truth', in *Mahatma and the Poet*, p.78.
25. Mahatma Gandhi, 'The Great Sentinel', in op.cit., pp. 87-92.
26. Rabindranath Tagore, 'The Call of Truth', in op.cit., p.76.
27. Kripalani, *Rabindranath Tagore*, pp.277-78.
28. Rabindranath to C.F.Andrews, *Letters to a Friend*, New York: 1929, p.143.
29. Ibid., p.92.
30. Rabindranath to Abala Bose, undated [1908], in *Prabasi*, [Bengali], 1345 B.S., p.466. Abala was the wife of scientist Jagadish Chandra Bose.
31. Rabindranath to Leonard Elmhirst, 19 December 1937, Elmhirst Papers, Dartington Hall, Devonshire, U.K. Elmhirst started the Sriniketan Institute of Rural Reconstruction in 1922 on the poet's invitation. See, Leonard Elmhirst, *Poet and Plowman*, Calcutta: 1975, p.16.
32. Rabindranath Tagore, 'The History and Ideals of Sriniketan', [transl.from the original Bengali by Marjorie Sykes]in *Modern Review*, November 1941, p.433.
33. Rabindranath Tagore, *Asramer-rup-o-bikash*, [Bengali], Calcutta:1967, pp.24-6, 47, 52-4.
34. Rabindranath, 'The Call of Truth', op.cit., p.84.
35. Interview with V.Gangadhar Menon on 27 May 1980 in Palghat, Kerala.
36. Interview with V.Gopala Reddy on 5 May 1982 in Nellore, Andhra Pradesh.
37. Interview with Mrinalini Sarabhai on 2 January 1980 in Ahmedabad.
38. Interview with Indira Gandhi on 12 April 1982 at the Prime Minister's Parliament House office in Delhi.
39. Mahatma Gandhi to Rabindranath, 5 May 1940, English Letters, R.B.A.
40. Rabindranath Tagore, 'Reflections on Non-cooperation', in *Mahatma and the Poet*, p. 61.
41. Rabindranath to C.F.Andrews, 3 October 1920 in Krishna Datta and Andrew Robinson, *Selected Letters of Rabindranath Tagore*, Cambridge: 1997, p. 240.
42. Rabindranath, *Visva-Bharati* [collected writings], p.32.
43. Rabindranath, 'Santiniketan School', ms.no.365, R.B.A.
44. Aditya Ohadedar, *Rabindra-bidushan itibritta*, Calcutta: 1986 and Dipan Chattopadhyaya, *Rabindrabirodhi samalochana*, Calcutta: 1994, both works cited in Dipesh Chakrabarty, *Provincializing Europe: Postcolonial Thought and Historical Difference*, Princeton: 2000, pp. 156-7.
45. Rabindranath Tagore, *Visva-Bharati*, [collected writings], p. 32.

Leela Samson

Imbibing Culture at Kalakshetra

In a letter written in 1944 to students who desired to join Kalakshetra, Rukmini Devi had said:

> Before you become a student, it is necessary for you to understand my aims and ideals in setting up this institute. I want you to know that this is not merely a place where you might learn some art, present yourself before the public and win recognition. Art is a divine gift and every artist a messenger of the Gods. Through Beauty alone can come true understanding. It is to encourage this that Kalakshetra is being founded. For without a spirit of dedication and a power to enter into the Spirit of ancient India, Kalakshetra would serve no useful purpose either to our motherland, India or to the world.

She believed that the supreme purpose of the Arts Academy was to encourage the living of beautiful lives—of lives refined, artistic, gracious, compassionate, true, noble and wise—everything that extolled beauty and eschewed ugliness. For her, the spirit of Beauty knew no distinctions of race, nation or faith. She had observed:

> The Academy will be still more happy to know that in its own humble way, it is helping to make more beautiful, more artistic, the lives of all. That in the education of the young, creative reverence for the Beautiful has a pre-eminent place, that ugliness begins to depart from daily life whether in the home or in the earning of one's livelihood, and that leisure finds decreasing satisfaction in the crude and vulgar. The world must turn away from those barbarisms of war, of greed and of cruelty, which still challenge its right to be called civilised.

Almost each of us who were drawn to Kalakshetra joined it to study dance or music, and perhaps we dreamt of becoming dancers and musicians. Soon we were made aware of the larger parameters of the learning process. As a child the learning process shapes you gently. Life in such an 'ashram' may be hard for someone who has been pre-conditioned, both physically and mentally. For a child, it is a happy and natural environment in which to grow and flower. One's appearance or physical comforts have no real worth for a child, especially if attention is not drawn to these things. A child is embarrassed because of the self-consciousness of parents and society. Fortunately for everyone concerned, parents did not see the naked feet of their children running around in the sand in Kalakshetra! Grubby they may have looked, but they were never too young to wash their own clothes!

Simplicity of form and structure; the reduction of life's needs to the essentials; a premium on cleanliness of the body and mind; the value of silence and of prayer; the importance of rigorous practice in the pursuit of perfection; reverence for life in every form; respect for the child and for the elderly—these were everyday lessons. They were not learnt easily because a child is unable to rationalise, and to understand their true worth. As soon as an awareness of the 'outside' world appears these lessons seem like an imposition. Each institute in the campus had morning prayers of every religion—the school, the arts academy, the Montessori children's school, the hostels. We 'believed' in all religions even before we knew what 'religion' meant! Every prayer was said by all. In the Besant Theosophical High School which we attended in the mornings, studies seemed part of games, singing, spinning and weaving, painting and some discipline in the form of Scouts and Guides. 'Individuality' and 'freedom of expression' were the two qualities I recall, as being granted to every child. No punishment was allowed.

However, when it came to dance and music classes in the afternoons, things were different. A tradition was being handed over to the child. An art was being taught. A reverence for Indian concepts of *bhakti* and *shraddha* had to be transferred. A knowledge of the philosophy of this land, its religions, its myths, its architectural norms, its poetic traditions, its musical forms, its scriptures—all these were seen as valid and necessary inputs to the learning of the dance. Discipline was therefore fundamental to the learning process. Respect and decorum were strictly maintained. Silence was valued. We were all better behaved in the Arts Academy than we were in School, although both these were on the same campus—one on each side of the hostels. An early consciousness seemed to evolve, about the value of what we were being taught. A definite philosophy was the backbone of the institute. One could feel it in the air.

In her inaugural address of the institute, Rukmini Devi proposed:

> We hope to attract artists from all over the world, for our Academy is international; artists in whom the spirit of Art shines and who know Art to be an expression of the power of Universal Life and growth. We often think of life in terms of Will and Wisdom, but often neglect life in its aspect of Beauty.

The spirit of nationalism and a desire to return to the roots of our culture was also evident. Rukmini Devi believed in the renaissance of Indian art and of Indian educational systems. She said that unless India learnt to pay reverence to her own arts, neither would she be worthy of *swaraj*, nor would she be able to take her rightful place among the nations of the world.

In the teaching or learning of an art form, a spirit of 'reverence' is essential. Not an empty ritual of reverence, but a genuine spirit of inspiration, wonder, fascination, even awe– call it what you may, must be transferred to the child. The reverence is both for the art form and for those who represent it. With the careful development of an eye for detail, a healthy respect for the complexity of the 'form' slowly grows in the child. Breaking down complex patterns of movement into several simple units learnt individually gives the child a sense of achievement. It is possible and also necessary to make each of these units singularly expressive and meaningful. When culled out successfully from the complex and ornate weave of the 'real' thing, it is a moment of truth for the teacher as well. To be able to see beauty in the small, in the insignificant, teaches you much about life; about the small, the insignificant, discarded, and the discriminated against. Shiva, in His garb wears all that is shunned by society as being dirty, repulsive and ugly. The perfect chemist, He transforms all these into symbols of the highest beauty. It is important when learning the 'big' things, to pay attention to, and to appreciate the value of the 'little things'.

One such thing, is the value of ceremony in our lives. In spite of the vast traditions of ceremony in our country—so much a part of India's religious practices, military traditions and societal celebrations—the urban, educated Indian has either discarded it or is self conscious about it, because they have forgotten its purpose. Ceremony when performed with grace is the blending of 'form' and 'spirit'. One must be guided by this grace of spirit in action. The beauty of such ceremony is that it invokes great power. All of us who have been witness to the 'Beating of the Retreat'—an old military tradition, know how beautifully history is encapsulated in that ceremony. No amount of classroom teaching or reading about it can give you the spirit of that moment at sundown, when man and nature resolve to put down arms and rest. Experiencing a thing is living it, knowing it. The teacher in so many of our educational establishments presumes power. This is so in the arts as well. In fact, all a child really needs are the materials; the opportunity and 'a loving hand' to guide him. Great teachers know this. The child learns himself.

II

What then, is 'a civilised world', a cultured world? Our definitions of war, of greed and of cruelty have been masterfully altered in our time. Perhaps this was so in every time. The difference is, that now we have brought war and greed and cruelty into our homes and pretend they do not exist, only because an outsider is not the perpetrator. No one dares to call this 'war'. No one can call this 'greed' or 'cruelty'? To the generation before us the Partition of India brought so much grief. We have many, many deep wounds of our own time that cut to the very bone. Do things ever change? Will they ever be different for our children and for theirs? It is rightly said—as we sow, so shall we reap. Each of us realises the truth of these words. The world over, we have made mistakes in correctly evaluating the larger community of people, states and nations and in truly appreciating their inherent differences. We are paying for this. Smaller communities, with different cultures are left out of the broad roads to progress. They are smothered by monolith, self-righteous 'Gods', who censure belief in the many other 'Gods', in the mannerisms and cultures they cannot understand. Alas, we live in a small world that demands conformity. God forbid, should your stride be faster or different, or that you do not choose the path, or that you choose not to move at all!

What about India? A land that has so much to give the world from its past. A people that have so much to give to the future. Is our culture strong enough for us to choose not a different path, but the right one? Most of us have no doubt that our culture is strong. The question is—are *we* strong enough? Have we enough faith in ourselves, in the culture we call our own? Or, in the striving to be part of a world culture, to be recognised as an aware, democratic citizen of the accepted world, have we forsaken what is ours? Has our particular culture made us united in spirit and compassionate, like the great Buddhas who walked this land? Or are we petty and impoverished descendants of those exalted men? Do we even know what treasures our culture has to offer? Does a modern, progressive education mean a distancing from one's own roots? It truly seems that while the others realise the strength and passion of their own identities, India slowly forgets.

"The needs of India are the development of a national spirit, and an education founded on Indian ideals—enriched, not dominated by the thought and culture of the West." Not an Indian, but an Irish woman, Dr. Annie Besant—a socialist, a Theosophist and a freedom fighter wrote these words in a letter to Babu Hirendra Nath Dutta, in 1905. She fought for the freedom of the human spirit—unmindful of the birth or nationality of those she fought for. She fought for India's freedom, more vociferously than any other, and loved this land more than her own. We do not even remember the great ones who won this precious independence for us. Listen to her words. Words of one not born on this land:

> To have a share in the winning of India's freedom, a share however small—what greater gift could come into hands which fold themselves in the cry of homage—Vande Mataram.

Nationalism was a religion above individual faiths. And there were not a few of these people in our country! The freedom they fought for, the freedom they gave us—was it merely to throw out the aggressor? Is there no other lesson to be learnt from their indomitable spirit, their selflessness, their non-aggression?

Ananda Coomaraswamy, a great Indologist, had observed in his book, *The Dance of Shiva*:

> Each race contributes something essential to the world's civilisation in the course of its own self-expression and self-realisation. The character built up in solving its own problems, in the experience of its own misfortunes, is itself a gift which each offers the world. The essential contribution of India then is simply her Indian-ness; her great humiliation would be to substitute or to have substituted for this own character or *svabhava* a cosmopolitan veneer, for then indeed she must come before the world empty-handed.

Do we believe for a minute that India was always radical? Our architects and sculptors, writers and poets, musicians and dancers—they paid homage to art, to nature, to love, to aspiration. Every independent thinker and philosopher walked this land and sowed the seed of his philosophy here. There was no shame in seeking a different path or in living by another set of values. Every man chose his 'God' and changed it at will, as long as that faith sustained him. This was so not only with religions, but with vocations and social contracts as well. We are not born to the bondage of 'man-made institutions'. Faith is not entitlement or privilege. It is duty and service. The only bondage is to birth and death. This is the truth. The rest is what one makes of it. Interpreting one's faith is the prerogative of every individual. It is private and directed inward, to an inner being. Now in India it is loud, vociferous, dogmatic and public.

Where has the one family of people gone? We all believe in teaching our children to become world citizens, to rise above petty differences of race, colour and creed. Yet nowhere are a people more conscious of the differences. We will not let our sons marry girls from minority communities. We would rather they were dead than bring that curse upon ourselves. We will not employ them. And we do not bow our heads in shame when we massacre them. In April 1914, Annie Besant wrote,

> In a few hours I step on board the good steamer Mantua, and say good-bye for a short time to India, the Motherland of my Master, sacred and beloved. Then, for a space, to dwell among the many dear and loving friends whom good *karma* has linked me with under other skies and among other scenes. How good it is to know that, in all lands, we who are the servants of the Holy Ones form but *one family*, whatever may be our outer differences of birth and colour—*fair augury of that happier day for earth, when brotherhood shall transcend all differences, and when mutual love and mutual respect shall bind into unity, the many varying types of the children of men.*

What faith in destiny and in mankind! What lofty thoughts and ideals!

We do not dare to dream even, in our time. What is it that makes us such small people—wrapped up in the ego, in individuality, in the self really, unable to spread our energies outwards, so that we may reach other people, heal their spirit, give some joy and comfort? Perhaps we simply do not have it to give. We are bereft ourselves! Lost in the acquisition of worldly wealth of one kind or another, unable to spare some part of our time for the healing and rejuvenation of our own souls. How can we serve others?

III

The acquisition of, not 'knowledge', but skill has become the hallmark of today's teaching and learning experience. The best teacher is one who can translate a skill to the student— effectively and fast. There is no time to stop and reflect. Acquiring is the password, and this is all that one can manage in the blur of our busy lives. The greed for art in one's life exists, but neither the time nor the patience to savour it when it is there. Yet we must have it.

Can we actually possess Beauty—natural or creative? Is it possible to 'have it' or own it? If art or beauty washes over one slowly and serves to make us more aware, more understanding, more gracious— then it has served its purpose. But neither the art, nor the artist, and certainly not the viewer have any intention that the experience of it be a personal expression of or the receiving of grace. The intention is to show art and to see art, rarely to experience it. I quote Rukmini Devi when she said,

> Any expression of grace is finally absorbed in the individual longing for Beauty. When that experience has taken place, the individual is no longer the 'creator', but has become his poetry; the musician has become music itself and the creator of a masterpiece has become the masterpiece itself.
>
> (Huizen, Holland—Dec.'54.)

In our society, when the artist and the so-called *rasika* or viewer are immersed in a game of 'one-upmanship', how far are the teacher and her pupil from it? Money is the only thing that counts. If you can buy a good education, you can buy art too. And you think you can buy the artist, as well. And perhaps this is true.

In December 1898, at the close of the annual convention of the Theosophical Society in Adyar, Madras, Annie Besant gave an impassioned address on 'Theosophy and the Future of India'. She said, " When the greatest in the nation live a life that is simple, frugal and holy in the discharge of their duty; then only, when leaders are spiritual, shall they obtain all else". While any of us who might aspire to serve our community or country in political life or otherwise, might scoff at such an idea, it is perhaps wise to be conscious of the fact that our country was and is considered to be a 'spiritual' force first—a reservoir of philosophies, arts, civilizations and cultures. This is the soul of India. It belongs in this sense to the world, to eternity. Its arts are eternally creative. There is an enduring form, an enduring truth. While it is old, it is also perpetually new. While it is ancient, it is also modern. There is nothing ephemeral about India's traditions.

Understanding this is important, in order that we be comfortable with our arts, with our culture. We are embarrassed because the progressive western approach would be to date our art forms of dance and music, as they have done theirs—modern, post modern and so on. Having fallen into that trap, we do not wish to be seen as believers in old traditions. If art can stir the depths of one's heart and produce harmony of vision and thought within, it is enough. It does not matter to which age it belongs. Our art has always been impersonal, however particular to the nuances of human nature the feeling expressed is. It does not warrant praise, or criticism. Only a capacity 'to feel'. Artists in India composed *kriti* upon *kriti* in praise of God. There was no sense of the individual ego. The composer did not put a name to his compositions, only a dedication to his God. It is through these dedications that we know who the composer might be. He wrote of things that moved him, that pained him. Yet it was not personal. It could be any of us.

True art anywhere, has no place for superficiality. Knowledge, devotion, creative imagination and idealism are the hallmarks of good art. Good taste and aesthetics is the icing on the cake—a gift from the Gods! An appreciation of one's culture comes through an appreciation of the arts and writings of our people. Culture serves to broaden the heart. It serves to destroy prejudice, crudity and divisiveness. Many amongst us are products of a rigid and unimaginative system of education. The cry for culture and for better moral values cannot come from crowded classrooms. They must come from an appreciation of nature, from recognition of the beauty of form and spirit, from sensitivity to the elements that make up our being. The artist can be the voice of the higher life and a symbol of a culture.

Mushirul Hasan

Aligarh Muslim University: recalling radical days

Ab yaad-i raftagaan ki bhi himmat nahin rahi
Yaaron ne kitni door basai hai bastiyaan

— Firaq Gorakhpuri

Memories of the past cannot be invoked
Friends have moved their abodes so far away...

I

Jawaharlal Nehru would have noticed quite a number of familiar faces in the sprawling convocation pandal. Next to him on the podium sat Nawab Mohammad Ismail Khan, the vice-chancellor of Aligarh Muslim University. Adorning the front row of seats in the audience were members of the Muslim landed gentry handsomely dressed in their black *achkans*. There were others as well on that wintry afternoon in January 1948, awed by the occasion and by the Prime Minister's presence. He was at Aligarh Muslim University on a mission of goodwill, to provide the healing touch, allay the fears of a beleaguered intelligentsia, and assure them of a safe future. Listening with rapt attention to his eloquent speech, the audience admired his breadth of vision, and felt relieved that the university, having fallen on evil days, would have its rightful place in Nehru's India.

Long after this visit, the story doing the rounds was that the university's saviour was no other than Nehru. This image of him stayed until the late sixties and early nineteen seventies, even though the university, tainted by its association with the Pakistan movement in the 1940s,[1] had shrugged off its past and moved into the present. Those privileged to be its students did not carry the cultural and ideological baggage of the Partition days; instead, they saw themselves as the inheritors of the great modernist and reformist legacy pioneered by Syed Ahmad Khan, the founder of the M.A.O. College. They were reminded of what Maulana Abul Kalam Azad, the first education minister of free India, had said about Syed Ahmad challenging traditional values and outmoded beliefs to further the forces of change. He had declared: "The battle was fought here in Aligarh and Aligarh is the visible embodiment of the victory of the forces of progress."

Vishwa Bharati had its Rabindranath Tagore, Banaras Hindu University its Madan Mohan Malaviya. On the other hand, Syed Ahmad was the Muslim communities' prized trophy. Quite rightly, Muhammad Iqbal described him as 'the first modern Muslim to catch a glimpse of the positive character of the age that was coming,' and 'the first Indian Muslim who felt the need for a fresh orientation of Islam and worked for it.'

Aligarh had its own share of writers, poets, artists, musicians, and scholars. And because India's history has a strong majoritarian perspective, and, in some respects a pronounced Bengali bias, most educated Indians have scarcely heard of them. With India's cultural histories being contested and fractured, the voices of 'Muslim' poets, writers and intellectuals (they themselves did not see themselves as Muslims *per se*) are either unheard or brutally stifled. The result is for everybody to see: Mirza Ghalib, India's greatest poet in the nineteenth century, is, today, in his own words, *Main andalib gulshan-i na-afrida hun* (I am the bulbul of the garden uncreated). Iqbal is dismissed as an 'Urdu' poet, whereas Tagore is said to represent the 'Indian' genius speaking the universal language of love and compassion. People know of Faiz Ahmad Faiz, but how many have heard of Hasrat Mohani, Yas Yagana Changezi, N.M. Rashid, and Firaq Gorakhpuri? With some notable exceptions, most progressive writers and poets in Urdu too have faded into oblivion.

II

This is a contentious story. Let me therefore revert to the confidence and buoyancy of Aligarh's campus life during my student days from 1964 to 1969. As Aligarh's first vice-chancellor after Independence, Zakir Husain's eclectic vision and breadth of outlook stood in sharp contrast to the growing parochial tendencies in the institutions located in Uttar Pradesh. He tried to disassociate the university from the Muslim League past, provide a modernist and radical thrust to it, and harness the younger teachers' intellectual energies to great effect. In 1948, the year Zakir Husain joined Aligarh, an atmosphere of gloom and uncertainty prevailed on campus. But when he left in 1956 as Bihar's governor, he had already turned things around. His able and energetic successor, B.H. Zaidi, had facilitated the smooth accession of the princely state of Rampur to the Union. Now, in his new role, he carried forth Zakir Husain's unfinished agenda. And because of the elegant and finely proportioned buildings built by him, including the library named after Maulana Azad, Kennedy House, the Polytechnic and the Engineering College, he became Aligarh's Shahjahan. These modern structures, combined with the grand courts of the late nineteenth century, reveal purpose and achievement.

Aligarh's Islamic content was, contrary to popular perception, next to nothing. Sure enough, the university conducted its teaching and research programmes in Urdu, Arabic, Persian, and Islamic Studies; but so also did other universities. Most students and teachers were, admittedlyMuslims, and yet the campus ethos was neither 'Muslim' nor Islamic *per se*. Hindu-Muslim tension in the city recurred, but this did not polarise our sentiments. Many of our teachers were non-Muslims; so were our best friends. I do not recall any of my Muslim teachers making us aware of our Muslim or Islamic identity. We read what our counterparts in Delhi, Allahabad, and Banaras did.

Oddly enough, the Shia-Sunni divide rather than Hindu-Muslim antagonism became more and more apparent to us. While the Medical College and the Engineering College recruited scores of non-Muslim teachers, the Sunni establishment resented the appointment of three Shia vice-chancellors—Zaidi, Ali Yavar Jung and Badruddin Tyabji after Zakir Husain. Over the years, I discovered the anti-Shia sentiment was equally pronounced in several other Muslim institutions. When, for example, my father joined the Jamia Millia Islamia in the mid-1960s to establish the history department, he was explicitly told by its vice-chancellor not to appoint 'communists' and 'Shias'. When I became pro-vice-chancellor in the same university in February 1992, anti-Shia feelings, though dormant for a while, were heightened during a protracted controversy over the next few years.

Aligarh was, admittedly, socially conservative. But it was not the hotbed of bigotry or religious intolerance. Girls observed *purdah*, but not as widely as one would imagine. Campus life did not exactly pulsate with new ideas, but spaces for expressing creative energies existed. Mohammad Habib (1895–1971), who had studied with D.S. Margoliouth at New College, Oxford, inspired an entire generation of students. Few teachers of history and political science can ever have had so many pupils who were later to win distinction as scholars. He retired in 1958, but contemporaries remember his gracious and courteous bearing, the eagerness of his talk, and the humility that endeared him to those who knew him well. Hamza Alavi, the eminent sociologist, had this to say:

> What saved my soul at Aligarh (1942–44): was the personal friendship and future kindness of that great historian, Professor Habib. I went there with a letter of introduction to Mrs. Habib from her cousin, Maryam Khala, the wife of the late Mr. Justice Hatim Tyabji, who were our close family friends. At Aligarh Prof. Habib stood ten feet tall in the midst of the mediocrity that surrounded him. He was a source of inspiration and knowledge.[2]

Hamza Alavi soon gravitated to radical circles, though his involvement with left politics began with the rather mundane matter of food.[3] He developed close friendships with many comrades, including Sajjad Zaheer and Sibte Hasan, but did not join the Communist Party "because of serious reservations about its blatantly undemocratic character."

The Aligarh historians promoted the study of medieval Indian life in different ways. Nurul Hasan, in particular, did much for furthering historical study. His writing talents dried up after he published a few seminal papers, including one on "Nur Jahan's Junta"; but he lent much intellectual support to young and upcoming Marxist historians like Irfan Habib, Athar Ali, and Iqtidar Alam Khan. He talked freely, with a touch of formality, in short incisive questions; he listened as easily and naturally as he spoke. His circle of friends was large. I remember the excitement when we set our eyes on E.J. Hobsbawm, S. Gopal, Romila Thapar, and Parthasarthy Gupta. Some of us still recall our endearing teacher Noman Siddiqi, who, in his laconic style, insisted on pronouncing Hobsbawm as "Hobbs-bom".

These historians wrote books that set new standards of scholarship. Moving away from elite perspectives and the communal claptrap, they brought alive the people's history through a study of agrarian relations, and the very many forms of exploitation in the rural hinterland. Satish Chandra published a major book on parties and politics in the Mughal court. My father Mohibbul Hasan had moved to Aligarh from Calcutta, and earned respect for his study of Tipu Sultan. K.A. Nizami, who dug deep into the social and religious history of the thirteenth and fourteenth centuries, excelled as a teacher; his main strength lay in his clear thinking, and his words carried weight. He turned to the Persian texts and followed the lead of the evidence, and rarely indulged in bold generalisations. His scholarship was to continue for many decades, though he became drawn into university politics for awhile.

The elegantly dressed cigar smoking Abdul Waheed Qureishy was great fun. He knew his Lewis Namier, Herbert Butterfield, and Dorothy Marshall. The only problem with him was that he rarely went beyond the reign of George III. We were left to read the rest of British history on our own, or seek the help of the two young lecturers, Raj Kumar Trivedi and Arshad Ali Azmi, who were also familiar with the secondary literature on Bismarck. Irfan Habib was, of course, the rising star on the intellectual firmament. Though self-effacing, we knew full well that his agrarian history of the Mughals was a masterly piece of work that made its readers think, and added a lively, stimulating interest in economic history. Irfan used to ride a bicycle then, as he does now. His extremely charming economist wife, Saira, drove an ambassador car.

We were fortunate in so far as the history department attracted leading scholars of medieval India from all over the country and from overseas. Amongst them I remember A.B.M. Habibullah, who taught at the University of Dacca; Mahdi Husain, a leading authority on Muhammad bin Tughlaq; and Hasan Askari, the legendary teacher from Patna. I remember them also because they stayed with us at Haider Villa. K.M. Ashraf, a brilliant historian who should have been teaching in Aligarh and not at Delhi's Kirori Mal College, knocked at our door virtually every morning to demand *pan* from my mother. Over the years he and my father had exchanged letters on political issues that were subsequently sent to his German wife in East Berlin.

Aligarh had a galaxy of scholars. K.G. Saiyidain profiles them in his book, *Mujhe kehna hai kuch apni zabaan se*, and so does Ale Ahmad Suroor's autobiography. Although they had retired long before our days, their reputation was intact. We heard of Hadi Hasan, the London-educated professor of Persian, Rashid Ahmad Siddiqi, the Urdu scholar with a pungent sense of humour, Haider Khan, the science professor, and Mukhtar Hamid Ali, the popular English teacher. It is worth mentioning that in the 60s, Abdul Alim, Munibur Rahman and Maqbul Ahmed, rather than the Islamists, dominated the departments of Arabic and Islamic Studies. Alim Sahib, a major disaster as vice-chancellor, had been a key figure in the Progressive Writers' Movement. Munib, a poet now settled in the United States, lived in London from 1947 to 1953 before joining Aligarh, whereas Maqbul, a specialist on West Asia, had been a pupil of Ms. Ann K.S. Lambton at the University of London. Both had European wives, who added a certain variety and depth to the social landscape. As children we visited Maqbul Sahib's house called "Allah wali Kothi", enjoyed the cookies his wife baked, and spent hours playing with their daughter Zohra and my brother Najmul Hasan's girlfriend.

My father had ceased to be a fiery revolutionary, but he was radical enough to draw left-wing intellectuals to Haider Villa. Here they dined frequently, partaking of the elaborate Lakhnavi cuisine cooked by my mother, drank whisky, and engaged in heated discussions. I remember V.G. Kiernan staying with us on a couple of occasions. In those days the Marxist intellectuals gathered to discuss what was a hotly debated issue: the great divide between Moscow and Peking. Victor Kiernan, who had translated Mohammad Iqbal and Faiz Ahmad Faiz into English, was Professor at the University of Edinburgh. He and my father spent many years together in Amritsar and Lahore, along with Faiz and M.D. Tasir, the poet and literary critic.

Moonis Raza, who headed the All India Students' Federation at Aligarh in the early 1940s and returned to the university as lecturer, dominated the political landscape until the late 1960s.[4] With his expansive style, he, more than anyone else, gave a much-needed sense of the value of discipline and direction to the study of geography in India. Though feudal in his habits and life style, he could also be frugal, austere, and unconventional in his ways. He was a most exuberant man, and seemed to put all his strength into whatever he said or did. His genial personality, remembered especially by his colleagues at the Jawaharlal Nehru University, opened doors to him wherever he went.

Moonis Sahib's brother, the sherwani-clad and pan-chewing Rahi Masoom Reza (1927–1992), became a leading Hindi writer and, in Bollywood, wrote songs and scripts, including the script for B.R. Chopra's television series, *Mahabharat*. In his Aligarh days he was a bohemian, radical and revolutionary. Indeed, he talked of

Yeh chiragh jaise lamhe kahin raiga na jayen
koi kwhab dekh dalo koi inquilab lao.

This is what he wrote as the introduction to his celebrated Hindi novel *Adha Gaon* (Half-A Village), now translated by Gillian Wright:

> The Jana Sangh says that Muslims are outsiders. How can I pre-sume to say they're lying? But I must say that I belong to Ghazipur. My bonds with Gangauli are unbreakable. It's not just a village, it's my home. Home....I will remain Saiyid Masoom Reza Abidi of Ghazipur, wherever my grandfather hailed from. And I give no one the right to say to me, 'Rahi! You don't belong to Gangauli, and so get out and go, say, to Rae Bareli.' Why should I go, sahib? I will not go.[5]

Moonis and Rahi were essentially kind-hearted, friendly and generous, though Moonis Sahib, or bhai as he was affectionately called, was prone to encouraging mediocrity during his long career as an academic administrator. He, then living in Vali Manzil, Badar Bagh, in close proximity to Khurshidul Islam, wrote my English speeches for debates; Rahi Sahib, reputed to be Aligarh's Casanova, dictated to me the Urdu version. Rahi Sahib harnessed his creative energies even after moving to Mumbai, following a marriage that raised many an eyebrow in Aligarh circles. Though Moonis Sahib won laurels as Rector of the Jawaharlal Nehru University he concluded his innings as Delhi University's vice-chancellor somewhat ingloriously.

III

Why were so many intellectuals in Aligarh drawn to Marxism? For one, the processes had begun in the 1920s when attempts were made to synthesise socialism with Islam. This was the legacy of the firebrand Urdu poet, Hasrat Mohani. In the 1930s, socialism was the new revelation that young idealists could invoke to exorcise communal rancours, by uniting the majority from all communities in a struggle against their common poverty, and to make independence a blessing to the poor as well as to the elite.[6] Their fervour played a considerable role in the widening gap between the 'left' and the 'right', as people began to say. The university had on its rolls Khwaja Ahmad Abbas, Sardar Jafri, Sibte Hasan, the writer who migrated to Pakistan, and Ansar Harvani, founder of the Student's Federation and a devoted follower of Subhas Chandra Bose.[7] Abbas and Ansar Harvani wrote their memoirs that, sadly, so few have read. These capture life at Aligarh vividly.

Eventually though, the radical trends, though kept alive in certain circles, were overwhelmed by the tide of Muslim nationalism. However, once the Aligarh architects of Muslim nationalism left for Pakistan, the socialists and the communists, encouraged by Zakir Husain, moved to Aligarh from many places in north India. Socialism carried the same poetic and romantic appeal as poetic blasphemy in the works of the Persian poets Hafiz, Mirza Ghalib, and Hasrat Mohani.[8] When *Hindustan* published Asrarul Haq Majaz's poem *Andheri Raat ka Musafir* ('The Traveller in the Dark Night'), the poem inspired his young readers. One line ran thus:

> *Khuda soya huai hai, Ahraman mehshar ba-daman hai*
> God is asleep and Ahirman comes bringing doomsday to him.

This is not to suggest that Aligarh had suddenly become the stormcentre of the Communist movement. It had not. The Students' Federation was still a tame affair, drawing only a handful at Al-Hamra, the study circle tucked away across the imposing Sulaiman Hall Gate. Internal factions reigned supreme, and endless ideological wrangling was the order of the day. As a result, the left front split into numerous fractions. The traditional elements in Aligarh society, spearheaded in the 1950s and 60s by the pro-vice chancellor, Dr. Yusuf Husain Khan, were strong—so much so that girls were prohibited from appearing on stage. The History Department had its own share of traditionalists, who were invariably pitted against the left historians. Hence, both Satish Chandra and Mohibbul Hasan had to leave Aligarh.

Amidst the cacophony of noises, it is quite remarkable that a number of women teachers and students occupied the cultural spaces. Though the butt of ridicule and criticism, the three Zaidi sisters, as they were known, actively organised *mushairas* and music concerts and staged plays. Unconventional in their demeanour and often provocative in their style, especially when one of them would light a cigarette in full public view, they were serious academics and at the same time, activists. Grand daughters of the leading poet and writer, Altaf Husain Ali a contemporary of Syed Ahmad Khan, Sabira, Sajida and Zahida broke away from family traditions to bring much richness to Aligarh's intellectual and cultural ambience. Ghazala Ansari was one of their colleagues, and her brother Ziaul Hasan was a communist working with the *Patriot* for years. So was her husband Anwar Ansari, a soft-spoken individual who belonged to Lucknow's traditional Firangi Mahal family. Although the Tyabji family in Bombay had established this trend of women breaking away from established family traditions in Bombay, it was not so common among Muslim elites in north India.

By the time I entered the university in 1964 the Progressive Writers' Movement had withered away. Yet, Aligarh had its share of Progressive Writers and poets. Prominent amongst them was Khurshidul Islam, overshadowed for a while by Rashid Ahmad Siddiqi, head of the department.[9] Ale Ahmad Suroor had also moved from Lucknow to Aligarh in the mid-1950s, often mistaken for my father owing to a striking resemblance. Moin Ahsan Jazbi was around, but his poetry had lost its old vigour; so was the young lecturer Khalilur Rahman Azmi, who had been stabbed, thrown out of the train, and left for dead during the Partition violence. We had easy access to Waheed Akhtar, a fine writer and poet who taught philosophy, and the brilliant up-coming poet Shaharyar whom I got to know well as a post-graduate student. Asghar Bilgrami, the political scientist, was one of our favourite teachers. Invariably, he talked of his days in Geneva and complained of Aligarh's stifling atmosphere. He, Jamal Khwaja, the philosophy professor, and Aulad Ahmad Siddiqi, the economist, extended their fulsome support to our liberal concerns. They patronised the Secular Society that was needlessly targeted by the CPI (M) group.

In 1968–69 the hub of cultural activities was Kennedy House, with its imposing mural by M.F. Husain. While the *muezzin* called the faithful to prayers, one could hear Beethoven and Mozart in one of its music rooms specially devoted to western classical music. Or, one had the option of listening to Indian classical music. For the all-night *qawwali* sessions, we'd go to the shrine of Barchi Bahadur, a little distance from the district court; for *nautanki*, Farid Faridi's favourite pastime, to the exhibition ground. Thanks to Asadur Rahman, the English lecturer and his vibrant wife Shaista Rahman, one had a fair mix of English plays. My brother took the part of Teiresias in *Oedipus Rex* of Sophocles, the lead role in Galsworthy's *She Stoops to Conquer* and acted *Gentleman Caller* in Tennese William's *Glass Menagerie*. He also acted in George Bernard Shaw's *Arms and the Man*. Rahman's departure to United States and joining Brooklyn College created a void in our lives. Lest I forget, the star performer then and later was, admittedly, Naseeruddin Shah. He and I took part in a Mock

Parliament session in Delhi, and in a debating competition held at Jaipur. Muzaffar Ali, then a painter, Asghar Wajahat, now a famous creative writer in Hindi, Madhosh Bilgrami, and Humayun Zafar Zaidi were a part of a lively literary group. They congregated at a friends house on Marris Road and exchanged their poems over rum and whisky.

Aligarh was the site of not just the annual *mushaira* held at the sprawling Exhibition Grounds across the railway line—the great divide between the town and gown—but equally within university precincts. Thus we had the good fortune of listening to Firaq Gorakhpuri, Makhdoom Mohiuddin, Akhtar-ul-Iman, Sardar Jafri, and Kaifi Azmi. I recall Makhdoom reciting *Ek Chambeli ke Manwa tale* at Al-Hamra, Firaq prefacing his *ghazal* with 'Bhaiyya-re' and Akhtar-ul Iman, the poet from Anglo-Arabic College (now Dr. Zakir Husain College) and Aligarh-educated, reciting the following lines from his poem 'The Footprint' or *Naqsh-i Pa*:

> Where have life's travellers gone?
> Nobody knows.
> What is this world?
> No beginning, no end.
> The shackles of time yet bind it so fast.
> Where can I stand free of those chains?

IV

Yet, Aligarh had its pitfalls. Facilities at the university were excellent, but, with few notable exceptions, the institution did not produce scholars or scientists of excellence. Most people were obsessed with the preservation of the university's 'minority' character, and their conversations centred round the future of the minorities. There were no bookshops, except the Naya Kitab Ghar, run by Kishen Singh, an enthusiast communist, and married to the sister of the surgeon Nasim Ansari, also a member of the Firangi Mahal family. Social life, too, was restricted. There were no restaurants and no decent cinema halls, except for Tasvir Mahal that screened English films only on Sundays. With limited avenues for self-expression, faculty members developed lazy habits. Comfort and leisure was all that mattered to them. Although Delhi was only eighty miles away, a distance covered by the Kalka Mail in just three hours, the capital seemed beyond the realm of most people's imagination.

The segregation of boys and girls was still maintained in lecture rooms—though the winds of change were beginning to alter attitudes. More and more young women from the Women's College would hop on a rickshaw and travel to the campus to take part in cultural and literary activities. It was difficult for them to visit hostels, but Barbara, later married to my brother Najmul and my friend Salma turned out to be more defiant. More often than not, opportunities of meeting one's girl friend were limited to Friday afternoons. That is when we would dress up and head towards the Women's College, a remarkable institution headed by an equally remarkable lady, Mumtaz Haider, the mother of Salman Haider, India's former Foreign Secretary. She was indulgent towards our group, and supported our activities, including the publication of a fortnightly magazine, *Domain*, edited by my brother (the first issue in 15 October 1967). Jokingly, she'd refer to us the English-speaking types as the 'East India Company'.

Though the forces of traditionalism were entrenched, they were hardly visible to us, the students. I had a taste of their strength much later in 1968, when the traditionalists, accusing me of being a communist and a pseudo-secularist, which I was not, mobilised their resources to defeat me in the Student's Union election. Of all persons, Muzaffar Alam, a Deoband *alim* and now Professor at the University of Chicago, issued a *fatwa* in my support. Whether this or the hard work put in by my liberal/secular friends tilted the balance in my favour or not is hard to tell. What brought comfort to all of us was the narrow margin of my defeat. Liberal and left wing teachers, who had predicted my defeat by a huge margin, expressed much joy at my performance. The Vice-Chancellor Ali Yavar Jung was particularly delighted, and soon, I became his unofficial ambassador to various educational institutions.

Ali Yavar Jung became, tragically, the victim of a massive conspiracy. A group of students, backed by teachers and by certain key administrators, organised a brutal assault on his life on 25 April 1965. Today, that incident reminds me of my own trials and tribulations at the Jamia Millia Islamia from April 1992 to September 1997. Ali Yavar Jung, a suave person with an extremely dignified appearance, was targeted, along with some left-wing teachers that were present at the meeting of the University Court. Ali Yavar Jung's courage and resource did not fail during this desperate time. Yet, this was Aligarh at its worst. Battered and bruised, I remember some of them turning up at my sister's wedding on the same evening.

This assault traumatised campus life for years to come. M.C. Chagla, the Education Minister, over-reacted; and the ensuing ordinances stifled Aligarh's otherwise liberal and democratic ethos. Thereafter, a retrograde legislation which the Prime Minister Indira Gandhi disapproved, was pushed through. Though left-wing intellectuals berated the ordinance, their support in the university had steadily eroded owing to personal squabbles and sectarian visions. Tired and aging leftist stalwarts faded into oblivion. Others moved elsewhere; Moonis Raza to Srinagar and Nurul Hasan to Delhi, first as member of Rajya Sabha and later as Minister of Education. Historians like Irfan Habib kept the CPI (M) flag flying doggedly; but most saw the prospect of a revolution fading before their eyes. This symbolised the death of a radical tradition.

Zakir Husain had claimed in 1955: 'The way Aligarh works, the way Aligarh thinks, the contribution Aligarh makes to Indian life ... will largely determine the place Mussalmans will occupy in the pattern of Indian life.' Aligarh has negotiated with its past and succeeded in creating a niche for itself in the country's academic structures. At the same time, its alumni face the uphill task of preparing the fraternity of teachers and students to meet the challenges of this millennium. They need to complete Syed Ahmad's unfinished agenda of fostering liberal and modernist ideas and take the lead, once and for all, in debating issues of education, social reforms and gender justice. They need to interpret Islam afresh in the light of world-wide intellectual currents, come to terms with the winds of change and guide the 120 million Muslims within the framework provided by India's democratic and secular constitution, and equip them to cope with the harsh realities of life. This is what the great visionary Syed Ahmad would have expected them to do. Marshall Hodgson observed over two decades ago, 'the problem of the Muslims of India is the problem of the Muslims in the world.'

Observed one of the university's alumni in 1976:

> Aligarh needs to be shaken out of the ennui that has set in. With India's largest population of educated, intelligent Muslims collected in one place, Aligarh can provide, by its example and its ideas, the lead to the rest of the community. Muslims will have to pull themselves together, end the search for scapegoats and do something to help themselves. Minorities can never survive on government doles.[10]

References and Notes

1. Mushirul Hasan, 'The Local Roots of the Pakistan Movement: The Aligarh Muslim University' in Mushirul Hasan *Islam in the Subcontinent: Muslims in a Plural Society* (Delhi, 2002).

2. *Friday Times*, Lahore, October 17–23, 1996.

3. This is how the story goes in the words of Hamza Alavi: 'I had hardly been there (in Aligarh) for a couple of months ... when we decided that the only way to get the food situation sorted out was to launch a campaign to clean up the food administration. That was in the late afternoon. First thing next morning, at 8 am, Bhola, our bearer, brought summons for me to appear before A.B.A. Haleem, the Pro-Vice-Chancellor, at 9 am....His opening words were: "You are a fool who has fallen amongst thieves!" He pointed out to me that I had no previous background in politics and that I should not get mixed up in matters that I did not understand. I had come from a 'Hindu background' (from Poona). I should be grateful that fate had been kind to me and brought me to that great centre of Muslim culture and Islamic traditions....What really stung me were his parting words. As I got up to leave him he shouted after me: "Remember, if you fail to take heed of what I have told you, and if you persist in your Hindu activities, I will see to it myself that you are kicked back to the Hindu background from which you come". I was livid. As I left his room, far from being humiliated, I said to myself: "These bastards must be fought". I went round and joined the AISF. 'That was the first political step of my life.'

4. This is what Hamza Alavi wrote to me on 7 July 1994: 'I had become an active member of the AISF at Aligarh. But, in the wake of the change in CPI policy, one day an order came from above instructing us to disband the AISF branch at Aligarh. Each of us was required to join the MSF individually. That may or may not have been a justified policy at the time. But I was outraged by the undemocratic manner in which it was imposed on us without the slightest attempt to engage us in a discussion. I was quite appalled by that dictatorial method. But for that, who knows, I might even have joined the CPI. As for the Aligarh AISF, Moonis Raza, who was one of our elders at Aligarh and a CPI leader, with a handful of his CPI comrades refused to fall in with the new line, and continued to operate an unofficial AISF, in defiance of "orders". But his ... AISF was clearly no longer of any significance for we did not even know of its continued existence. It evidently operated in a clandestine way.'

5. Rahi Masoom Reza, *The Feuding Families of Village Gangauli*. Translated from the Hindi by Gillian Wright (New Delhi, 1991), pp. 290–1.

6. Faiz Ahmed Faiz, *Poems by Faiz*. Translated with an Introduction and Notes by V.G. Kiernan, Delhi, 2000 paperback edn., p. 23.

7. K.A. Abbas, *I Am Not An Island: An Experiment in Autobiography* (New Delhi, 1977), pp. 74–5.

8. Nasim Ansari, *Choosing to Stay: Memoirs of an Indian Muslim*, translated from Urdu by Ralph Russell, New Delhi, 1999, p. 30.

9. This is how Ralph Russell describes his meeting with Khurshidul Islam in 1949: 'There were several things I liked about him. Most of all, I suppose, it pleased me that he met me on warm, friendly, equal terms, without any trace of servility or of any desire to impress, and without any sort of formality. I liked his voice; I liked the ease and clarity with which he spoke Urdu; and I liked the thoughtfulness and coherence of the views he expressed.' Ralph Russell, 'Urdu & 1', *The Annual of Urdu Studies* (University of Wisconsin-Madison), Number 2, 1996, p.22.

10. Najmul Hasan, *Reporting India and its Neighbours* (Delhi, 1989), p. 323.

Krishna Kumar

A Memory of Coming to Life

I

U nder Gandhi's leadership, the struggle against colonial rule evolved into an interesting sketch of what one might reasonably call a national culture. Those born between the second and the fourth decade of the twentieth century—roughly between 1915 and 1935—appear to have had a good chance to get acculturated into this during their childhood and youth in many parts of India. By the early 1940s, it was already a little too late as the embryonic stirrings of what I am trying to commemorate as a national culture were facing formidable challenges, if they were not already a fading force. Apparently, the social forces harnessed by the national movement under the Congress leapt into a make-believe maturity under Gandhi's charismatic and nurturant authority. When that authority started to wane, these forces receded into their juvenile state.

Independent India, with the elderly and de-graced Gandhi assassinated by a valid representative of the reaction he had triggered, was left with a state without a cultural life backing it. Tagore had warned Gandhi about this possibility with cold precision, but there was little Gandhi could have done without stopping to be himself. Given the cleavages between his upbringing or socialisation and his agenda, one is hardly surprised by the limits of what he achieved; rather, one is shocked. Subsequent to the diminution of his authority, and finally his forced disappearance, the social forces he had unleashed exhibited the lack of intrinsic motivation and the skills to conserve what they had attained. The stirrings of a national culture Indian society had heard in its deeper mind started to sink. A barren sound of the state's drum, under Nehru's sincere command, continued to remind the people that they had had a singing class.

Before I proceed to portray the substance of the fleeting phenomenon I have identified, I would like to devote some space to explicating the two terms, 'culture' and 'national'. Not that there are not enough definitions around, but in the kind of conditions that prevail in India today there is no harm in recalling the commonplace. That culture and the nation are both always in the making—and not just in the so-called developing societies—can no more be regarded as an everyday truth. Children are being told to feel proud of India because it had a glorious culture in ancient times. In this ethos, it may feel strange to be reminded of the ordinary fact that cultures thrive on tacit knowledge, and therefore, the need to indulge in explicit glorification betokens death.

We live in the age of documentation, an activity that necessarily implies the fear of losing something. It also contradicts the principle of knowledge, about life and the world (including aspects beyond our examining reach and reachable only with the help of imagination), which marks a living culture. The bulk of it must be tacit, and accessible only by sharing both space and life. Turning this larger part of the knowledge that a culture inheres into a description runs the risk of sounding absurd. Essentialisation, often through a process of reification, threatens to distort the proportions of ordinary matters beyond recognition. When words become the primary instrument of talking *about* a culture, the universe of tacitly held understandings— held obviously in a web of relationships—is turned into a rational struggle.

This unfortunate transformation is at the heart of the difficulty underlying the relationship between culture and education. The difficulty is so great that even decent, great theorists of education like Dewey and Tagore face it gingerly; others generally avoid it. The basic trouble is that education in modern conditions is a highly literate exercise: it depends so much on words that cannot safeguard against essentialising whatever it deals with. The only safeguard education can offer are uncertain resources like the teacher's personality and the ethos of the institution. These resources become inaccessible when the teachers' selection, training and conditions of work cease to require more than bureaucratic handling; and when the idea of an ethos becomes so unfashionable that the internet is presented as an alternative to libraries and gardens are maintained for announcing status, not for giving children a chance to look after plants and insects.

Luckily both Gandhi and Tagore were aware of the tenuous linkage between education and culture, though their writing on this subject is shrouded in contemporary discourses.[1] Their ideas, and even more their practices, are important for us because education is in modern societies a prime instrument of what is customarily referred to as nation-building. If nations need a cultural sketch to live in, the instrumental value of education for pencilling such a sketch will stay limited so long as teaching and learning are literacy-centred. Indeed, the use of education for nation-building turns out to be quite self-evidently dangerous when nation-building is undertaken by hostile neighbours like India and Pakistan. In both, education has become a ready-to-use tool for the destruction of culture. How these rather well-built nations will survive without living cultures is anybody's guess. But let me return to making one more point about culture which I have borrowed from Mahadevi Verma.

She makes a distinction between the *nirmit* and the *nirmanadhin* aspects of culture and favours attention to the latter. We can translate these two Hindi terms of hers as, respectively, the 'finished' or 'built-up' and that which is 'under construction'. The former aspect of a culture commands admiration but symbolizes the principle of decay, literally because something already completed can only decline, whereas the latter aspect symbolises change and growth, suggesting hope. The distinction assumes remarkable complexity when we place it in the context of Mahadevi's definition of culture as a self-renewing energy. Culture, she says, is the means by which life in society purges or refines itself and which preserves the qualities born in the course of the purging. This is as close as I could get to translating Mahadevi's tight Hindi prose; but I can do better by putting my own metaphorical gloss over it. We can elucidate her definition by regarding culture as a soap which rinses away the impurities resulting from the daily struggle of living; miraculously, the soap is made from the used, dirty rinse-water. In this peculiar chemistry of culture, the messier or richer the rinse-water, the more effective the soap. On the firm cybernetic ground of this metaphor stands the argument that a culture must remain mostly 'under-construction', or else it will hasten its own death.

Now to apply this logic of Mahadevi to retracing the Indian project, we notice that it concerned a gigantic reinvention by means of the intermixture of cultural specificities and the reduction of inequities. The chances of a *national* culture taking a form—without hurting other forms or substituting them, or in any way claiming to become *the* national culture—depended on the scale and the subtlety with which the intermixing would occur and the willingness with which inequities would be reduced. Implicit in these processes was the opening of religious, linguistic, and ethnic borders, the hastening of measures like land redistribution and the inclusion of Dalits in the apparatuses of the state and civil society. Directly hurting some and making many chronically sullen were necessary parts of the game initiated by the national movement, well before Gandhi's arrival. He made it look real, that is all; and that is what made the deadly difference. Angry and nervous about the rise of the downtrodden, the upper caste Hindu communities politicised themselves into a kind of counter-consciousness which nurtured the dream of an alternative national culture. It fed the already active search for cover among the Muslim elite.

Once formed, the state of free India offered security for individual freedom and an isolated mechanism for social justice. Neither was smoothly reconcilable with caste and patriarchy, both of which had sanction in religion. A voluntary and vast war on socially inherited structures of allegiance was the core national culture that surfaced between the second and the fourth decades of the twentieth century, shaping the socialisation of countless individuals. Nationalism clearly offered a far wider programme than independence, and Gandhi's idea of *swaraj* was of a moral responsibility to rule ourselves differently from how the British had ruled us. Many people who grew up during those decades, especially women, lived life in ways not recognised earlier; others dreamed.

Tagore's delineation of the 'heaven of freedom' sketches that dream in two strokes: 'where the mind is without fear and the head is held high'. Gandhi's contribution towards making both these components of Tagore's dream a reality is a historical fact that probably no critic of his will choose to deny. He made common men and women capable of taking the mighty British empire in their stride. This he did by selecting such ordinary things as salt and cloths a symbolic venues for fighting against colonialism. But apart from the symbols he chose, his style—both in writing and living—had the gift of what Calvino (with, of course, no reference to Gandhi) calls 'lightness' in his last book, *Six Memos for the Next Millennium*. In the first memo Calvino explains lightness as 'a value rather than a defect' in the context of his own efforts to 'remove weight, sometimes from people, sometimes from heavenly bodies, sometimes... from the structure of stories and from language'.[2] Calvino's memos were prepared in 1984; in Gandhiana we find plenty of examples that Calvino would have approved. His photograph taken outside the Buckingham Palace or the one with his hand on Lady Mountbatten's shoulder as they enter the Viceregal Lodge (both pictures are given in Louis Fisher's book on Gandhi)[3] offer us vivid examples of his determination (it hardly matters whether it was conscious or not) to take weight off powerful people. His confidence in his own dignity made the British look a little silly, and starkly unfair. This is how his own body and conduct became like salt and khadi—easy-to-read haikus of India's pride. Today we can hardly grasp this language without making a special effort simply because we have come a long way. Our children are now said to be in the need of being told about the Vedas and what mathematics they might contain, not to mention the Hindu ability to kill large numbers of Muslims in street encounters as displayed in Gujarat, in order to feel self-confident and secure. Gandhi's way was subtler.

The same could be said of his writing, if additional proof was needed to make the point. That it is possible to break out is conveyed in *Hind Swaraj*, not so much by meaning or assertion as by a cacophony of disagreements. I can imagine Gandhi's personality to be a bit like this book: ridiculously bold, yet so modest and graceful as to distract people from the extreme nature of his disapproval of established truths. Ambivalence was a necessary part of his strategy, and so was frequent shifting of position. This last characteristic has made Gandhi a victim of all-round appropriation; currently, it is the Hindu Right's turn; never mind that they killed him. They and their sympathisers can plentifully quote him on cow slaughter, Sanskrit, the varna system, and so on. One thing they cannot afford to imitate is his lightness which permitted him to be so inventive, and the total lack of which makes them so stodgy. Gandhi put people together around the hallucination of a nation no one could define except by saying it was worth trying out. People who acquired an instant citizenship of the India run by Gandhi's stick included energetic young minds like Nehru and a few million others who must have felt a little dizzy, yet driven.

Now *that* is precisely what Tagore was worried about. Popular upsurge was fine, he thought, but without a cultivated mind to hold it, a dangerous rebound could occur. These are his words from an article on the *charkha* cult written in 1925.[4]

> Some strong and wide-spread intoxication of belief among a vast
> number of men can suddenly produce a convenient uniformity

of purpose, immense and powerful. It seems for the moment a miracle of a wholesale conversion; and a catastrophic phenomenon of this nature stuns our rational mind, raising high some hope of easy realisation which is very much like a boom in the business market. The amazingly immediate success is no criterion of its reality,—the very dimension of its triumph having a dangerous effect of producing a sudden and universal eclipse of our judgement. Human nature has its elasticity, and in the name of urgency, it can be forced towards a particular direction far beyond its normal and wholesome limits. But the rebound is sure to follow, and the consequent disillusionment will leave behind it a desert track of demoralisation. We have had our experience of this in the tremendous exultation lately produced by the imaginary easy prospect of Hindu-Muslim unity. And therefore I am afraid of a blind faith on a very large scale in the *charkha* in the country, which is so liable to succumb to the lure of short cuts when pointed out by a personality about whose moral earnestness they can have no doubt.

These were thoughts appropriate for a pedagogue. Tagore's awareness that learning takes time, that there is no substitute for it, extended to the infrastructure of custom and hierarchy, poverty and drudgery that predated colonial rule and were consolidated by it. Tagore was an artist as well, and his pedagogic experiments were unique in the emphasis they placed on the training of sensibility. Tagore and Gandhi came from two rather different universes of early socialisation, and they acted and responded to many situations in dissimilar ways, but they recognised and prioritised the same issues as India's problems. Gandhi's campaign mode apparently filled Tagore with both awe and suspicion—awe for its splendid success, and suspicion in its residues. Tagore was afraid that Indian society will not change all that much under Gandhi's magic; it would only acquire a memory of coming to life.

II

The job of managing memory is normally done in modern conditions by the system of education. It is a difficult job, but who needs to be reminded of that in the year 2002 when the highest court in the land has failed to protect India's children from resolute and unscrupulous manipulators of memory? To preserve the rich and complex memory of the national culture brought alive in the

Gandhi era of the freedom struggle was a stupendous task. An unreformed colonial system of education was simply not up to it. If God were to initiate an inquiry into the poor performance of secularism in India, surely one of the key terms of reference will be why education was *not* perceived as the central agency for consolidating secularism. Those providing intellectual inputs in the state's enterprise of promoting secularism also showed little interest, and even less insight, in education. You can read whichever author you prefer on this matter, you will find that education is nobody's concern. Of course, each one of them occasionally chants education as a *mantra*, but its tedious complexity as a means and the details of the task involved in reforming it remain unrecognised, almost as if these are boring matters, suitable for lesser minds to handle. One cannot help saying that the superficiality of educational policy and discussion reveals the colonised character of the secular discourse itself. And from this viewpoint, what India has gone through over the last decade, from Ayodhya to Gujarat, is simply the price paid for a backlog.

In all likelihood, the payment will have to continue. As I indicated earlier, the transformative national culture demanded engagement with a varied range of issues, from land reforms to language planning. Education was a key challenge inasmuch as its character would determine whether society could absorb modernity without losing the 'tacit' property of culture (in the sense explained earlier). Both Gandhi and Tagore had worked out models of educational planning which emphasised the tacit aspect of learning. Gandhi's model suggested the use of crafts for this; Tagore's model featured an aesthetic core. Instead of trying to synthesise the two, national policy ignored both, and from the mid-1960s (the turning point being the report of the Kothari Commission) candidly advocated a book-centred approach to school teaching. [5] Not just Gandhi and Tagore, other philosophical resources too, such as Sri Aurobindo and Krishnamurty, were ignored.

Those in charge of educational planning appeared to have no interest in or patience for the philosophical basis of education. For them, education was a crude instrument of nation-building, and nation-building itself meant what Tagore would have called the cultivation of a national ego. By the early 1980s it was clear that education, like radio and television, was of concern to the state merely as a means of propaganda. And we know all too well by now that propaganda was needed in plenty, to hide India's national failure on the welfare front and to highlight its irreversible march towards becoming a nuclear power. The memory of a *nirmanadhin* national culture was finally fading and militaristic nationalism, by definition devoid of any creative principle, was taking over.

There is historical irony in this development. Of the two national projects born in Partition, the Indian project claimed to be more imaginative because it repudiated, and not just shunned, the application of religion as a binding force. As a new nation, Pakistan was based precisely on that applicability of religion, but soon enough it slipped into using religion to cover the state's failure to provide welfare to the people and its own capitulation to global imperialism. It is a strange fact of our times that Pakistan's religio-militaristic nationalism is setting the tone for us, rather than Indian nationalism—with its promise of democratic social change—serving as an inspiration for Pakistan.[6] Both neglected educational reform, permitting their poverty of historical common sense to be perpetuated by a ramshackle system of school education fit only for use as a propaganda machine.

III

In India, some of us are inconsolably pained these days because our propaganda machine has been stolen by those who have an altogether different script to propagate. In this moment of grief, it is easy for us to overlook the pathetic state of our system of education, irrespective of the shoddy and vicious sense of history that is about to be dispersed through it. Culture and history are among the most sensitive areas of learning because, while dealing with them, schools must engage with the child's socialisation at home. All colonial systems of education have the tendency to isolate the child at school from the living reality of daily practices witnessed at home. Curricular arrangements reflecting this tendency benefit from superficial training of teachers, their low economic status, and the predominance of prescribed textbooks and centralised examinations. By overlooking this inner world of education, Indian state planners permitted the penetration of schools by ideological forces inimical to the Constitution and its intellectual heritage. In Pakistan, the post-colonial state compromised with religious revivalists all too soon, allowing what little liberal substance the colonial dispensation had to die out.

The two national trajectories differ, but their points of arrival are remarkably similar. It is all too clear that South Asia is now a ready-to-use battleground for two matched militaristic nationalisms. Notwithstanding the fact that India is still a functioning democracy and Pakistan has failed to become one, they both have joined the list of the world's biggest buyers of modern, sophisticated weapons. And, of course, they are both proud owners of nuclear weapons of mass destruction. As inheritors of what undoubtedly was the greatest national movement in the entire colonial world, they both owe an explanation to the world. The explanation must come in two parts: one, How did they fritter away the moral legacy of the freedom struggle?; two, How did they end up becoming a major threat to world peace and potential perpetrators of regional suicide?

References and Notes

1. In her *Gandhi, His Gift of the Fight* (Hoshangabad: Friends Rural Centre, 1987), Marjorie Sykes provides some comparative insights into Gandhi and Tagore's ideas. She had worked with both.
2. Italo Calvino, *Six Memos for the New Millennium* (New York: Vintage, 1988) p.3.
3. Louis Fischer, *The Life of Mahatma Gandhi* (1951; London: Granada, 1982).
4. Sabyasachi Bhatacharya (ed.), *The Mahatma and the Poet* (New Delhi: National Book Trust, 1997) p.101-102.
5. For a discussion of this turning point, see my 'Agricultural Modernisation and Education: Contours of a Point of Departure' in *Economic & Political Weekly* (Vol. 31, Nos. 35-37, special number, 1996) pp. 2367-2373. The Kothari Commission report was written during 1964-66.
6. For an understanding of the complex interlocking of Indo-Pak memories and perceptions, and for a comparative study of the textbooks of history the children of the two countries are required to read, see my *Prejudice and Pride* (New Delhi: Viking/Penguin, 2001).

III
VOICES: AFFIRMING PLURALITY

U.P. GOVERNMENT, HAVING FAILED TO NAME THEIR PROVINCE "ARYAVARTA" ARE REPORTED TO BE ADOPTING THE NEXT BEST NAME.

MARCH OF TIME in Shankar's Weekly November 27, 1949

Alok Rai

The Persistence of Hindustani

The ghost of Hindustani continues to haunt the language debate in our country. Whenever the matter of Hindi and Urdu is discussed, it has been observed, tempers fray and voices rise— and then, inevitably, the name of Hindustani is brought up as a pacific compromise. It has been playing this role, *unsuccessfully*, for a long time now. This essay is an attempt to see whether this ghost can finally be laid to rest—if only to free ourselves to attend to the real issues for which the name can only be, after all, but a nominal solution.

A ghostly continuity implies a prior unghostly existence... but with Hindustani, its being appears to have been, at best, ectoplasmic from the very outset, always hovering on the edge of existence and, indeed, frequently falling off it altogether. Thus, on the 9th November 1948 in the Constituent Assembly Ghanshyam Singh Gupta reported:

> I was in search of simple Hindustani. I could not find it in the constitutional proceedings, I could not find it in the law books.... The official proceedings of this House are published in 3 languages: English, Hindi and Urdu. I read English, I read Hindi and I got read (sic) Urdu with the idea that I might be able to find what they call simple Hindustani. I could not find it. Urdu was Urdu and Hindi was Hindi. There was no such thing as simple Hindustani.... It is only in the bazaar that I could find simple Hindustani. When we cannot have simple Hindustani even in the elementary school books, how can our laws be made in it?[1]

Ironically, though, the very volumes that record these momentous debates describe the vernacular in which both Seth Govind Das and Maulana Hasrat Mohani, among others, addressed the Assembly as 'Hindustani'. But at the end of these debates, when the 'Schedule' of Indian languages is being drawn up, the list of 14 languages does not include this same Hindustani![2] Like another famous ghost, Hindustani too might have something important to tell us.

II

Scholars of nationalism distinguish between two broad kinds. The first of these may be characterised as geographical-territorial; the second, associated primarily with the name of the 19th century German thinker Herder, is cultural-linguistic. There is a further distinction to be found in the literature—that between patriotism and nationalism proper. Thus, patriotism is the affective commitment to a particular place and its ways of being; and nationalism, on this account the bad sister, so to speak, is the assertion of the *superiority* of one's own particular 'nation' against other competing 'nations'. These 'nations' may be, and often are, found (discovered/invented) within the same geographical-territorial domain. Then again, these categories are both fluid and overlapping, and there is the residual and inescapable ambiguity of the term 'nation' itself—is it something 'given' or 'achieved'?—which renders this terrain both intellectually and politically treacherous.

The inherent 'naturalness' of the Indian landmass lends itself easily to illusions of divine ordination. After all, one has only to look at the rhythmic elegance of the Indian subcontinental landmass, clearly demarcated from the rest of Asia by high mountain ranges and, somewhat messily, by the north-western deserts, washed by three seas, by the dark waters of the Bay of Bengal and the blue waters of the Arabian Sea—to fall prey to some version of the thought that God '*intended*' India. Variations on this theme may be found all the way from the Vishnupurana to modern times. From this purely aesthetic point of view, the violence of Partition was more than merely physical—it rent asunder that which God had, manifestly, Formed.

In the course of history, however, this, and such, 'naturalness' has had little persuasive appeal, except for those who are its beneficiaries. Thus, our colonial masters, for instance, were unlikely to abandon the colonial enterprise of 'civilising' India merely on the aesthetic grounds that their presence here was an intrusion into something that was already sufficient and complete. Even as God rested, satisfied with his handiwork, having pared his fingernails, the mischievous Brits stole in… In other words, the geographical-territorial version of nationalism had to be supplemented, during the course of the Independence struggle, by other linguistic and cultural forms, which drew on more immediate loyalties, and therefore commanded greater mobilisational force. Thus, the emergence of the freedom movement is also the period during which different cultural and linguistic regions begin to acquire a self-conscious regional awareness. The tension between the regional and the supra-regional—if not yet, or always, or consensually, 'national'—is familiar to all students of the evolution of our modern being. The inherent and exhilarating (and sometimes infuriating) diversity of India lends itself being configured in different ways in order to yield different 'unities', different and competing 'ideas of India'.

But for all that cacophony and contention, there was general agreement on the idea that there must be *one* national language. After the first flirtations with polite 'memorandum' nationalism, it was realised that the communicational-mobilisational needs of the movement required that this national language be one that would be accessible to the broad masses of the Indian people. Gandhi is often credited with the political initiation of this idea; but forms of this are to be found much before Gandhi's advent into Indian politics, in the writings of sundry forward-looking thinkers, particularly from Bengal. Thus, speaking on 14 Sept 1949, Purushottam Das Tandon, the Hindi ideologue, reminded the Constituent Assembly:

> We have been speaking of a national language for years and years. It is not a new subject before the House. It was in the 19th century that this idea of a national language took shape in Bengal, not in U.P. or Bihar...

Lakshmi Kant Maitra, representing Bengal, grumbled: "We have been amply rewarded for all that!"[3]

The fact is that for all the unanimity on the question of the desirability of having *one* national language, the question of what that language would be often came close to wrecking the constitution-making process altogether. One can only imagine what went into the making of the exasperation that T.T.Krishnamachari voiced: "Has anybody in the House given one moment of thought to those of us in this House, who have been merely gaping unintelligently because we could not understand what is being said?" TTK was assured by a Kannadiga friend that 'there was not much substance in the Hindi speeches that have been made', but he went on nevertheless to "convey a warning on behalf of the people of the South... there are already elements in South India who want separation and it is up to us to tax the maximum strength we have to keeping those elements down, and my honourable friends in U.P. do not help us in any way by flogging their idea 'Hindi Imperialism' to the maximum extent possible. Sir, it is up to my friends in U.P. to have a whole-India; it is up to them to have a Hindi-India...'[4]

Although the Hindi of Seth Govind Das and 'Rajarshi' Purushottam Das Tandon was vociferously urged upon the Constituent Assembly as the inescapable instrument of national unity, it soon revealed itself as a threat to such unity. The wise people who were running the Constituent Assembly managed to save the situation by deferring the question of language until the very end, when most of the Constitution was in the bag already, and members were reluctant to abandon the whole project, or start all over again.

However, the universally and consensually acceptable 'national' language, prior to the convening of the Constituent Assembly, was not Hindi but Hindustani. There, as we have remarked already, it continued to lead its ghostly existence, hovering between being and non-being. G.A.Grierson, in his monumental *Linguistic Survey of India* (1916) declared that "Hindustani is so well-known a language that it would be a waste of space to give more than the merest sketch of its grammar".[5] Only a few decades later, people doubted whether it existed at all. To be fair to him, what Govind Das said is that 'the question of Hindustani ... exists no more.'[6] However, irrespective of whether it is exaggerated reports of a demise that we are dealing with, or life after death, the fact of the matter is that 'the question of Hindustani' refuses to lie down and stay dead, so to speak.

It isn't only Hindi fanatics who have denied the existence of anything such as Hindustani—like the Gupta who went looking for simple Hindustani and failed to find it. There are the liberal Hindi protagonists who see, in the very name of Hindustani, the insinuation that their Hindi is distinct from the generous people's language—thus, for them, Hindustani is encompassed in Hindi. Likewise, for a liberal Urdu scholar like S.R. Faruqi, Hindustani does not exist except as the index of a malign attempt to confine the name of Urdu to the 'high' Urdu register, heavy with Arabo-Persian borrowings, and deny Urdu's claim to the people's language which Faruqi also calls Urdu. Thus, while the hybrid linguistic *domain* of Hindustani is anathema to the purists on both sides, its *name* is denied by liberal Hindi-and Urdu-wallahs who are both eager to annex the domain.

III

It might be interesting, at this point, to look at the evolution of the name Hindustani. The colonial origins of the name are well-known. It seemed entirely logical for the colonisers to assume that the people of the place that they had conquered—Hindustan—should have a language that could be called Hindustani. Apparently, the name 'Hindustani' was not unknown even before the advent of the British— although, obviously, only outsiders could feel the need to name the unknown language(s) of the strangers whom they encountered in the land of Hind. Thus, there are sundry occurrences in 16th and 17th century Persian texts.[7] But the name of Hindustani never caught on among the locals, as it were. Indeed, Gilchrist, writing in the late 18th century, went on to say that he would use the name Hindustani in preference to all other names "of the popular speech of the country ... *whether the people here constantly do so or not"*[8.]

The interesting question here concerns the limits of colonial knowledge, and also the limits of the effectivity of colonial knowledge—and, indeed, colonial ignorance.[9] Thus, the ascription of a unity, albeit false—and a misnomer—on the intercommunicating languages and dialects of the people, *particularly as this translated into administrative practice and publishing activity*, could hardly be without effect. Thus, the colonial authorisation of the name of 'Hindustani' was bound to be something akin to a self-fulfilling prophecy, with an ambiguous impact on the *fact* or real existence of Hindustani, as a language-system that enabled at least contigual communication even in pre-colonial times, particularly in alliance with modern communication technologies. Gilchrist cites the famous Orientalist, H.T.Colebrooke on the existence of an

> elegant language which is used in every part of Hindoostan and the dukhin, which is the common vehicle of intercourse among all well-educated natives and among the illiterate also, in many provinces of India; and which is almost everywhere intelligible to some among the inhabitants of every village...[10]

This language, which could be called Urdu, and Hindi, can only be Hindustani, capacious and tolerant as it spans the range from the speech of 'well-educated natives' down to the demotic dialects of diverse peoples.

The name of Hindustani, however, remained confined to colonial usage, in the main, until we come to the latter half of the 19th century. Once it became crucial for the emergent Hindi-Hindu savarna proto-elite in the period after 1857 to make space for themselves in the colonial administration11—the shared and overlapping linguistic space had to be divided and split up. Then, the name Hindustani could mean either that overlapping part of the continuum which was common to both Hindi and Urdu—which was no fun at all if one was thinking of making space for oneself in the zero-sum game of the colonial administration. Or Hindustani could mean that part of the continuum which was neither Hindi nor Urdu—in which case it disappeared altogether, as it did for Mr Ghanshyam Gupta. As the politics of dissension gathered steam, and—mixing metaphors madly—snowballed and ramified, 'Hindustani' came to denominate the terminological compromise which was advocated by Gandhi, among others. However, compromise was the last thing anybody had on their mind at that time. 'Hindustani' left both the combatants dissatisfied and suspicious: each saw the name as a Trojan horse for the other side—even as it sought, with manifest contradiction, both to distance itself from, and to claim, also for its democratic legitimacy, the common terrain! In this kind of force-field, Gandhi's compromise formulation—'Hindi or Hindustani' was doomed to failure. That *or* could connote either alterity or identity. It could mean either that Hindi was the same as Hindustani, so the mullah was up in arms; or that Hindustani was an alternative to Hindi, so the pandits, quite as pugnacious, would have none of it.

Census data offers a comic—also tragic—illustration of the fate of Hindustani in our troubled times. Thus, between 1931 and 1951, the numbers of people claiming Hindustani as their mother tongue in U.P. declined by 86.4 %, and by 98.5% in the period 1951–1961. Similar catastrophic declines—disappearing millions!—reflect little more than the communalisation of linguistic identities. Comparable figures are reported from M.P. and Andhra Pradesh.[12] Hindustani isn't the only language-description to have got caught up in the politics of identity. Thus, in the 1941 census for Punjab, language statistics were not collected—because it turned out that there were no Punjabi speakers there at all: the Muslims claimed Urdu as their mother tongue, and all the others claimed Hindi![13] The 1971 census still recognised Hindustani, albeit grouping it under Hindi—but subsequent censuses have eliminated Hindustani altogether. The terminological difficulty is so acute that one is tempted to abandon the name altogether—except that there is something valuable in the idea of Hindustani that continues to haunt us—as opposed to the reality of it, which is at best ambiguous.

IV

In terms of cultural recovery there is a further wrinkle that must be factored into our thinking about Hindustani. As far as the colonial origins or adoption of the name are concerned—that is at worst an indication of pacific intent, an attempt to deny and hopefully reverse, by means of a nominal initiative, the emerging linguistic divide between Hindi and Urdu, the gathering, spiralling extremisms—a far cry indeed from the 'divide and rule' strategy too easily discerned by semi-literate nationalists. But in his great 1879 Dictionary of Hindustani, Fallon cites this usage by way of illustrating the meaning of 'bhuccha' or yokel: "Kaisa bhuccha hai, Hindustani nahin jaanta." I suspect that there is a whole, still unravelling, social history packed into that remark.

Of course it is important to understand the hostility that the name of Hindustani provoked among the Hindi protagonists in terms of the greed and envy of a hungry proto-elite—but there is something else there also, and that has to do with the social profile of Hindustani. As the Fallon quote indicates, Hindustani was the language of urbanity: it was the language of the socially dominant Avadh elite. The OED, Second Edition, identifies Hindustani as 'the language of the Muslim conquerors of Hindustan, being a form of Hindi with a large admixture of Arabic, Persian, and other foreign elements; also called Urdu...' S.R.Faruqi, op.cit., is rightly critical of this identification with the 'Muslim conquerors'—after all, they came from different places, and used different languages—but the association of Hindustani with urbanity and contiguity to feudal power structures is less easily dispelled. The Avadh elite comprised both Muslims and Hindus, and while its social position implied that it, and therefore its language, was associated with education and modernity and a shared (composite) culture, it was also, inevitably, associated with social privilege. And the hostility that that privilege provoked in the upstart Hindi proto-elite—relatively rustic, excluded from the feudal-aristocratic world of the Avadh elite—was easily extended to the whole cultural package. It is entirely understandable that the Hindi counter-elite, politicking for a place in the sun, against the already ensconced Avadh elite, had no love for this cultural package. But when the politics gathered pace, it turns out, neither? did significant sections of the Avadh elite—i.e. those that powered the Muslim League.[14] The conflation of Hindustani with Urdu, and then of Urdu with Muslim, was the retrospectively ineluctable consequence of this political dialectic.

Of course it would be unfair to saddle Hindustani with the entire poisonous history. Hindustani was also the language of popular mobilisation, of affective communication, then and now. Much of the poetry of the freedom movement, in this part of the country, is in a language that can be identified as Hindustani: it is also, be it said, often the work of people who are beneficiaries of privilege—but so must every other movement be in a society in which merely to rise above a bare, animal existence is already an indication of privilege. But the fact that Hindustani was imbricated—but not complicit—with the Avadh feudal order meant that a whole range of cultural possibilities could be represented as being tainted, even as it enabled the Hindi counter-elite—primarily upper-caste and conservative, even reactionary—to pretend to a democratic, popular legitimacy whose consequences are all around us even today.

Summing up in his account of the constitutional debate a propos, Granville Austin remarks, Partition killed Hindustani.[15] The implied antithesis between the two explains the continued lure, the ghostly persistence of Hindustani—as something that might assist in the process of recovery from the cultural consequences of Partition. But the chances don't look too good. In a recent paper, Hindustani was described, sensitively, as not quite a language, but rather a zone of 'anxiety' between Hindi and Urdu.[16] This is a pity, because a large part of the power and delight of Hindustani consists precisely in the way it enables the skilled user to play with polymorphous perversity, so to speak, over the entire range, from fairly tatsama Sanskrit all the way to fluent Persian and guttural Arabic, providing cross-border frissons to a genuinely multilingual community. Classical examples might start with the multilingual puzzles of Amir Khusrau, but other examples abound, right down to our own times. The delegitimising of this glorious linguistic domain—particularly in the pedagogical apparatuses of the State—chokes this play and renders the anxious victim-learners dull, pompous and pedestrian. Unbending, inhumane politics is the inevitable corollary. On the recoil from all this, Hindustani presents itself—on the ramparts, at the hour of the wolf—as a utopian symbol, a point of desire, something light, bright and distant from our sphere of sorrow—to coin a phrase!

Hamlet, beware! I yield to none in my love for this, my, language. And have often been tempted by the thought—something of an occupational hazard for wordsmiths—that some kind of linguistic initiative might provide the trigger for change—a revolution made by poets. More realistically, however, I suggest that the yearning for Hindustani is a kind of symptom of our political condition, a revulsion against the purist, intolerant attitudes that inform the politics of the Hindu Right. Like a litmus paper, this recurrent yearning can at best register change, and perhaps the hope for change—but the transformation itself will have to happen in the real, material world.

Sensitive observers realise that the stalemate between the English elite and the Hindi elite that purports to challenge it holds us all hostage—the fact that the privileged speak for 'secularism' and the intolerant and communal speak for 'democracy' poisons our necessary public discourse about both these vital ideas. It is at this point that the possibility of Hindustani presents itself, as the natural vehicle of popular democracy as well as of secularism.

References

1. *Constituent Assembly Debates*, hereafter CAD, vol. VII, p. 358.
2. This is an alphabetical listing, starting with Assamese and ending with Urdu at no: 13. Sanskrit, an evident afterthought, figures as no: 10A! CAD, X, p.14911.
3. CAD, IX, p.1450.
4. CAD, VII, p.235.
5. LSI, vol. 9, part 1, p.50.
6. CAD, VI, p.222.
7. Shamsur Rahman Faruqi, *Early Urdu Literary Culture and History*, OUP, 2001, p.30.
8. cited, S.R.Faruqi, *op. cit.*, p.32; italics added.
9. David Lelyveld, "the Fate of Hindustani: Colonial Knowledge and the Project of a National Language", in Carol A. Breckenridge and Peter van der Veer, ed. *Orientalism and the Postcolonial Predicament*, OUP, 1994.
10. Alok Rai, *Hindi Nationalism*, Orient Longman, 2000, p.13.
11. This is a long story. See my Hindi Nationalism or Christopher King, One Language, Two Scripts, OUP, 1994.
12. L.M. Khubchandani, "Togetherness-Otherness of Hindi", unpublished paper presented at the National Seminar organised by the Mahatma Gandhi Hindi Vishwavidyalaya on "Zicr: Language, Culture and Technology in October 2002.
13. Source: Sardar Hukam Singh, CAD, IX, p.1440.
14. Ayesha Jalal and Anil Seal, "Alternative to Partition: Muslim Politics between the Wars", *Modern Asian Studies*, 15, 1881.
15. Granville Austin, *The Indian Constitution*, OUP, 1966, p.302.
16. S. Imtiaz Hasnain and K.S.Rajyashree, "Hindustani as an anxiety between Hindi-Urdu commitment", unpublished paper presented at the 2002 ZICR conference, aforementioned.

Neera Chandhoke

Holding the Nation Together

I

Towards the end of the twentieth century, theorists were admitting with some regret that the nation-state had proved one of history's most serious mistakes. And they had reason to feel this way. The decade of the 1990s had witnessed some truly horrendous tragedies, all in the name of nationalism and national identity. Bosnia, Kosovo, Rwanda, Burundi, Sri Lanka, were just some of the countries that have been torn apart by narrow chauvinistic xenophobia parading in the guise of national identity. People spoke of the tragedies that had been enacted in these God-forsaken places in hushed tones and suppressed voices. In the same period India experienced the rise of a sectarian and divisive majoritarian agenda. The agenda openly and aggressively sought to build a cultural nation out of the debris of the Babri mosque brought down with great glee in 1992 by the *kar sevaks*, even as they chanted the name of the God Ram. Canada was to see the referendum on the separation of Quebec from the rest of the country being defeated by a narrow margin. The once great USSR was divided and further subdivided into a number of competing nations. All over the world, human beings justified their inhumanity towards other human beings by citing the cause of nationalism. Something had gone seriously wrong with the project of the nation state.

It is not surprising that scholars and political commentators looked for other ways in which the inhabitants of a particular territory could live together in some measure of peace if not harmony. Preoccupation with this particular problem generated a burgeoning industry in the form of anguished scholarly outpourings and political analysis. Attempts to negotiate the problem led to several formulations ranging from multiculturalism to minority rights, to looser versions of the nation that could accommodate overlapping identities, to cosmopolitanism, to supra-national formations and sub-national groupings. In the process the issue of identities, whether real or constructed, came to dominate the field of conceptual analysis. The themes of nation, nationalism and national identity dominated the discourse in anthropology, sociology, literature, political theory, and history.

In retrospect there were two issues that came to be of particular concern to analysts. The first was the inability of the same nation that had been carved out of disparate histories and sociologies in the colonised world in the mid-twentieth century to deliver basic goods to its people. The nationalist dream had simply petered out; and the promises of the nation state had been compromised. Nowhere was this sense of betrayal expressed more strongly than in the literary genre of the postcolonial novel, for instance in Gabriel Garcia Marquez's *Love in the Time of Cholera*. The literary critic Jean Franco suggests that Marquez who had already begun to pillorise and parody the nation in his other writings, specifically makes the 'private' the centre of his writing in this novel. Even as the `apocalyptic landscape of decay and cadavers bear the scars of modernisation', the `protagonists enacting their anachronistic love story can no longer represent anything beyond their own moral passions'. *Love in the Time of Cholera*, argues Franco, `marked the dissolution of a once totalising myth which is now replaced by private fantasies lived out amidst private disasters'[1]. The novel that during the struggle for decolonisation had created the nation in fervid imaginations was now to deliberately deconstruct the nation for these very imaginations. It revolted against the betrayal of the national vision.

The second theme that preoccupied political energies and harnessed scholarship was dismay—at the way in which the state had sought to build a nation out of a welter of different ways of life which had existed in pre-modern societies. Everywhere the attempt to construct a nation out of societies that contained a number of cultural, religious and language groups had resulted in the flattening out of different identities, and consequent homogenisation. But, as scholars were to point out, identities do not just go away. In time these identities were to reassert themselves in the form of what came to be known as the global 'ethnic explosion'.

The idea of *natio,* which had come to us from ancient Rome, was submerged in the idea of *ethnie,* which had come to us from ancient Greece.

Civic nations as exemplified in the French model of the nation state, which posited the sovereignty of a category called 'the people' had been overtaken by notions of what Michael Ignatieff called the nationhood of 'blood and belonging'. Civic nationalism based on citizenship rights had been overtaken by ethnic nationalism based on ethnic ties—whether these be of religion or language. Therefore, when the Tamils in Sri Lanka revolted against Sinhala domination, it was in the name of the linguistic nation. When Serbians sought to cleanse the country of Muslims, it was also in the name of the nation. When the Hutus sought to build a nation in Rwanda it was at the expense of the Tutsis. And when Hindu nationalists created the monster of Hindu communalism to put the minorities in their place, it was also in the name of the nation. History and its textbooks have been written and re-written in the name of the nation, mythologies have been created and recreated in the name of the nation, and symbols and icons have been worked and reworked in the name of the nation. Terms such as nation, nationalism, and nation-ness have acquired a trajectory of their own; a trajectory that often outstrips the imaginings of those who had sought to build the nation in the first place.

Scholars struggling to find an answer to the problem sought to link up the phenomenon of deprivation, the non-ability of the nation state to deliver, and the phenomenon of the global ethnic explosion. People had revolted against the betrayal of promises and against the phenomenon of hope belied under the banner of nationalism. Often under the clothes of nationalism lurked the wolf of economic and political demands. There is something in this. However, the question that arises at this particular moment is the following: why do people react in the way they do, burning, and killing and raping, and generally indulging in blood letting in response to political, economic, and social deprivation? There are after all other ways to express discontent. Why does protest against the policies of the state take this particular form of hatred towards the other community, of calls to annihilate the other community? Why does civil society turn inwards upon itself and target its own people, instead of targeting the non-performing state?

II

These are troublesome questions that do not permit of easy answers. But if we think about it, there is something vexatious about the construction of the *hyphen* between the nation and the state. There is also something troublesome about the construction of the nation itself. In other words, both these constructions are arbitrary. The problem perhaps lies here.

Take the idea that every nation should have its own state, a suggestion that comes down to us through the history of Europe. But if we look closely, the converse is true. For through history we find that it is the *state that demands a nation*. To put it differently, pre-occupation with building a nation was to intensify in the exact political moment when the modern state was to become the dominant mode of political organisation. If we hyphenate the nation with the state, one problem is solved—that of political allegiance to the state. The nation after all throughout history has been considered to be the exclusive source of all allegiance, loyalty, and political passions. Every citizen, Rousseau had observed in pre-Revolutionary France, must be taught to love his own country. "That love makes up his entire existence: he has eyes only for the fatherland, lives only for the fatherland... the moment he has no fatherland, he is no more". This suggestion acquired somewhat the status of a Talmudic injunction for all the states seeking to build strong nations.

This presupposition was to have an interesting political spin off. Every state tries to become a nation simply because nation-ness makes the task of garnering legitimacy relatively easy. After all collective allegiance can with some felicity transform itself into political obligation, which in turn generates legitimacy. Further, nationhood not only generates legitimacy; it also secures effective political institutions. The capacity of state institutions to function effectively can be greatly imperilled when particularistic identities jostle for space and power through competing rhetoric—resulting in instability, discontent, and anomie. To put it differently, the state can be effective and legitimate only when a strong undergrid of nation-ness supports it. The formulation proved so attractive that the *hyphen*, which connects the conceptual worlds of the nation and the state [the nation-state] came to rule politics across the world. By the beginning of the twentieth century the hyphen was to prove astonishingly influential.

Predictably, states across the world have tried to weld diversified languages and belief systems into one nation—by the imposition of one language for instance. Only two and a half percent of Italians spoke the 'national' language at the time when the country was unified while the others spoke a number of dialects. The very leadership that had unified Italy now set out to create Italians through the policies of one language, or the politics of linguistic nationalism. Equally, in 1789 fifty percent of the French people did not speak French at all: only 12 to 13 percent spoke it correctly, and in northern and southern France virtually no one spoke French. The French nation was created out of the politics of speaking French, which meant in principle that regional dialects were wiped out.

Something of the same kind happened in India. Consider that the people of India speak languages or dialects that belong to five linguistic families: Indo-Aryan, Dravidian, Austro-Asiatic, Tibeto-Burman, and Andamanese. The 1991 census found that 30.4 percent of the people speak Hindi, the numbers being 258.4 million. 7.7 percent of the people, i.e. that is 65.5 million people speak Bengali. 7.6 percent of the population or 64.6 million people speak Marathi. 39.1 million people speak Gujarati, which amounts to 4.6 percent of the population; 30.6 million speak Oriya amounting to 3.6 percent of the population, 21.3 million or 2.5 percent of the population is Punjabi speaking, and 13.6 million or 1.6 percent of the population speaks Assamese. Among the Dravidian languages, 73.1 million people or 8.6 percent of the population speaks Telugu, 59.5 million or 7 percent of the people speak Tamil, 34 million or 4 percent of the people speak Kannada, and 33.2 million or 3.9 percent of the people speak Malayalam. 21.3 million or 2.5 percent of Indians speak English and 45 million or 5.3 percent speak Urdu. The largest group in India thus speaks Hindi or related dialects, followed by Telugu, Marathi, and Bengali speakers. These figures represent however a handful of languages spoken in India, which according to the 1961 census numbered above 1650. The 1971 census records mother tongues that are not included within the Eighth Schedule of the Constitution such as Bhili, Dogri, Gondi, Khandeshi, Oraon, Santali, and Tulu.

When we look at the languages that have commanded the country historically, we find that the domination of a language has little to do with the numbers that speak it, and more to do with other reasons such as the exigencies of statehood and power. In the pre-colonial period for instance two languages eclipsed other languages. The first of these languages is Sanskrit. Semantically the origin of many languages in the country, it has been traditionally the language of higher learning, the language of classical texts, of religious rituals, of literature, poetry, drama, music, and of the literati. During the Mughal era however, matters changed. Raja Todar Mall, the revenue minister of Emperor Akbar, was to make Persian the language of official records in the last decades of the sixteenth century. Therefore, though Sanskrit was not displaced from its position as the language of classical discourse, increasingly it was Persian that came to command the country as the language of the court, of administration, of the judiciary, of diplomacy and also as the language of poetry, literature, and historiography. Since it was the language of administration, upwardly mobile Indians opted to learn Persian.

Whereas both Sanskrit and Persian remained confined to the intelligentsia, increasingly a third was to eclipse others as the language of everyday life in northern India. This was Urdu, founded by the poet Mir in 1752 who called it *Urdu-e-Mu'alla* or courtly language. But actually Urdu, which derives from the Turkish word *Ortu*, [a military camp] was developed in the cantonments and in the bazaars. Evolving from *Khari Boli*, which is a branch of Hindi spoken in the region, and which owes its origins to one of the linguistic families of Sanskrit. Urdu is a *patois* where a Persian-Arabic vocabulary has been grafted onto to a *prakrit* syntax and grammar. For these reasons a variety of people across religious and regional identities took to the language. Urdu acquired a still more communicable avatar in the form of Hindustani, which could be written in both the Persian-Arabic as well as in the devanagari script. In effect, Urdu in its avatar as Hindustani became a link language in large parts of northern India.

During the colonial era the linguistic map of India was to alter drastically. By the nineteenth century it was a language from another continent, English, that came to overwhelm the country not only as the language of administration, but that of learning, educational institutions, and communication. The origins of the dominance of English lie of course in the linguistic practices of the colonial power, in the pompous, insufferable, and infamous minutes of T.B Macaulay. In 1835 he was to write:

> I have no knowledge of either Sanskrit or Arabic. But I have done what I could to form a correct estimate of their value. I have read translations of the most celebrated Arabic and Sanskrit works. I have conversed both here and at home with men distinguished

by their proficiency in the Eastern tongues. I am quite ready to take the Oriental learning at the valuation of the Orientalists themselves. I have never found one among them who could deny that a single shelf of a good European library was worth the whole native literature of India and Arabia.

Lord William Bentinck, the Governor-General of India in the 1830s, was to follow this rather rash and offensive conclusion to its logical end. In 1835 he ordered that Western learning and science should constitute the content of higher education, and that the language of instruction should be English. Rapidly English became, as Persian had been a century earlier, the language of power. Till today we witness millions of Indians rushing to get their children educated in the English language. Macaulay's minutes reaped rich dividends as people forgot their own languages—to learn a language that belonged to the historical evolution of another country. In fact, English was to become the link language of the members of the Indian National Congress, as evinced in the fact that all the resolutions of the Congress were passed in English.

Matters were different when it came to building an entity called the Indian nation. By the turn of the twentieth century, even as millions of Indians began to mobilise for the freedom of the country from colonial rule, we see simultaneously the construction of the Indian nation through the politics of linguistic nationalism. The effort to construct the nation linguistically was to prove contradictory. On the one hand a movement for the hegemony of Hindi as the national language made its appearance in North India. But on the other, a twist in the tale emerged. For although the case for Hindi was primarily propelled by movements anxious to emancipate the country from the influence of alien English, and though the idea of Hindi as the national language constituted an integral part of the national vision, increasingly it acquired a communal complexion. The movement was simultaneously to position itself against Urdu and Hindustani as the spoken language of the people—simply because Urdu was identified with Islam. Despite the efforts of Gandhiji who wanted Hindustani written in both the scripts as the link language of India, and who wanted scripts to resemble the spoken word, the spoken language of the people was once again subordinated to the language of nation building. Commonly used words like *padho* [study] were replaced by an archaic word like *adhyayan;* and *trikon,* the triangle, was replaced by *tribhuj,* even as Hindi was purged of its Urdu components.

Urdu, once the language of the courts, of the judicial system, of the bureaucracy, and of literary transactions, has today been excluded from the benefits that should be attached to a creative language. If the language has survived it is because of its usage in the Bombay film industry, as the language of love, as the language of longing, as the language of grief. But it is no longer a language of everyday life which is connected to the street, the job, the bazaar, the coffee house, public meetings, and all other institutions that constitute the public sphere of civil society. In the process the spoken language of the people, Hindustani, was stripped of its vitality and vibrancy. If one aspect of the movement for Hindi was connected to the politics of emancipation from colonial rule and colonised mentalities, the other aspect revealed a stark communal face. In time the idea of Hindi-Hindu-Hindustan posited not only a close link between a language and nationhood, but also between language and religion.

III

The politics of linguistic nationalism bred its own contradictions. Regional language movements that appeared on the political horizon were to contest the claim that Hindi was the national language, on the grounds that other languages were also national. The resurgence of regional languages that was to consolidate both linguistic as well as regional identities was in time to catapult the issue of linguistic states onto the political horizon. But that is another story. What is important is that attempts to pose Hindi as the national/ official language has proved one of the most contentious of political issues in the country. This has raised vital issues on what can be considered national and what is not national. Can only the national be official or can the two be separate? In other words, who has the right to define the nation?

Ambedkar has confessed that at the time of the discussion of the draft constitution, there was no article that proved more controversial than the one that deals with the issue of Hindi as the national language. He said,

> No article produced more opposition. No article, more heat. After a prolonged discussion, when the question was put, the vote was 78 against 78. The tie could not be resolved. After a long discussion when the question was put to the assembly once more the result

was 77 against 78 for Hindi. Hindi won its place as national language by one vote.

As suggested above, the drive to make Hindi the national
language and the language of pan-Indian integration began in the
last decades of the nineteenth century. One of the major proponents
of Hindi as the national language was B.G Tilak who incidentally also
was to support the principle of linguistic provinces. At a meeting of
the Nagari Pracharini Sabha at Benaras in December 1905, he was to
suggest that "if you want to draw a nation together, there is no force
more powerful than a common language for all". He also pleaded for
a common script for all Indian languages, that is devanagari. Gandhiji
also extended his support to the movement to make Hindi the national
language. As early as 1909 he was to write in the *Hind Swaraj*: "A
universal language for India should be Hindi". But by 1917 he was
strongly arguing the case for adopting Hindustani as the national
language—because Hindustani was neither Hindi nor Urdu, neither
highly Sanskritised nor highly Arabised. Anxious to pre-empt a
communal divide on the issue, Gandhiji stressed this point in speech
after speech and editorial after editorial, dismissing in the meanwhile
the problems that were likely to be encountered by non-Hindi speaking
groups in the south and in Bengal. He was to write,

> A spirit that is so exclusive and narrow as to want every form of
> speech to be perpetuated and developed, "is anti-national and
> anti-universal. All underdeveloped and unwritten dialects
> should...be sacrificed and merged in the great Hindustani stream.
> It would be a sacrifice...not a suicide.

This suggestion expectedly proved problematic because it was
simply not acceptable in South India. South Indians naturally felt that
Hindi speakers would get an unfair advantage in jobs and in power.
On the other hand the choice of Hindi as the national language would
institutionalise the identity of the Hindi speaking people as the national
identity, and that would be to deny the status of 'national' to other
languages. Nor was Hindi for them an antique language like many
Dravidian languages. Even as resolutions in session after session of
the meetings of the Congress spoke of Hindi being the national
language when the country was free, opposition mounted in non-
Hindi speaking states.

This was exacerbated in 1925 when under the insistence of
Gandhiji, the constitution of the Congress was amended to read that,

"[t]he proceedings of the Congress shall be conducted as far as possible in Hindustani. The English language or any provincial language may be used if the speaker is unable to speak Hindustani". Simultaneously a sustained drive to introduce Hindi in the south was initiated by Gandhiji and Rajagopalchari, and triggered off an expected backlash. As early as 1937, when the Congress-led provincial government mandated Hindi instruction in primary schools in the south, Tamil nationalists united under Dravidian leadership to activate agitation— a pattern that was to be repeated right up to the late 1960s. But during his visits to South India Gandhiji continued to insist that Tamils should study Hindustani, and the *Dakshin Bharat Hindi Prachar Sabha* was established for the purpose. Even Rajaji, who was an ardent Tamil nationalist, was to support Gandhiji in this endeavour. In time the cleavage was to adopt formidable proportions; between the insistence of the Congress leadership in Tamil Nadu that Hindi was a symbol of national integration, and the resentment articulated by many Tamil nationalists that the imposition of Hindi led to the devaluation of the language and culture of the region.

In the 1930s the first anti-Hindi agitation led by the Dravidian leadership took the form of the threat of secession and the formation of the Dravida Nadu. In fact, the rise of the Dravidian leadership, the formation of the Dravidra Munnetra Kazhagam in 1949, and the decline of the Congress in Tamil Nadu was closely allied to the agitation against the imposition of Hindi on Tamil Nadu. This Dravidian leadership connected with attempts to maintain Brahmanical domination over the region. Therefore, even as the Constituent Assembly decided that Hindi in the devanagari script was to be the official language, the implementation of Hindi was postponed till 1965. It was provided that language commissions would be set up in 1955 and in 1960 to oversee the phasing out of English and the progress of Hindi as the official language. In the meanwhile English would continue as the official language of the union, and states in the union would use their regional languages. Regional languages were designated as 'official' languages by incorporation in the Eighth Schedule of the Constitution.

Even as the Constitutional provision laid down that the central government should take steps to introduce Hindi as the national language by 1965, non-Hindi speaking groups prepared for a massive confrontation, particularly in Tamil Nadu. Delegates from the south opposed the Congress, which stated that whereas the use of Hindi as the all India official language would not be obligatory, it will be encouraged for purposes of inter state and state-centre communication and trade. They opposed the move as alien, detrimental to regional languages, and undemocratic. In a rancorous mood T.A. Ramalingam Chettiar of Tamil Nadu warned that the south was faced with

> 'a matter of life and death...If there is the feeling of having obtained liberty, freedom and all that, there is very little of it felt in the south. Sir, coming here to the capital in the northern-most part of the country, and feeling ourselves as strangers in this land, we do not feel that we are a nation to whom the whole thing belongs. It is not even the things that are said—we have given up our language in favour of Hindi—but the way in which the Hindi-speaking people treat us and the way in which they want to demand things which is more galling'.

By 1963 the anti-Hindi agitation in Tamil Nadu assumed appalling proportions even as the deadline year of 1965 drew nearer. The DMK, which was formed in 1949 upon the twin planks of Tamil nationalism and anti-Brahmanism/anti-Hindi, was to launch protest after protest from 1963 onwards. Those portions of the Constitution that dealt with the official language were burnt in the streets, and students unions and political parties joined the massive protests against the decision to impose Hindi. The call of the DMK before 26th January 1965 was marked by public mourning and the hoisting of black flags in many Tamil homes and public places. Books written in Hindi were burnt, government offices and transport were attacked and seven protestors committed suicide. The Congress government in the state responded with coercion and 66 people were reportedly killed in police firing. By the middle of the 1960s, even as the Central government prevaricated upon the continued use of English, even as agitation rocked the region, the DMK leadership lost control over the movement.

IV

The escalating protest over Hindi made it impossible to institute monolingualism in the country, and the central leadership compromised on the issue. The Official Languages Act in 1963 represents this spirit of compromise. Whereas Hindi would become the official language of the country in 1965, English would continue as an 'associate additional official language'. A Parliamentary Review Committee would consider after ten years whether English should be retained if sufficient progress in extending the domain of Hindi as the official language had not been made. Prime Minister Nehru made a commitment not to impose Hindi on non-Hindi speaking people in the country. But the south of the country continued to be rocked by discontent. This was exacerbated by the 1964 directive issued by the Home Ministry under Gulzarilal Nanda [a Hindi-wallah] to all ministries, that they should report on the progress of the implementation of Hindi for official purposes and indicate what steps they proposed to undertake to see that Hindi became the official language in 1965.

On the 26th of January 1965 when Hindi became the official language, riots erupted in Tamil Nadu. 60 people were killed in police firing and two youths committed self-immolation. After a series of inter-party discussions the central government in 1965 assured the various states that Hindi would not be imposed upon them, and that they could continue to use English for official purposes. This became the Official Languages Amendment Act of 1967, which provided for the following. First, that Hindi and English would be used in Parliament. Secondly, the central government would use Hindi in its communication with Hindi speaking states and English for communicating with non-Hindi speaking states. Thirdly, all policies relating to language have been brought within the state list under the power of the state government. Fourthly, articles 29 and 30 of the fundamental rights chapter of the Constitution protect minority languages. The Commission for Linguistic Minorities acts as a watchdog for protecting the languages of linguistic minorities within states.

Fifthly, the major languages of India listed in the Eighth Schedule are treated as official languages. The original Eighth Schedule contained 14 languages: Assamese, Bangla, Gujarati, Hindi, Kashmiri, Kannada, Marathi, Malayalam, Oriya, Punjabi, Tamil, Telugu, Urdu, and Sanskrit. Today the Eighth Schedule lists 18 languages, having incorporated Konkani, Nepali, and Manipuri and Sindhi. Sindhi was added to the Eighth Schedule via the 21st constitutional amendment in 1967, and the other three in 1992. The inclusion of languages in the Eighth Schedule has again been the result of massive political mobilisation around the issue, which in turn has been facilitated by one of the provisions in the schedule. This states that if any group sufficiently large in number moves the state to include its language for administrative and educational purposes, this can be done consequent upon a directive from the President of India. As in the case of linguistic states, whereas the government of India has shown some responsiveness to mobilisation on language in civil society, it retains the discretion of deciding whether the demand is legitimate, and whether a sufficiently large number back the demand.

Certainly the listing of 18 languages in the Eighth Schedule as official languages is a wise move, for it recognises and validates the multilingual character of Indian society. But this is not to say that the formula is entirely unproblematic. One major defect is that no criterion for the inclusion or exclusion of languages has been specified. It is *implied* that major languages, which have literary scripts and traditions of their own, which are used in newspapers and radio broadcasts, and which are spoken by people in large contiguous areas, are candidates for inclusion. Secondly, classical languages of culture and heritage, and languages that are considered to be a resource or a root language for modern languages, such as Sanskrit, also find place in the Eighth Schedule. Thirdly if a language is recognised as an official language in the states, such as Konkani in Goa and Manipuri in Manipur, it is included in the Eighth Schedule. And fourthly if a sufficiently large movement backs the demand that a language be included in the schedule, the demand has been conceded as in the case of Sindhi and Nepali.

But conversely if a language is not backed by popular mobilisation, if it is not the official language of a state, if it is not seen as a root language, or if does not have a literary tradition or script that is recognised by society, it does not find place in the Eighth Schedule— even though there may be very good reasons for granting it the status of an official language.

For instance neither Santhali, which is spoken by 3,000,000 people, nor Maithili, which is widely spoken, is included in the Schedule. The anomaly is that whereas Sanskrit with about 2500 speakers finds place in the Eighth Schedule, several tribal languages like Bhil and Santhali with millions of speakers do not. Other valid questions can be raised. If languages with literary and cultural traditions find place in the Eighth Schedule, why are Braj and Rajasthani not included? Braj, Rajasthani, and Awadhi, are the languages of a great tradition but they are subsumed under Hindi, whereas Konkani is regarded as distinct from Marathi. Further, whereas in the linguistic re-organisation of states Punjab came to be known on the basis of Punjabi, and Tamil

Nadu got its Tamil, Kashmiri, which is both a literary as well as a majority language did not go to Kashmir. Kashmir got Urdu, which logically should have gone to U.P.

The politics of linguistic nationalism should have run their course by now, but they continue to propel political anxiety. Consider for instance that as recently as the 28th of September 1989, bitter riots erupted in Badaun in Uttar Pradesh around the decision of the state government to make Urdu the second language of the state. This of course has a history. On the 8th of October 1947, the state government of what was then the United Provinces, had opted to make Hindi the state language even before the Constituent Assembly had taken a decision on official languages. Arguably, by the decision to allot Hindi written in the devanagari script, the status of the official language of U.P. made Urdu redundant in the very region where it was spoken. Since then the communal divide has intensified in North India; the decision to restore Urdu its status as the second language in what is now Uttar Pradesh (1989) was to spark off communal riots in the name of language riots. Fortunately however, the rioting remained confined to Badaun and did not spill over the border as most communal riots are prone to do in the country. But the riots proved that a point-linguistic nationalism has the capacity to arouse atavistic emotions. This is an uncomfortable reality that has again and again faced the country—through its pre Independence as well as post independence times.

In sum, attempts to build nations out of a highly disparate people, and attempts to construct a hyphen between the state and the nation, often rebound on the proponents of linguistic nationalism. For nationalism and nations like the proverbial amoebae reproduces itself through fragmentation and multiplication. It is not difficult to imagine that if the Central Government had not given in to the demands of the Tamil nationalists in the mid-1960s, we may have witnessed a Sri-Lankan kind of situation, which has catapulted out of hand by outstripping the original demands of the Tamil nationalists.

To put it differently, attempts to tinker with the lives of people in order to build homogenous nations have almost everywhere proved counterproductive, even in the home of the nation-state that is Western Europe. The massive presence of immigrant populations in these countries has thrown into sharp relief innumerable questions of how people belong and who belongs to this entity called the nation-state. For the nation state demands the kind of conformity that steamrolls the images of the people of who they are and how they belong to their country.

Perhaps if leaderships leave people to live out their lives with others in some degree of autonomy, we may find something that approximates a nation. Consider for instance, that despite great differences, the people of India have over the course of time come to speak a common language. This common language may be the language of commodity, the language of cricket, the language of the Bombay film and its music, the language of dress codes, the language of cuisine, or the language of icons—whether these be Sachin Tendulkar, or Subbulakshmi, or Bimsen Joshi, or M.F Hussain or indeed Amitabh Bachan. We do not have to be ordered to speak a common language, just as we do not need to be ordered to follow a common religion. The people of India can forge ties of belonging by themselves without any kind of social engineering that has rebounded so badly on various leaderships. Something that approximates a nation is quite capable of holding itself together—through means that have never been envisaged by cultural entrepreneurs and inventors.

References and Notes

1. Jean Franco (1989) 'The Nation as Imagined Community' in H Aram Veeser edited *The New Historicism* (New York, Routledge) pp 204–212 in pp 207, and 208.

Kapila Vatsyayan

Plural Cultures, Monolithic Structures*

I

On the one hand, it is said that everyone is coming closer and that we are all members, equal or otherwise, of a single global family—'global village' we call it. On the other, perhaps never before, have so many big or middling wars been fought on the basis of race, colour, ethnicity, language, religion and cultural identity. By some accounts ten times more people have been killed in these wars than during the Second World War. Every moment there are clashes between groups, adjacent and remote, not explicitly on the basis of political ideology but on the basis of race, colour, ethnicity, language and religion. A second deeper look invariably brings to surface the economic inequalities and motivations of power: these are neatly camouflaged. These are the implicit and explicit levels of tension and conflict. It would appear that just at the moment of the shrinking of all differences into a single homogenised village without differentiation, there is an outburst of intolerance and violence with each other and against each other. Most parts of the world appear to have been affected by this twin phenomenon of coming together and falling apart. Also, it would appear that the countries which were erstwhile colonies and are now political independent nation-states, are more inflicted with this malady, of course with outstanding exceptions.

* The Zaidi Memorial Lecture, delivered at the India International Centre on 19 January 2002

It is against the background of this consciousness, as also the awareness that monolithic or certainly single models of development that have been adopted, that one is obliged to ask the question whether there is an intrinsic inability of clearly defined cultures to live with each other in harmony. Or, are the tensions and conflicts the result in part, if not whole, in the imposition or acceptance of models of development and governance which are uniform, fixed, rigid, linear and unidimensional? Is the problem with 'cultures' or is it with structures of governance?

Underlying this paper is an attempt to try and comprehend the characteristics of societies with plural cultures—clearly distinguishing them from those others who are today called multi-cultural on account of recent immigration, but were and are basically mono-cultures. It is also an attempt to identify once again the texture of these plural-culture societies who have existed for centuries as a network of honeycombed units, clear and distinct but in a relationship of give and take. Was there co-existence or was there always a confrontation between the several groups called tribes in Africa? Did the Tutus and Tutsi always fight? Was this the case of several groups of Indonesia and of course the countless groups and communities in India? Were the Kukis always at war with the Meiteis? Even a minute's attention will reveal that there was space for a fluidity of identities.

Without elaborating upon other parts of world, relevant as their situation is to ours in India, let me begin with ourselves: all those who have lived and been part of the civilisation called Indian, and those who are now citizens of the nation-state called India. I shall attempt to identify the diverse levels of this plurality as also refer to the measures adopted to categorise this plurality for purposes of territorial demarcation, administrative boundaries and citizenship rights and duties, education, economic and social development. In the very exercise of the descriptive account there are bound to emerge a number of issues which are relevant for our purpose of understanding both the cultures, as also the yardsticks for classification evolved for governing these societies.

II

Primary and self evident is the physical, geographical entity known as India. Its very land mass is so situated that a natural boundary as also paths of communication are created. The youngest of the geological mountains, the Himalayas, are both a natural boundary as also a natural pathway. More, this is a unique continuous range from the north-west to the south-east. Here there is immense bio-diversity. While plurality through mobility from the north-south movement was facilitated, there was as much geo-physical and cultural movement from the north-west to the south-east. This is as true of the flora, fauna, high altitudes, the forest covers, as also the people: the Gujjars Bakarwalas and the Kirats and Nishadas of ancient India. Perhaps nowhere else as many rivers flow from a single mountain system.

The river systems give rise to the civilisations which develop from them, today identified by their popular and debatable terms— Indus, Ganges and now Saraswati. The rivers and the foothills of the mountains provide the geo-physical basis of agricultural societies of great antiquity. Again the movement is from the north-west to the south-east generally. Through their meandering paths at different altitudes and contours, the rivers have flowed separately and sometimes together. The confluences and meeting of different tributaries to make confluences (*Sangam*) Prayag, is a common phenomenon. The people who have lived along these rivers have similarly led distinct lifestyles; they have come together to mingle, co-exist and then move on their different paths. Further south, the landscape has provided the space and place for contrasting groups of people and their lifestyles shaped by environment and agriculture function. The desert dwellers comprise numerous groups but they are not 'static' for ever. They move from desert lands to fertile lands, from the west to the east, from the west to the south-west. Middle India, with its extensive forests, is again both a place for meeting as also mobility. Further south the Vindhyas once again become a natural demarcation, as also a route for communication. The same is true of the seas that surround us on the east and west. The oceans provide the boundaries, and are also the channels of communication both with the west and the east.

Altogether each geo-physical region of India is an eco-zone closely connected with others, adjacent and remote. The consciousness of the connection between the mountains and the oceans, the forests and the rivers, the deserts and the marshlands has been responsible for a large body of literature which has conceived of the land as a large coherent unit with plurality and inter-dependence. The very ecology of the country has been responsible for the development of major concepts of unity and multiplicity, of interdependence of one region with the other. Major myths revolving around the ocean, the mountains, the rivers, the forest, the flora and fauna evolved. The one message was interconnectivity.

All this description of primary and self evident geo-physical landscape would be an irrelevant exercise were it not for the fact that the non-cognisance of the eco-zones, the plurality of the methods by which eco-balances were maintained has been the cause of much disruption. Our first paradox of plural cultures and monolithic structures appears here. The history of the non-cognisance of the plurality as also interdependence of regions is rather long. It cannot be elaborated upon here. Nevertheless let me draw attention only to one or two aspects of the recent debate on issues of environment: the natural and human landscape and the processes of development.

We are all aware of humanity's concern with the threat to the environment. Conferences have been held in Stockholm, Rio de Janeiro and now Japan. Issues of greenhouse effect, global warming, depletion of the ozone layer have been raised. Alternate sources of energy have been discussed. However, few have identified in these conferences that underlying this situation of imbalance in the environment is not only the fact of an unequal distribution of natural resources but also the more basic question of man's attitude to Nature. The modern world has believed and subscribed to the view that man is the most important and dominant species of the universe. This is a fundamental philosophic premise built on the basis of a progressive evolutionary model and a deterministic science. A mighty edifice of a modern civilisation has developed on this premise. Man is considered as the most dominant amongst life forms, and thus the most empowered to exploit and modify natural rhythms.

In clear contrast to this view, among large parts of humanity largely from all those cultures which are considered under-developed or developing and those with plural societal structures, there was the faith and assertion that man is one amongst all life forms. He is not dominant, even if he/she is special. Flora, fauna, even stones and inanimate life are as important. This is patently clear from the myths and legends of the people of America, Africa, Asia, the aborigines of Australia and of course India. In India whether at the highest textual tradition of the Vedas or the myths—legends of the Nagas, the Marias and Murias, the Mukkuvars, the Bhils or Santhals, the Ho's, Oraons, and Saoras, there was and continues to be an acute consciousness of

Man-Nature relationship. Man identified and communicated with ocean, mountains, rivers, forest plants and animals and birds. He considered it his sacred duty not to assault Nature. Understandably all these perceptions were couched in a multiplicity of vocabularies and lifestyles directly related to the environment.

Though not couched in scientific terms and therefore often dismissed as superstition, it was a layperson's or collective community's understanding of the two issues which we discuss today in international forums: bio-diversity and ecological balances. Many strategies were identified to ensure both bio-diversity and ecological balances. After a detour through mono-models of cultivation, single seed plantation, water management through construction of large dams and other monolithic structures of development, some scientists and planners have realised that there was some sense in the affirmation of these cultures in plural ways in the principle of bio-diversity and in maintaining eco-balances through a variety of strategies. Now there is a cry for conserving bio-diversity, plural methods of water conservation and all that we understand by the term alternate models of development. Each of these recent recommendations refer to sustainable development. Basic to all suggested alternate paradigms of development there is the concern for maintaining eco-balances and protecting the environment.

It is in this context of environment and need for sustaining eco-balances that the Indian worldview and the commitment of small cohesive groups becomes again relevant. India believed, and continues to do so, that man was only one amongst all life forms; that there were multiple ways by which an order could be sustained. Further that nothing was absolute or static. Negation of these perceptions in the actual organisation of land distribution and management has created serious disruptions. The common land, the fallow land, the common water resource was the responsibility of all. Certain locations both of land and water were considered sacred. In this connection let me draw attention to a recent study on Bio-diversity Management sponsored by UNESCO. This global study comes to the conclusion that many cultures in all their plurality evolved certain notions of the sacred. These notions of the 'sacred' were the strategies for conserving bio-diversity. Many traditional societies all over the world value a large number of plant species from the wild for a variety of reasons, for food, fibre, shelter or medicine. Arising out of the close forest-human linkage, the protected refugia of the natural ecologies in a given region has existed as sacred groves. These groves are managed through a variety of ways in different parts of India. The concept of the sacred grove ranges from identifying a species, for example the peepal (*ficus religiosa*) and tulsi to a given eco-system and human made agro-ecosystems and village eco-systems.

In turn all this leads to the concept of the sacred landscape. One of the best examples of this sacred landscape was that recognised along the course of the Ganges, originating from the high mountains of the Garhwal Himalayas in the north-west, travelling through the plain of Uttar Pradesh and West Bengal and draining into the bay of Bengal. The plains with human habitation represent a set of inter-connected eco-systems types bound together by the river. The humans are or should be only one part of the integral eco-systems. We know that non-recognition of this aspect has resulted in the pollution of the Ganges and the degradation of forests and lands. Mindless, unlinear progress or haphazard industrialisation has led to a situation where human survival is threatened. Inability to comprehend the integrated system has caused major malfunctions. The Bio-sphere Reserve concept of UNESCO is actually a modern version of the sacred landscape concept of small cohesive societies of the so-called under-developed world. It is known as much to the Australian aborigines as to the native Americans as to the countries of the Mediterranean, Africa and Meso-America, as to the countless groups called tribal and village societies in India. The question to be asked is, was cognisance taken of their consciousness in development models? The answer is a clear 'No'. The disruptions caused are both obvious and alarming.

III

The plurality of natural landscapes is matched by the plurality of human landscapes, and indeed the human species itself. Elementary and self evident is not only the plurality but the plurality of criteria adopted to classify and categorise this plurality. Of course there is a staggering plurality of racial types; this is all too well known. However we have also to recognise that often we have continued to adopt nineteenth century anthropological yardsticks. We have spoken not only of the evolution of man, but have divided the human race according to physiognomy, blood groups and the rest. This is well known in the discipline of physical anthropology. These theories of racial distinctions were not restricted to physical characteristics but they went further to identify character. Racial discrimination and the appellation of the white, black, brown and yellow races was a logical corollary of theory in the evolution and legitimisation of power structures. India accepted the criterion, even if with modifications and protests. It is not at all necessary even to mention Gandhiji's being thrown out of the train on account of pigmentation and power. There is then the classification which implies history and linguistic grouping. The earlier debate on the Aryans and the recent discourse on the Aryans and their homeland is one outstanding example. In addition to speaking about the Australoids, Mongoloids, Negroids, we speak about Aryans and Dravidians. The very mention of the division evokes a vision of many centuries, with an unsaid acceptance of racial distinctions. This is closely linked to the plurality of linguistic grouping and family of languages. We shall speak about this later.

Next, we classify all these or some racial groups according to social structure, broadly following the *varna* and *jati* grouping of some ancient Indian texts. Further the social structure is quantified on the basis of 'caste', again a term of recent origin, and categorise the population of practically the whole land on the basis of caste and those outside the caste system. Further the same population is classified in terms of functions but implied in the classification is an evolutionary evaluative criterion based on some historical notions of civilisation. Hunter, gatherers, village societies (*grama*), city (*nagar*) and mega cities—denote a hierarchy, not merely the differentiation of life-function, modes of agriculture, and trade. The same population is then classified on the basis of languages and what are termed as dialects. The history of the classification of languages and dialects also carries with it a special type of discourse on linguistic structures.

We further divide the same population on the basis of 'religion', that is, institutional religion and arrive at a demographic profile of Hindus, Muslims, Sikhs, Zoroastrians, Christians, Jews and so on. To all these classifications is added understandably the economic criteria, and therefore the division into the below poverty line, above poverty line, lower and higher income groups. The same population is as naturally classified into the illiterate and literate, implying a stage of evolution from pre-literate to literate societies. The gender demographic classification is natural and basic.

Can any statistical exercise of numbers set up a one to one correspondence between one category and another? For example, are all Aryans brahmins and all Dravidians non-brahmins or shudras of the social system? Do all forest-dwellers speak the same language? The absurdity of these questions is as patent as the complexity of defining what constitutes the total cultural identification of an individual or a group. We are back to our initial statement of the geophysical landscape and the human landscape. Each local space and place, each region has its own very special processes of overlapping categories, symbiosis or semiotics. A distinctive personality can be identified by taking all these factors into account. However, the acceptance of any single yardstick immediately results in distortions of reality.

This jig-saw puzzle of plurality and the yardsticks of adopting criteria for measuring plurality is an issue which has not been addressed with the sophistication that it deserves. It appears that there is both an element of generalising and essentialising a single criterion of race, language, social structure or religion. The essentialising has resulted in some major disruptions—not only at the political level but also at the social level. Each individual or group comprised multi-identities; also the identities were fluid and changing. This allowed for co-existence and reciprocity. Any external categorisation, or attempt to give or demand a single identity on the basis of either race or language of religion meant that there was no room for accommodation or manoeuvre. The situation worsened because the structures co-related identity with fixed territory and privileges. On the one hand nation-states are theoretically constructed on the basis of individual rights, eschewing all classification on the basis of caste, creed, race, language, spoken or written, and of course religion. On the other, these very identities have been used to demarcate 'place' and privilege one group above another. Naturally tensions and conflicts have increased.

As illustrations let us take the case of social structure and the volatile question of 'caste' and the categories called SC, ST and OBC. Only two questions may be asked, amongst many others. First, was the *varna* system an absolute fixed system in the original concept, and was there was any possibility of inter-connection and mobility, and even transgression? Second, that as and when any hierarchical rigidity manifested itself, was the corrective mechanism social or political, that is, through governance? As regards the first, the famous *Purusasukta* of the Rig Veda is often quoted, to establish that the system was fixed and purely hierarchical. A careful reading of the hymn will make it clear that this hymn invokes the image of a Cosmic Man, a paradigmatical model of the universe. All aspects are taken into account. No doubt that the brahmins are compared to the head, the limbs to the kshatriyas and the stomach to the vaishyas and feet to the shudras—but is it not true that a human being cannot be complete without each of these parts of the body? Can one live without the stomach, that is food and all materiality, can anyone be mobile without limbs, walk without feet and have direction without a mind? If we take the original hymn in its entirety into consideration, and not insulate the parts, then it is clear that the hymn sets up a model of inter-dependence of the parts and the whole. It alludes to an interdependent structure and not of either of aggregating or insulating any part. It is a metaphor of an inter-connected structure. Indeed, one commentary asks the question, whether a society can walk without feet, can man live without food?

While this is not the occasion to dwell on the original conception, it is necessary to mention that no culture venerates feet as much as the Indian culture. Also as and when transgressions took place, there were systems of legitimisation or the recognition of excellence. Valmiki, the author of the *Ramayana*, was a shudra, and Satyakema the thinker was born of doubtful parenthood. More, while brain power did assume hierarchical power, it was not absolute. As and when hierarchy was imposed, invariably there were powerful social movements of dissent and protest. There was a call for the establishment of a new social order. The history of the pervasive bhakti movement in medieval India from the south to the north, east to the west, speaks of the voices of ironsmiths, cobblers and weavers who raised their voice against inequalities. We read and venerate a Kabir, Rahim, Manivachanar.

Much later in the nineteenth century when oppression and hierarchy again surfaced, there were the social reform movements which eschewed caste distinctions: the Arya Samaj, Brahmo Samaj and many others. These facts are so well known that they need no recounting. Nevertheless, it is necessary to point out that these were social reform movements of the people, what we would call civil society today. These were not acts of governance by the political state. The reform movements aimed at breaking insulation, facilitating movement with an insistence on equalisation of social status and not a mechanical representation of numbers in power structure. This distinction is fine, but real and meaningful. Gandhiji's movement of the removal of untouchability also aimed at social equality, not the representation through numbers.

While the number of castes, jatis, categories of brahmins, kshatriyas, vaishya and shudras were and are innumerable, there was a measure of plurality and social intercourse. The colonial state, by recognising these social structure identities for administrative purposes and privileging and underprivileging others, gave a fixity to a flexible network. Alas, the nation-state of political free India, instead of fostering the idea of nationalism by eschewing these identities for political purposes [and fostering social reform movements] has used, almost exploited, these identities for purposes of political mobilisation. A sphere of life which was best left to the inner dynamism of its self-organising system of complex social structures has been made the vehicle of empowerment, in a system which should have eschewed these identities. It is not necessary for me to mention that over these decades, these identities have been exploited ruthlessly in a race for numerical strength, and power. As a result, the social structure originally envisaged as an interconnected integral system itself split. There is irreversible fragmentation.

What is true of the constituents of what is called caste-society is even more true of that category of the population whom we have by consensus called Scheduled Castes, Scheduled Tribes and the OBC. The history of the nomenclature of SC, ST is revealing and educative. Yes, there were groups of people who were considered low and were disempowered. However, were the groups or their identities fixed and never changing, was there no overlap? It is well known that some were considered Scheduled Caste in one region but were part of the general caste structure in another region. Different configurations could be formed. It was an act of governance of the raja which notified these identities, these 'fixed' identities for ever.

Thus there was the category not only of the martial races in the caste system, but a category called criminal tribes. Now, could there be such a fact as being criminal from birth? The ridiculousness of some of these classifications has alas been perpetuated, by changing the nomenclature of criminal tribes to 'denotified' tribes. No more needs to be added. It would appear that with good intentions but not sufficient thought and perceptions, the fluid and changing overlapping identities of societal structures were given permanent fixed single identities—for purposes of administration and governance, and not greater social interaction and mobility. There was no recognition of optimum skills and the special creative faculties of some of these communities.

In the context of the SC/ST/OBC, perhaps only one aspect may be highlighted. It is accepted that the crafts sector of India is a foreign exchange earner, with everyday reports of the increase in exports. The creators and makers of these crafts are mostly, if not all, either SC or ST or OBC. In statistical terms nearly 15 to 20 per cent from amongst the SC/ST are hereditary craftsmen, called workers of the craft sector. We do not call them 'artists' because they do not give individual signatures. They are not industrial workers because they are not mechanical replicators. They are the highly creative skilled givers of an Indian identity in which we all take pride. We export this creativity and display it on our person as clothes, jewellery and decoration in homes. We also use this creativity by recycling the forms and techniques at sophisticated levels in the urban milieu. However, by adopting another set of criteria of literacy or economic status, we classify them as 'backward'.

Besides the crafts sector, there is the section of Indian population we call traditional and folk artists. These are the Bhavais of Gujarat, the Langas and Manganers of Rajasthan, the Theyyam dancers of Kerala, the Terukuthu dancers of Tamilnadu, the Tolapavakoothu puppet artists of Kerala, the Marias of Madhya Pradesh, the Ho's and Oraons of Bihar, the Bodos of Assam, the several groups of Nagas of Arunachal Pradesh, Mizoram, the Riangas of Tripura, to mention only a few. In addition there are the Purulia, Seraikala and Mayurbhanja dancers of Bengal, Bihar and Orissa, and the traditional musicians and dancers, and puppeteers. In socio-economic classification, they are labelled as Scheduled Castes and Scheduled Tribes and backward. In cultural terms, they are the highly gifted artists of India—the givers of an Indian identity. Any sensitive appraisal of their creativity and the cultural context of their social status, reveals that they were given a higher social status on certain occasions. In short, social identity was not static or fixed. The case of the Seraikala dancers becoming brahmins for the month of Vaisakh is an outstanding example. There are many others.

By recognising only a single identity of caste or SC/ST, there has been disempowerment. This is a very complex issue of plural identities and one-dimensional classification systems. They can hope to have social status and empowerment only if they were to enter the single monolithic structure of standardised education and employment in bureaucratic jobs. Is this not a paradox?

IV

Let me introduce another paradox. Indians sometimes are apologetic about the multilingual Indian state; at other times they take pride in the plurality of languages and literature. Also, sometimes an inflexible one to one correspondence is established between race and language, or place and language. Do all Aryans speak Sanskrit or the Indo-European/Indo-Aryan languages? Do all Dravidians speak and write only Dravidian languages? Do all those living in Tamilnadu speak only Tamil, or those in Kerala speak Malayalam? In short, while the plurality of linguistic families is a self-evident fact and the contours/development of languages can be generally identified, no categorical statement can be made on the absolute purity of a language, its insularity and lack of interaction, and the exact geographical space which it now occupies.

Languages like the river systems flowed and also co-mingled. Sometimes large lakes were formed, and at other times, single streams. This is the history of languages, and what we term as dialects. Plurality comprised language families, but multiplicity of expression existed within a family, of Hindi/Maithili/Kaithi/Rajasthani, as also mutual interaction Hindi-Urdu, Telugu-Tamil, Sanskrit-Malayalam. Recognition of this plurality and multiplicity was logical. However, as in the case of castes and the SC/ST, the succeeding Census reports and the initial survey of 1908 by Grierson, in the very nature and criteria adopted for languages, speakers and dialects resulted in giving a fixity to a changing fluid phenomena. Also it gave absolute priority to the written over the oral.

In the formation of states, a territory was identified with a single language, and the population was considered to be the speakers of a single language. Now each of these is a partial truth, and not the whole truth. The written and oral were two strong parallel streams in the Indian tradition, whether the *sruti* of the Vedas, which by purpose was not written or the rich corpus of Santhali, Mundari, etc. While most people used a language in an area, there were strong pockets of other languages: Telugu speakers in Tamilnadu, Tamil speakers in Kerala, Konkani speakers in Maharashtra. Finally many, if not most people, were not mono-lingual but bi-lingual. Even these simplistic examples make clear that language and race, language and religion, and language and territory could not be set up in a frozen one-to-one equivalence.

Any discerning person realises sooner or later that India is not an aggregation of linguistic groups as in Europe. At all times it is a multiplication of several socio-cultural historical factors; resultantly there is the co-existence of plural language identities in an individual or group. You speak one language at home, another in the courtyard, a third in the street and a fourth in office. Each of these co-exists with ease. There is an overlap of a partial universe in a single person or group. The plurality has given richness, vibrancy and a continued potential for creativity. However, with the ever-increasing pressure of legitimisation and prioritisation of language as an instrument of upward mobility in white collared jobs, it has also led to the shrinking of differences in languages, as also an inability to cross boundaries effectively. The plurality of languages, our classification systems, and the boundaries of geographical / political states have led to the complex and almost unresolvable issues of mother tongue, national language and foreign languages in the educational system.

In our categories, we have to touch upon the most obvious and much discussed reality of India as a multi-religious country. Religion is however defined and identified as institutional religion. The entire division of the population into Hindu, Muslims, Sikhs, Parsis, Jews, Christians and majority-minority is on the premise that all those who are not Muslims, Sikhs, Parsis, Jews, Christians are Hindus. And yet in anthropology and philosophy we speak of a category of people who are 'animists' and atheists. Also we have categories of the Wahabee Sikhs, Sufis and a host of others—not to speak of Buddhists, Jains and others. As in other spheres, while there was distinctiveness and some exclusivity, there were many overlaps of identities. Whether in Indonesia or India there was no contradiction in being a devout Muslim and equally dedicated to the story of *Ramayana* as the Wayang Ustads of Java; or to be a Muslim musician and sing of Hari OM as Bade Gulam Ali did; or to play the Naubat before the temple of Shiva. Besides, the history of Indian temple building and mosque architecture clearly manifests cooperation and reciprocity: the Govind-Deva temple of Vrindavana is an example of such cooperation and fusion of styles. There are countless other examples. Treatises of music in Persian speak of both distinctive identities as also overlayerings and assimilation.

The *Risale-Raga darpana* is one example. The transmission system through the *Daggar bani* is indicative of the overlapping of religions and cultural identity.

These multiple identities were scattered throughout India. Although there were dogmatic tendencies, they were contained by as also contested by the inclusive open movements. Also there was reciprocity in social conduct. Regional or local identity took precedence. By essentialising these identities into fixed identities and juxtaposing them against each other, the foundations of conflict were laid. The Indian character of religious identities gradually began to give place only to the fundamentalism of dogma and doctrine.

V

I turn now to the area of education and the parameters of making a division between the literate and illiterate. Although abject poverty and deprivation is certainly related to illiteracy and illiteracy has to be eliminated, not all illiterates are uneducated or uncultured. The craftsmen, traditional artists, and artisans have already been mentioned. In our demographic profiles we took no note of the oral system of transmission of knowledge still prevalent, not only in India but also in many parts of Asia and Africa. By not taking cognisance of this system or the variety of knowledge systems still extant, the educational system was restricted to the teaching of the 3Rs and only minimal cerebral skills. It is not necessary to delineate upon the history of the foundation of the present system of education as a consequent upon the debate between the Anglicans and the Orientalists. The educational system was to prepare Indians for white collared jobs, to put it gently.

Over these decades, we have certainly educated a large number of people, and have achieved great heights in some domains; but the process of education at the primary and secondary level has become a tool of alienation and uprooting from local cultural contexts. Also there is the largest percentage of the educated unemployed, while at the same time there is a dearth of teachers at the primary and elementary level. The prophetic but demoniac minutes of the Hunter and Wood report has become a reality. The report had said: "By not recognising the indigenous system of education, for jobs, we shall have shrunk the system, so that it will shed of its own accord, without our being held responsible". Our parameters of quantifying the illiterate and literate, the educated in the `modern system of education' and others in the traditional or non-formal system has marginalised the illiterate but educated through the oral system, and those others in specialised disciplines of the earlier knowledge systems. Here also the plurality of educational systems and pedagogical tools have been assessed by the application of a single monolithic yardstick. Plurality of approaches in their cultural context had characterised the earlier systems. A single model has more or less replaced these.

We must also remember that plurality and flexibility was solidly grounded in speculative thought and theoretical models of Indian civilisation. From earliest times there was an unequivocal commitment to plurality of paths: from the first articulations of the Vedas to the medieval poets and thinkers, the varied schools of philosophy, the mathematical systems. There was differentiation and plurality, but with interconnections in the pursuit of knowledge. Different configurations could be formed in space and time, and there was room for exceptions, as also transgression. At the level of social organisation, the plurality could be regulated through a variety of strategies. This was the theoretical level. At the operational level there were rigidities and distortions; but correctives came from the civil society, not the state.

It was into this situation of long continuities and changes that India, like some other countries, experienced as a civilisation the impact of another worldview, which came with the era of enlightenment, political colonisation, and intellectual transformation, Newtonian mechanistic determinism, Cartesian dualism, as also the entire baggage of positivism. This was internalised by the many, in a slow but a sure process. They largely accepted the categories evolved in the West at a particular moment in history. While this is not the occasion to dwell on the evolution of categories and acceptance of derived models, it has to be recognised that these schools of thought greatly influenced the development of structures of governance, administration, and the education of nation-states.

In addition there was the concomitant counterpart of the Orientalist discourse. We also viewed ourselves in terms of the categories evolved in the construct of the Orient. Thus although we struggled for political independence and attained it, when it came to governance we accepted—by compulsion or volition—the left-behind baggage of the intellectual discourse, as also the linear single monolithic models. Resultantly, the alternate or indigenous knowledge systems were devalued, and their plural institutional systems marginalised. A holistic tradition began to fragment.

Mahatma Gandhi, more than anyone else, was acutely conscious of the fact that *selfhood*, that is, *Swarajya* could be gained only by a self-cleansing system and a discarding of previous structures. He advocated a system of self governance at local levels. We have today after decades recognised it in the model of alternate modernity. The educational programme was the pivot of local self governance and micro-level village economies. He envisaged an equalisation of potentials of each constituent. Boundaries of caste, religion, class, language could be broken in ways other than through a single linear model of economic development. However, his vision was not realised. The history is too well known. Others, even those who shared this vision, were compelled to accept the structures left behind. Thus while the goals were new and idealistic, the vehicles were not only old but inappropriate and ill-suited for the vast majority of the people inhabiting a subcontinent of plural cultures.

This was the case not only for India but other erstwhile colonies with plural cultures. Resultantly, the mismatch between the generic or the genetic self-nature of plural cultures and monolithic single models (called 'universal'), at the level of intellection, education and governance led to conflict and tension between and amongst groups and levels of society. We recognised it sometimes as the voice of the disempowered, at other times as ethnicity, and at other times as economic disparities. However, few nation states persevered with the objective of evolving appropriate and more suitable models of development for plural culture societies. The rhetoric of distinctiveness and uniqueness was matched by an over-riding compulsion to become equal members of a global society—that was fast becoming a homogenised mass of an unipolar model called an universal model for development. We opted by choice or compulsion to assess and evaluate ourselves on the basis of the dominant discourse of other lands. Indeed the choices were difficult and the paths tortuous. The eco-cultural balance was disturbed. The more we tried to put fluid living cultures into monolithic homogenised structures, the greater the tensions, and violence.

VI

The subject is vast and complex. In the modern context, at this end, let me restrict myself only to a few examples of how the fluidity and plurality was replaced by a 'fixity' and contrived uniformity which gave rise to disjunctions. One amongst them was the use of common land and water resources and was a well known fluid structure. The pattern of the Bengal Land Settlement Act, and others in the pre-independent era has been followed uniformly in many parts of India by Acts and Ordinance. The history of settlements in and around the Jagannath temple and others in Tamilnadu is revealing. The notion of 'sacredness' was a strategy for conservation and societal responsibility. The moment both became the property of the state or individuals there was trouble and turmoil. The balance of eco-zones and human habitation could not be maintained through single uniform models of state action, without involving and empowering those who both communicated with and were the users and beneficiaries of these primary resources.

Let me now briefly turn to the subject of education and the structures of the educational system. Education is crucial for a democracy, but what kind of education? Can a single monolithic model either in structure or curriculum meet the needs of societies of plural cultures of long continuities? Again, it was Gandhiji who spoke as early as 1908 about a new and more appropriate system of education. Hind Swarajya articulated his total philosophy. Education, *Bunyadi Talim* was a central pivot. From a different but related point of view, Tagore formulated a policy of Lokashiksha in 1930. He modified it sometime during his last days in 1944. Both advocated and stressed the need for the natural integration of the 'head' and the 'hand', and the cultural specific of the plural educational models. Distant but also relevant was Aurobindo's call for the integrated self of the physical, mental and spiritual faculties. Gandhi's Wardha scheme was part of his larger economic model. Tagore called for the inculcation of a total being, and he did not envisage a divide between Sriniketan and Shantiniketan.

Independent India in the first decade adopted *Bunyadi Talim*, Basic Education. It was discarded or rejected, as was bound to happen in the absence of the economic and social underpinnings. A number of commissions were set up for educational reforms, as for example. the Mudaliar Commission, the Radhakrishnan Commission, the Kothari

Commission. Each of them made valuable suggestions including diversification of structures and curricula. However, at the implementation stage, there was the outmoded top-down approach. While the Constitution of India provides for free and compulsory elementary education, we are far from the goal; what is more, the content of the education with an emphasis on only the 3 Rs and cerebral skills dissociated the learner from his/her cultural roots.

Many years ago a blue print was made to make the single teacher schools into two-teacher schools. It was recommended that the second teacher may be from the traditional craftsmen—the potter, the ironsmith, the cobbler etc., literate or illiterate. The recommendations were not accepted, nor modifications made in the nature of planning at the micro-level with an integrated approach. Even this brief narration makes it clear that primary and elementary education in a vast country with plural geo-physical environment, cultures has to be matched with plural structures and diversity of approaches for different situations. The replication of a single model for all parts of India, from the Himalayas to the Arabian Sea, deserts to marshlands, with differentiation in societal structures, could not be viable, as it has not been. There are other instances within polytechnic and university systems where there is a dysjunction between the vibrant creativity and productivity of the sector, called non-formal or traditional, and the institutional structures established by the state. Through the system white collared jobs naturally became the only aspiration.

Finally, the issue of structure, content and pedagogical methods of education cannot be dissociated from the administrative system that a country adopts for governance. As mentioned before, Gandhiji wished to completely re-haul if not reject the system. Jawaharlal Nehru wanted to reform the system. Morarji Desai headed an Administrative Reforms Commission. Smt. Indira Gandhi had a love-hate relationship with it and therefore often bypassed the system. Rajiv Gandhi wanted radical changes. And yet the strongest monolithic structure is the administrative system, with or without the rusted iron frame of the administrative services. The fundamental question is, does the uniform administrative system take into account plurality, and is there space and place for flexibility and initiative? The answers to both questions are unfortunately in the negative. However, the tripartite balance of the administrative, executive, judiciary and legislative cannot be ignored in any discussion on plural cultures and monolithic structures.

Pertinently many analysts and observers have spoken about these issues and challenges. More than ever before there is a sizeable body of opinion which recommends a plurality of models for organising and governing plural societies. A different intellectual framework emanating from within South Asian (Indian) methods, cultures and knowledge systems must be used, both for analysing the complex realities and the processes of change. In this exercise it is evident that many conventional or derived notions will have to be given up. It is possible to do so, and the time is ripe for it. India has the great potential and human resource for it. The challenge is of a sensitive comprehension and a skillful harnessing of these multifaceted energies, of plural sources of creativity.

Makarand Paranjape

Reworlding Homes: colonialism, 'national' culture, and post-national India

I

It is quite clear by now that Indian nationalism was quite different from its European predecessors and that it was certainly not a 'derivative discourse'. European nationalism may be said to have two major trajectories. The first, born out of the age of revolutions and of the European Enlightenment, defined the nation as an aggregate of citizens, whose consent to be thus governed defined the nation. The second was the post-Enlightenment idea, influenced by German Idealism and Romanticism, of the nation as made up of a *volk*, a people with a distinct ethnic, linguistic, or cultural identity. Indian ideas of the nation, on the other hand, were characterised by their emphasis on *desh* or locality, region, and territory, *jati* or birth, tribe, community, and *praja* or the people, subjects, or citizens. Incidentally, the word *praja*, which M. K. Gandhi often used for the nation, includes in its various meaning both the citizens and the rulers of a state. It is also interesting to note that it is related etymologically to the nation, because of common Indo-European roots.

Indian nationalism was different from European nationalism because the former was born out of a struggle with the latter, or of that extension of the latter which found its way to India as imperialism. An external challenge and threat were thus its first defining feature. Its second defining feature was an internal struggle with its own traditions and social arrangements, the most virulent of which was movement of politico-religious separatism that caused the Partition.

For most part, I shall confine myself to the first of these defining features, that is, India's struggle with Western imperialism. And at the very heart of this clash of cultures—the collision between British imperialism and Indian society—were questions of autonomy, self-hood, or to use a Gandhian word, *swaraj*. I would even go so far as to say that the whole project of imagining or forging a nation was but a subset of this larger question of autonomy or *swaraj*.

In other words, I would argue that power and resistance to power, which might be seen as the dominant tropes of the encounter between the colonisers and the colonised, embody, in the final analysis, a struggle for autonomy, for selfhood, and for *swaraj*. These exertions over the content of a new individuality and a new collectivity were really about creating the condition for an economic, political, social, and cultural order in which the humanity, dignity, equality, and autonomy of the individual could be maintained. That is why it seems to me important to get the vocabulary and the idioms of these struggles right, not to annex them to other discourses because, were we to do so, we shall have lost our own autonomy even before we begin to explore the principal actors and texts involved. Words like *swaraj* have a resonance and dimension which is irreducible to any other synonym or substitute. While we need to be critical in the usage of such words, to reject them altogether is tantamount to cultural suicide. In other words, not only is it important for us to define the terms of discourse at the beginning, but also to frame them in a culturally responsible and rooted manner.

If we agree to use cultural coded terms like svaraj, we will at once recognise that the issue of translation is at the very core of our concerns. That is because we have to grapple with two or more languages of being, two or more ways of seeing the world, two or more systems of cognition. To erase this multiplicity and difference is to deny the complexity of this encounter, to reduce it to this or that usually political motive. It is to do violence to our own past and present, not to speak of irreparable damage to our future. We must therefore be cognisant of two or more modes of being and reference, without collapsing the one into the other. This requires a kind of critical perspectivism that has a sort of double or multiple vision, the capacity simultaneously to have a dual focus.

If so, what is the relationship between the *ghar* and the *bahir*, to invoke the title of Rabindranath Tagore's famous novel, between the inner and the outer, the private and the public, the personal and the political, psycho-spiritual and the socio-economic, the native and the colonial, the Indian and the Western—in a word, between the home and the world? It is clear that there is no obvious conflict or dichotomy between the two, that they are not mutually exclusive. Instead, there seems to be continuous interrelationship between the two. The personal is the political, as is all too familiar to us by now. The quest for conjugal happiness in *Ghare Baire* (1916) is thus directly lined to the struggle for a new India. Why is this point of such great importance? That's because the world is out of joint and to set it right requires the kind of reorientation which will also transform the most personal of relationships. This is what Tagore suggests to us.

But we must see these two poles as not being related dialectically as much as dialogically. In dialectics, one side cancels or supercedes the other before it is in turn cancelled or superceded. Such a mechanism of endless opposition does not produce the kind of breakthrough in which both can not only co-exist but get transformed. I would prefer to see the interpenetration of opposites in a manner which is dialogic so that what is produced is not antithesis versus thesis but a sort of third space. This third space is not Homi Bhabha's interstitial space between the nation and nationlessness, a sort of grey area that the diaspora is supposed to occupy. Rather, to me, it is the possibility inherent in the here and now of every situation of conflict or competition, a finger of hope pointing to what is neither oppressed or oppressive, neither victimiser nor victim, neither dominant nor subordinate, but something else, something autonomous without being either subservient or repressive. This is the space of non-violent action, of autonomy, and of svaraj.

II

Having suggested what I see as the crucial tropes or recurrent motifs of the encounters between the colonisers and the colonised, I would like very briefly to examine how they are played out in nineteenth and early twentieth century Bengal. Such an exercise is, no doubt, fraught with the great risk of over-simplification or reduction, but we still need to attempt it for heuristic reasons if for nothing else.

It would be good to start with Rammohun Roy, an emblematic figure in the Bengal renaissance and the creation of Indian modernity.

Placed at the very beginning of the Indo-British encounter, his life and work offer a telling narrative of the progress of colonialism in India. What is noteworthy is that 'progress' in this case is really a regress. No wonder that in Roy we find greater possibilities of autonomy and *swaraj* than in a later figure like Michael Madhusudan Dutta. This is because imperialism is not yet established and instutionalised in Rammohun's time. Those who wish to see a unilinear progression of imperialistic hegemony will therefore be disappointed. Just as the conservatives who ruled Britain had a greater respect for the native cultures of India than the liberals and utilitarians who followed them, the beginnings of British paramountcy in India actually afforded greater spaces for native agency than the later decades of empire when the barriers between the rulers and the ruled were cast, so to speak, in concrete. What makes Bengal so interesting is that it offers the entire colonial spectrum in graphic clarity from its beginnings to its demise.

But to revert to Rammohun for a while, I would characterise his letter to Lord Amherst as a substantiation of a certain position in the Indo-British encounter. I would call this the insufficiency thesis. Rammohun's basic argument is that traditional knowledge in India, whether it is *vyakaran* or Vedanta, is inadequate. What is required for the progress of India, therefore, is the infusion of Western knowledge, which can only be done through English. Of course, it is crucial to distinguish Rammohun's position from that of Macaulay's. Rammohun by no means indulges in a blanket condemnation or dismissal of all the intellectual traditions of India as did Macaulay. Yes, the tone of his description of traditional learning in India is satirical bordering on the contemptuous. He does discredit this knowledge as being inconsequential to the point of being farcical and ridiculous. But unlike Macaulay, he does not believe that the solution lies in absorbing European literature. Rather, he asks for Chemistry, Astronomy, and other practical arts and sciences. Rammohun wants a revolution in India not too different from what happened in Europe. He is therefore an indigenous champion of an Enlightenment that cannot, when we examine world history, be considered the sole preserve of Europeans.

This insufficiency thesis finds its most vocal supporters in what came loosely to be called the Young Bengal group. Though its members were rather different and distinctive, we might pick up Michael Madhusudan Dutta as a good representative. While Rammohun resisted conversion to Christianity, but Christianised, rationalised, and modernised Hinduism, Madhusudan went over completely, even risking loss of patrimony and disinheritance. His return to Bengal and Bengali after an unsuccessful foray into complete Anglicisation has often been seen as the classic embodiment of the recurrent pattern of the loss and recovery of the self under colonialism. Whether the loss was total in the first place is debatable as is the question of the nature and extent of the recovery. What is more certain, however, is that there is no simple passage possible between the world of the colonised to the world of the colonisers. Is Madhusudan's rewriting of the *Ramayana* more than simply a critique of tradition? By making the manly Meghnad the hero who is outwitted and defeated by the more effeminate and devious Rama and Lakshmana, is he doing more than just inverting the power structure of the traditional epic? Can't Rama and Lakshmana also be seen in place of the British in India, who came in to trade but stayed to rule? While these questions remain, it is clear that by and large Madhusudan considered Hindu society to be morally bankrupt and culturally decadent. A new creation could take place only with a substantial rupture with the past. The rotten trunk of the old Hindu civilisation would have to be cut off before something new and better emerged.

One might argue, to complicate matters, that Rammohun's outward resistance concealed an inner surrender to the West, while Madhusudan's outward subjection masked an inner rebellion. Further, that in a given life cycle, one character would very likely embody more than one position or, more likely, run through the whole gamut of responses to the dominant from abject surrender to fiery rebellion. What is more likely, however, is a certain range, a spectrum of intellectual and professional negotiations within which each character functions. It is this range that I have tried to identify and emphasise.

Sri Ramakrishna, to take another fascinating example, an unlettered but vastly gifted spiritual giant, who was also endowed with a definite sense of a grander purpose, may be seen as exemplifying the opposite position of the cultural and intellectual self-sufficiency of India. From a rustic and non-literary background, he nevertheless shows a great erudition in the older tradition of oral wisdom. That this was actually a classical tradition, not just a subaltern one, is clear when we see the number and quality of his preceptors, starting with the Bhairavi Brahmani and ending with his formal Vedantic guru, Totapuri. The order of sannyasins that he inspired was thus an offshoot of the much older tradition of intellectual leadership instituted in the Sankaracharya order. That he could tame, domesticate, and transform a modern positivist like Narendranath Dutta can be read as the allegory of the triumph of tradition over modernity.

I once heard a swami of the Ramakrishna order pose an interesting question. All *avatars*, said he, came to slay some *asura* or the other. Which one did Sri Ramakrishna slay? The startling answer was, the *asura* of materialism. Whether we agree with this assessment or not, we can be reasonably certain that one of the causes of the decline of the Brahmo Samaj was its reintegration into a modernised and reconstructed Hinduism that Sri Ramakrishna was instrumental in inspiring. Not just Vivekananda, but Keshub Chunder Sen, and a whole generation of Western educated 'progressive' young men came under Ramakrishna's spell. Not just the dignity but the inventiveness of Indian traditions was demonstrated. Ramakrishna reinvented Hinduism in terms of the *sarva dharma samabhava*, that Gandhi and Vinoba later made the fulcrum of a new national consensus.

Between these two poles of insufficiency and self-sufficiency are a host of interesting and challenging figures. Bankim, on the one hand, who is seen nowadays as the progenitor of a certain kind of Hindu communalism, but who was more properly a moderniser and proto anti-colonialist, not to speak of the father of modern Bengali prose. Not just Bankim, but Vivekananda, Sri Aurobindo, and Subhas Chandra Bose all represent a certain masculinist type of resistance to colonialism. Aurobindo's project, ultimately, went much beyond revolutionary anti-imperialism to a kind of transformative futurism or spiritual evolutionism that would result in a mutation in human consciousness and unalterable metamorphosis in terrestrial life. Bose's authoritarian militarism still has its adherents, but was unable to dislodge Gandhian pacifism as the dominant ideology of the nationalist bourgeoisie. But perhaps the most interesting intermediate figure is Tagore.

III

In Tagore's work and thought we see an attempt to attain a balance between these two positions. Cultures are seen neither as sufficient or as insufficient in themselves but always in a process of negotiation and evolution. The static, the rigid, the fixed, the mechanical come under disapproval. In his lectures on nationalism, for instance, Tagore attacks the mechanistic and aggressive urge to power that he saw as the European nation's characteristic and defining feature. Of course, we must also keep in mind that what Tagore means by nationalism in these lectures is actually that extension of the national that expresses itself as the imperial. In other words, though the lectures criticise nationalism, their real subject is imperialism. Tagore was one of the several makers of modern India. Like Gandhi, Nehru, and Maulana Azad, Tagore wanted the Indian experiment in nation building to be somewhat different from the European one. The nation that he envisaged would steer clear of the narrow and exclusivist prejudices of states defined by a single identity, whether of language, religion, or ethnicity. At the same time, the universalism that he promoted did not imply either a capitulation to Western culture nor the erasure of the local, regional, or the national. An authentic cultural position did not mean a fanatical rejection of the Other, nor an ingratiating submission to it. Neither collaboration nor conflict was the sole recourse of a vibrant and self-confident culture, but rather a continuous engagement with the particulars of a given situation. Coercion, consent, and resistance did not exist in different compartments for Tagore, but were deeply intertwined.

Such a careful and critical mediation between political extremes is seen at work in *Gora* (1909). Through his eponymous protagonist, Tagore rejects both the extremes of Hindu fanaticism and comprador elitism. The first part of the book shows the inadequacy of the former, while British imperialism comes under attack later, somewhat indirectly. It is only when Gora goes to the countryside that the unmasking of empire takes place and he finds the brutal face of British rule exposed. The oppression of the peasants and the economic pauperisation of the villages opens his eyes to the structural realities of imperialism behind the rather polite façade of paternalistic collaboration offered to the native bourgeoisie. From being a 'good subject', Gora becomes a bad subject and finds himself in jail. When he returns, he is disgusted to discover that he has become a national hero. Gora's long disappearance from the text serves to give the other characters the space to resolve their complicated personal and social relationships. Gora, in turn, discovers what has been his own fatal flaw—the suppression and disregard of the other half of India, its woman. It is now that Suchorita's face appears in his mind's eye, merging with that of his mother, Anandamoyi, who is of course Mother

India herself. He clearly understands that a new India can only be created by including and recognising its women. This will have to be a collaborative and cooperative project, harnessing the agencies and energies of both the sexes, not a hyper-masculinist imposition of the will of a strong man on the passive and compliant masses.

Gora is an earlier text than *Ghare Baire*. Tagore uses two couples to work out his vision of a new India. Binoy and Lalita serve not only as foils to Gora and Suchorita, but are perhaps the mainstay of the book. Binoy, not Gora, is the real hero, because Binoy is closer to the average person. The character of Gora is later transformed into that of Sandeep. The extremism of both comes under disapproval. In *Gora* Tagore tells us that what appears to be most Hindu is actually least so. It is a foreign element masquerading as the authentic internal one. The West that we internalise is the real enemy, more dangerous than the West out there. Tamed of its Semitic zeal, such an element may coexist with the others in a larger rainbow of many cultures that is India. But when it strives to dominate, taking over the whole spectrum of political and cultural possibilities, it must be opposed and neutralised. This only Suchorita's feminine sexual energy can do. Without her, Gora's cultural nationalism would turn pathological and destructive, not only to his own household, but to the nation in the making.

Gora ends with the major characters preparing for a long journey outside Calcutta. Their actions have raised a storm which must be allowed to subside before they can return. The seeds of a new society are to be nursed in another soil before they can be transplanted back. Tagore explores three formulae of nationalism in *Gora*. Hindu nationalism, based as it is upon an unrepentant and unreformed tradition, is rejected as is the slavish and imitative collaboration with British raj that is represented by both Baradasundari and Haran Babu. The latter is an especially inapt, not to speak of inept, prospective groom for Suchorita because he would stifle and obliterate her self, not for some higher cause but for the sake of his own already bloated ego. Such idolatry is intolerable to Tagore. Gora's own formula for what constitutes a true Indian is not cumulative. It is not the Punjab plus Sind plus Gujarat plus Maratha and so on that we celebrate in our national anthem penned by none other than Tagore himself; instead, it is arrived via negative, *neti neti*, neither Punjab, nor Sind, nor Bangla, nor Brahmin, nor Dalit, and so on. What is left, of course, is a sort of basic common denominator of humanity, shorn of all caste marks or identity tags. The real Indian is simply the essential man or woman. Paresh Babu, Anandamoyi, and the two young couples qualify as the inheritors of an authentic Indian tradition as well as the progenitors of the new Indian nation. Together they form the basis of a new society that is yet to emerge fully as the novel ends.

Today, after he has been canonised and idolised so incontrovertibly, it is difficult to imagine just how much Tagore was reviled and abused in his life time. In one of this last essays on Tagore, Nirad C. Choudhury describes the poet's life as a lonely struggle against personal loss, economic difficulty, and public scorn. He was not spared even when he died; his funeral turned into a fiasco, with unruly mobs disrupting the solemnity of the occasion. Certainly, *Ghare Baire* too invoked decades of criticism and abuse from varieties of readers and critics. Tagore was accused of having written a book promoting immorality and adultery. He was dubbed anti-national and anti-Hindu. Yet, I believe that it is only in this kind of intrepid and sometimes unpleasant mediation with various aspects of our complex realities that the quest for autonomy, whether personal or social, can be sought.

While proposing these three paradigms of our interaction with the colonising West, I do not wish to valorise any particular approach as more valid or effective. Each paradigm is, moreover, much more ambivalent than it appears at first. This is because the whole field of culture is complex and involved. Neither Indian attitudes to British rule, nor British attitudes to India can be encapsulated into any easy formulae. Yet, these are the broad patterns that recur repeatedly, which I have tried to identify. Our discussion cannot be complete, however, without invoking a person who does not figure as prominently in the Bengali imagination as he does in the national. I refer, of course, to Mohandas Karamchand Gandhi. With Ashis Nandy and others I believe that it is in Gandhi that all the currents of India's quest for modernity and nationhood intersect most graphically. While I have written elsewhere about Gandhi's approach to these questions, I might just say that what he represents is the curious paradox of an upholder of tradition also being its greatest critic and a critic of modernity who is also the most radically modern person of his times. Gandhi's modernity was, I must put it somewhat curiously, already *post*modern. He wanted to create a modernity that was not so much anti-modern, but drastically *non*modern. Of course, he failed, but before that he had thoroughly re-engineered Indian traditions so profoundly and irrevocably that not only is there no going back, but the way forward is also unalterably civic and secular. Gandhi tried to reworld the home in ways that would at once make us at home in the world and also make the world a non-threatening, homely place.

IV

If *Gora* is the novel of Indian nationalism, then O.V.Vijayan's *Khasakkinte Itihasam* (1969) may be considered the novel of post-nationalism.

When O.V. Vijayan turned to write it, he was turning away from his project of writing *the* 'revolutionary' novel of the 1950s at the instance of the Comrade-President of the Malabar District Board of Teachers. The Comrade had urged him to put more '*Inquilab*' into his next project after expressing mild praise for Vijayan's already published short stories. However, something quite eventful happened to intervene between the Comrade-President's advice and the great revolutionary novel that Vijayan was setting out to write. This was the invasion of Hungary by the Soviet Union in 1956, when Soviet tanks rolled into Budapest, and the killing of Imre Nagy in 1958. A disillusioned Vijayan turned away from the master narrative of universal socialism to the legends of a remote village in Kerala, Thasarak.

What did Thasarak, immortalised as Khasak, offer Ravi, the protagonist of the novel? An escape from modernity, from the relentless telescope of the Florentine, always turned outward, to those realms of the inner spirit which alone have the key to escape the inexorable cycle of births and deaths? At any rate, fleeing from the original sin of post-Enlightenment rationality, Ravi finds a magical world in Khasak. Here the local legends, respected by both Muslims and Hindus, offer a counter to progress or the march of Hegelian History. If modernity, as Max Weber said, stands for the inevitable disenchantment of the world, Khasak is the place where its relentless logic is circumvented or swallowed up. Ravi is re-enchanted by Khasak. Here he atones for his sin of incest, a sin which had dogged him in his previous life and blocked any meaningful relationship or commitment. The scourge of small pox catches up with him even in remote Khasak, like bad karma from which there is no escape. But in Khasak, this orphaned child, who becomes the object of his step mother's desire because his father is a paralysed old man, now finds a whole bevy of mothers, who with their own breast milk heal the scabs of his raging fever. At last, he mates the houri of Khasak, Maimoona herself, with her translucent skin embroidered with the blue veins. In the last scene of the novel, Ravi waits to return to the world, as the rain sweeps over him, uniting him with the whole cosmos in its cleansing embrace. The ending is ambivalent, hinting at both a death and a resurrection.

The ethos of Khasak has been nurtured by the same 'tender absurdities' that both Hindus and Muslims share. Much as mischief makers like the Mulla or Sivaraman Nair try to get them to quarrel, the social fabric of Khasak remains intact and unrent. This is because "The history of Khasak was the great oral legend; that, and a shared indigence held Khasak together" (*The Legends of Khasak* 96). The two nation theory is defeated by the dwarf cretin Apu Kili who nonchalantly switches from wearing a tuft to a fez, until his hair grows back, and the lice return. Similarly, Nizam Ali turns away from the Allah Pticha, the Mulla, first to become a capitalist, then a communist, and finally the Khazi of the legendary Sheikh. As the Khazi, quite in opposition to the Mulla's madrassa, he encourages the new primary school, which Ravi has come to run as the first modern teacher for Khasak's first school. When the Mulla dies, he gives the call to prayer after seven long years.

Ravi's school is in Sivaraman Nair's seeding house, the place of love and imagination. Here the old legends of Khasak and the new narrative of modern education blend to offer at least a temporary hope for the new nation that has emerged from the ashes of colonialism and the carnage of the Partition. Vijayan's Khasak thus provides an arresting antidote to the grand narrative of nationalism

V

All the protagonists of my narrative happen to be Hindu, upper-caste men, such as I myself am. Where are the subaltern voices, one might rightfully ask? Why have I not dealt with women, with religious and ethnic minorities, with Dalits and other subalterns? Today when the marketing of margins has become almost de rigueur, what I have attempted is certainly risky if not unfashionable. However, I hope that mine is a critical conservatism, not an unthinking one. Without attempting an elaborate defense, I will simply say that it is only today that we might consider makers of modern India as conservatives. In their own time, they were all of them pretty reformative, if not radical. They were driven by an energy that can only be considered progressive in its own time. That they were mostly concerned with upper-caste, Hindu India must be admitted, though, again, here Gandhi is an exception, which is precisely why he is so threatening to a certain brand of Dalit politics. For that matter, Gandhi was equally threatening to Hindu fanatics.

The dominant culture of modern India whose contours I have tried to sketch was, I admit, primarily concerned with the terms of India's relationship with British imperialism specifically and Western modernity in general. Once this relationship was defined so as to ensure a certain modicum of dignity and autonomy for India in the comity of nations of the world, other, intra-national readjustments were bound to follow. The builders of modern India were trying to re- right/ write a relationship of structural inequality with the West. Once this was effected, they were sure that gender, caste and religious equalities could also be achieved as an irreversible consequence of an anti-imperialistic nationalism. That is why, when we turn from the narratives of dominant culture to that of, say, the women, we find a distinct shift in the emphasis. The role, status, position, and subjectivity of women within the Hindu patriarchy is the central concern of the women writers, rather than questions of colonialism proper. Similarly, Dalit and other subaltern texts are primarily concerned with justice and equality within Indian society, even if this means going outside the Hindu fold. However, I would argue that these micro concerns are inextricably interlinked with the bigger questions that I have alluded to of autonomy, selfhood, and *swaraj* in the context of British imperialism. There is no former without the latter.

Dominant culture needs to be studied not just for its absences and erasures as is the prevalent practice today, but also for its presences and additions. From Rammohun Roy to Mahatama Gandhi to Ashis Nandy the mainstream intellectual and cultural tradition of modern India has tried to forge not so much a counter-modernity, but an alternative modernity that while it was distinctly Indian, also had universal aspirations. This they did not so much by synthesising the East and the West, the home and the world, the inner and the outer, the traditional and the modern, the spiritual and the scientific, the female and the male, the Hindu and the Muslim, the Brahmin and the Dalit, and so on, but by constantly mediating and negotiating between the two to produce something other. This other was not a hybrid, not some kind of mongrel in-betweeness, but a third world without the pejorative associations of that term. A crucial methodological instrument in this process was translation, both as an actual practice and as a metaphor of a larger way of apprehending our reality. Translation was a way of 'reworlding' the home and of domesticating the world. That is why in our contemporary postcolonial practice, I consider translation to be crucial, not just in our reading of translated texts, but also in our preserving the double vision that comes from having more than one register of thought.

The makers of modern India—from Rammohun Roy to O.V. Vijayan—tried to rewrite the monolinguality of modernity and imperialism in our own multiple tongues and voices. The cacophony that ensued had the capacity of transforming modernity itself, rendering it polyphonic and chaotic. From the universe of rationality, the attempt was made to create a 'multiverse' of dissonant wisdom. In the process, various paradigms of coping with the dominant West were tried out—of these, the insufficiency and the self-sufficiency thesis are significant. But even more significant was a position that refused to argue from either of these positions, but included them both. Tagore and Gandhi, in their own rather different ways, can be cited as examples of this method. But what they share with their other contemporaries and predecessors like Rammohun Roy, Bankim, Ramakrishna, Vivekananda, Vidyasagar, Aurobindo, Bose and others is a deep and abiding concern for the autonomy, self-hood, and *swaraj*.

The habitus of this new society is provisionally the nation state, but also civil society and community life based on equality, justice, and plurality. Gandhi's *Ram Rajya*, I would thus argue, is a deeply secular idea that is at once designed to capture the imagination of the masses in a vocabulary comprehensible to them, but also to present the vision of a new, radically modern state. This intermingling of an apparent unworldliness with such this-worldliness becomes the locus of a new home for an India that has broken its colonial shackles and is ready to assert her own sense of selfhood and dignity once again. Because it is only upon the restoration of our selfhood and dignity that we can say that we are at home in this world, not beggars, slaves, or aliens in it.

Rukmini Bhaya Nair

Poetry as an Expression of National Crisis: a preface and three poems

In the immediate aftermath of 9/11, America's radio-stations, television channels, newspapers and magazines all reported that they were flooded by an unprecedented tide of poems. It was as if the grief and national outrage felt by the people at large found its most spontaneous, if not necessarily most considered, expression in poetry. In fact, it appears that this 'turn to poetry' in times of national crisis may be an intriguingly primeval feature of modern societies, otherwise wedded to far more visually gripping forms of expression— such as film and television, or even the fine arts, such as painting and music.

Can poetry then be thought of as a 'natural' barometer of our emotional responses to national crisis? If so, then the implication appears to be that even the most sceptical amongst us, who in general regard the idea of borders and boundaries as some sort of bureaucratic legerdemain, still instinctively acknowledge at such moments that we 'belong' to the country. We cannot but take collective responsibility for events such as the recent carnage in Gujarat. It is here that W.H. Auden's famous line, `Poetry makes nothing happen; it survives' returns to haunt us—for, as a testament of survival, poetry is also about *threats* to survival, to community life. When a 'national culture' embodies— or fails to embody—that self-protective and inclusive urge to survive and, just as importantly, enable *others* survive—poetry swings into action as an urgent critique of the failures of civil society.

It is not an accident that our Prime Ministers with views as politically diverse as Vishwanath Pratap Singh and Atal Bihari Vajpayee, have been poets. Rather, their turning of crises into poems may indicate that they are part of a long-standing tradition that frankly admits to the subterranean connections between political culture and poetic expression. While this is not the appropriate occasion to go into this thesis in greater detail, I would tentatively suggest that these poets belong to a culture where statecraft, philosophical 'musings' and poetry go together. Among the Greeks, it was different. Plato, for example, staunchly maintained that the 'old quarrel between poetry and philosophy' could *never* be resolved; hence, he had no option but to recommend the banning of poets from his Ideal Republic. Poets were just too much of a risk for the state; they were far too prone to creating crises and disturbing the mental equilibrium of the populace. In India's composite history, however, whether in the Mughal or Maurya courts, poems have always been—and, interestingly, continue to be—natural forums where politicians present their individual 'solutions' to endemic national problems that may have been left murkily unresolved in their professional world of *realpolitik*.

Each of the three poems which follow this brief excursus into the relationship between poetry and the anxieties of state are, with one exception, to appear in my new collection, *Yellow Hibiscus* (2003). They were written in the successive years 1999, 2000 and 2001 in response to my own, often inchoate, reactions to India's convulsions.

The first poem, simply called *Buddha*, was written after the destruction of the Bamiyan Buddhas in February, 2001. India's connections with Afghanistan, as we know, date at least as far back as the figure of Gandhari in the *Mahabharata*, whose name derives from the city of Kandahar, via the figure of Rabindranath Tagore's unforgettable *Kabuliwallah*, right up to the present. Although my 'model' in this poem was actually an old Burmese Buddha who sits on my desk, in each of these figures I saw, once again, a response to violence that appeared—in the depths of its capacity to absorb anger—ultimately unbeatable. Such an impregnably non-violent resistance to the bitterest intolerance has conventionally been considered an integral part of 'our national culture', both as political strategy and as a mindset—but this principle has also been alarmingly contravened in recent times.

When 2000 dawned, one recalls the atavistic frenzy of millennial celebrations across all national borders. 9/11 and the destruction of the Bamiyan Buddhas were at the time still events waiting to erupt—and for a brief period, calm reigned. The third poem in this 'set', called *Seasons Greetings to a Reader in a New Millennium*, is based on the commonly felt impulse, on centennial dates like these, to assess one's own life and times in the light of the future. And a typical metaphor for the crisis that signals the end of an era is, of course, the passing of seasons. Thus Tagore in his famous *1400 Sal*, for instance, summons up a distant spring morning, disingenuously enquiring: *Who are you, reader, reading my poems a hundred years hence*, while Thomas Hardy hears a song-bird's note of hope amidst the bleak gloom of a wintry English landscape in *The Darkling Thrush*. But despite these fine effusions, any verses delivered on cue still tend to remain suspect. For, how can a genuine poem so seasonally appear on time? Yet, as I see it, the line is thin between the implied insincerity of writing *for* the occasion and the passion of writing *on* all occasions. Maybe this is an illusion, but it allows a degree of tolerance both of one's own and others' productions—a quality that is supposed to be, as we've just said, intrinsic to our 'national ethos'. From such a writer's perspective, it has to be this 'utopian' intellectual openness that is perhaps the most crucial feature of an 'Indian poetics' broadly defined.

Finally, the last poem in this selection is from the beginning of my book *The Ayodhya Cantos*, published in 1999, which has as its central theme the pulling down of the Babri Masjid in 1992—certainly an episode which reflected a major national crisis. However, even though my story in that long allegory was set in Ayodhya, it began, oddly enough, in Gujarat—so, today, it almost seems as if the poem was prophetic! This poem was written after a friend described to me how she once travelled through the Gujarat deserts in the height of summer with the temperature touching 47 degrees centigrade. Yet, when she looked out of her car window, what she appeared to see was a landscape covered in glittering snow! . What the eye saw—namely, the salt dunes of Gujarat, site of Gandhi's heroic 'salt-satyagraha'— and what the body felt, seemed quite contradictory—and yet they were one. From this insight sprang this 'Prologue' to the Ayodhya verses, entitled Journey from Baroda which tries to describe some of the syncretic traditions that have gone into the making of modern India—symbolised by the figures of a Sufi ascetic, Meerabai and Mahatma Gandhi. If we are ever to survive the violent crises to which the Indian people have repeatedly been subjected in recent times, it is surely to such pluralist visions that we must return.

BUDDHA (2001)

Face shuttered
Eyes down!
The folds of his
Shoulder-cloth
Mimic his frown...

        Waterfall of gems
        Like a gush of tears!
        Uncontrollable
        The weeping
        In his silent ears...

Hands cupped
Begging for alms!
The rich world's
Shining in those
Empty palms...

        Lips that contain
        All forms of enmity
        Infinite desire!
        And the sag
        Of gravity...

A man who speaks
With his eyes
Hears with his hands...
Lifts you effortless
To paradise!

SEASONS GREETINGS TO A READER IN A NEW
MILLENNIUM (2000)

Spring

when you restore
my poetry
in the museums
of the future
do not try too hard
for a perfect fit...

cracks ran between
these shards
even in their own
time and the lines
made so little sense
that people laughed!

as for the script
it was always un-
decipherable
how can I explain
a form that is whole
only when broken?

but finger these
fragments lightly
in the spring-time
of the future and
they will speak to you
in your own tongue...

Summer

as galaxies unwind in
the heat of the night
I send you further
despatches on freedom
an idea that swings
in the terrorist breeze...

some call it poetic justice
this body I think mine
is more remote than yours
and time explodes in our guts
as when the universe began
blowing us away—apart.

love's starry tentacles shed
and the tiger-skin of intellect
a poem flits into the dark—
its hoot like an escaped
convict's and its maimed
wing brushing your cheek...

Autumn

on our subcontinent
we deal in infinity
not just our gods
but gossip and silver-
tongued brutalities
everything is repeated...

the leaves fall twice
from the trees and this
second time that dry
scrunch under your feet
is the sound of my poetry
being ground into dust...

Winter

against these cruel white terraces
of paper you are invisible—look!

but sure as a young mountain-
goat
this poem will still track you
down
one day it will find its greenest
pasture...

JOURNEY FROM BARODA (1999)

Sand

If you wish to cross
The deserts of Gujarat

      Let your mind freeze

The sand is a tiger
Yellow and shadowy

      It leaps at your car
      On the metalled road

And in the desperate
Heat of that meeting

      You let your mind freeze.

Sea

Blue arm of the Arab sea
Flung across the coast

      Rests at Jamnagar, caresses
      At Gir, dim forest fortresses

And wanton in that darkness
The sea tells its secrets

      So let your mind freeze
      From Baroda to Porbundar

Where sea embraces desert
Let your mind freeze.

Salt

And then you will see snow!
Great crystal piles of it

> Glittering in drifts, dunes
> Cold as distant Karakoram

Of the many forms of water
Steam, ice and fallow rain

> The snow in Kathiawar
> Is a gift from the sea

Residue of the purest salt
It lets your mind freeze.

Sufi

Crossing the snowy desert, a man changes

> Not keeping to the road
> Shacking up with bearded strangers
> Sharing a Sufi's ganja

You follow his path
As if it were your own

> But in the end the Sufi leaves you
> There is no reason why he should have stayed

He told you things you knew already

That the stars in the desert sky
Are more numerous than its grains of sand
And that we have more foolish questions
Than these infinities put together

It is not his wisdom he leaves behind
But his voice, breaking on a doha

His voice lives in the desert

You hear him speak
Among the snow dunes

The brittle intellect is like a glass
We see through it but cannot pass.

Meera Bai

Another time, a woman dances by

No one has seen her face
But when she sings
She surrounds you in bright swirls
Chunarias, ghunghats, odhnis,
All the scandalous cloths, the scents of the desert

Her name is Meera

She is nothing like the Sufi
She does not know the colour white, she has never seen
Grey, even in a man's beard, a woman's hair
Never

Still, you remember the many forms of water
And you forgive her
You have not seen her face but you want to touch her

Then she throws back her veil

Her face is fat and pock-marked
How can you touch her?
How can you not?

Her voice is the voice of the desert
She is a tiger
She is snow
She is lascivious flesh, a creature of veils and anklets

You have to possess her, touch her
Though you know you will be burnt
As soon as you take her

False snow, flaming poet!
Scorched salt of the desert
Flamboyant Meera taunts you
Tempts you with her raddled skin

Perhaps she will shed it when you enter her
Like her loose untethered clothes, like the lithe
Side-winding desert snake, her childish rattle
Announces death, this woman who is a trophy tiger
Whose hide hangs, shamed, in some rich hall
Still stiff with resistance, untamed

She stands beside a shallow salt-pit, alone

Poorer than anyone you've ever known, she is Venus
Harvesting the sea, denuded lover
Deprived, depraved, utterly captivating
How can you resist her?

She is the spirit of Dandi

Her pride puts her beyond your reach
Beyond acrimony, and far beyond desire

Meera Bai, *bhootni*
Does not ask for your manhood
Since when did freedom lie in the tick of a penis?
She wants you to believe in the colours of the desert
In promises, poems, marches, the gentleness of tigers
She wants you to trust your soul, her body

That is how she wants you

And when, finally, finally, you look into her urgent eyes
You see neither sea nor desert, but yourself
Capable of anything, a Sufi, a secure wanderer, a laughing ghost

Then pock-marked Meera sings of victories, lovely and confident
Calling out this question to the stars

> *Where does diffidence begin*
> *But in this space beneath the skin?*

Mahatma Gandhi

There is a man at Porbunder who can answer any question
He stands on the sea-front
Wearing spectacles and a knowing look
Mounted on a pedestal, so that he can see
Farther and better than anyone

If the truth be told, he is only half a man, a bust
Also, he is made of stone, but these are points of details
The truth is that just half of him
Is equal to most questions

Why do sphinxes flourish in deserts?

Because questions grow, abundant cacti
Or rarest peonies, in the desert air

Gandhi is the greatest of sphinxes

He understands the value of salt
That it stands for forces
Greater than hunger
For taste, for grace

On the scratch surface of the desert
In the rough business of living
Salt's showy masquerade as snow
Signifies that beauty springs, defiant
From our most destitute pastures

The Mahatma knows green life
Grows out of the desert
Disguised as lifeless sand

And he guesses why this sand
Still glints, unquiet, in your hair

But he says nothing

You have travelled from Vadodara to consult him
Come through the desert, gathering questions
Meera's rhetorical barbs, the Sufi's sceptic thrusts

No man is alone after a desert journey
In the midst of *chai, pakora,* neighbourly gossip
The Sufi hangs out with you, Meera stands at your elbow

They join in your conversation with the half man
Add their challenges to yours
Voices of the desert
They speak
When the world is silent

And hearing in his head those voices
Anticipating their questions
The Mahatma

Lets his mind freeze

Over the many forms of water
He lets his mind freeze

Whose *bhakti* is greater
The Sufi's transcending his mind
Or Meera's abandoning her body?
Which the fake, Meera who is a tiger or the scholarly
Hashish-eater, a Sufi who deciphers heavenly bodies?

Are you really wiser than them, Great Sphinx, or only crazier?
Which half of you is more important, this bust which gazes
Out to sea, or the phantom limbs we cannot observe?

When will you march towards Dandi again, defying the thugs?
What is illusory, the snow that you imagine you have seen
Or the salt you think you've walked on but never tasted?

The Sphinx keeps his counsel

You would have to assume
From his frozen attitude
That the half man had
No use for his voice

None

His invisible hand
Keeps an invisible spinning wheel busy

He is actually weaving his answer
Concentrating on the fine mesh
Delicate as snow, or the pattern
Of sand on your palm when you lean
The weight of your body
Against the desert

He makes you an answer with his hands
It is all a labour of love, he says
Wordless, at your journey's end

He speaks of *bhakti*

The thread of truth binds you to me
It ties the desert to the open sea.

Ram Rahman

The Theatre of the Streets

The documentary tradition has an important position in the history of photography. While contemporary developments in new media, and in particular, digital manipulation, have altered the context of the straight, documentary photograph, it retains its power as a formidable formal visual medium.

Our culture is particularly rich for the photographer who has an eye for the spontaneous and phenomenally layered visual theatre that we seem to create with a throwaway ease. We surround ourselves with images, reflecting a mass visual language tradition much stronger than the written word—perhaps because mass formal literacy is a distant goal. As a photographer, I revel in the way we inscribe our public and private histories on the very walls and spaces of our public life.

Surrounded on all sides by religious, political and social icons and messages, we create a public frieze of our collective cultural consciousness—which is as loaded with signs and meanings as any analytical work by a social scientist or political thinker. I am convinced that this visual epic, with its trace of the memory of religious and political icons and events and sites of charged meaning, is much more complex than in most other cultures around the world. We are in that moment of transition—the handmade sign co-exists with the more sophisticated print and digital poster—and soon we will lose the liveliness of the handcrafted.

The photographic medium is ideally suited to notations of this cacophony with its isolated framing and freezing of the moment—signposting and recording a people's commentary. The humour, pathos and irony of this street theatre is truly a 'Democratic Forest' as the American photographer William Eggleston has so aptly titled his book!

Theatre of the Streets

PHOTO ESSAY by RAM RAHMAN

GANDHI, India Day, Madison Avenue, New York, 2001

CUTOUTS, Delhi, 1995

STALIN, Ernakulam, 1987

GANDHI MARCH, Delhi, 1995

Connaught Place, Delhi, 1999

INDIRA GANDHI, Delhi, 1989

MAULANA AZAD, Connaught Place, Delhi, 1997

Daryaganj, Delhi, 1999

Calcutta, 2000

Red Fort, Delhi, 1995

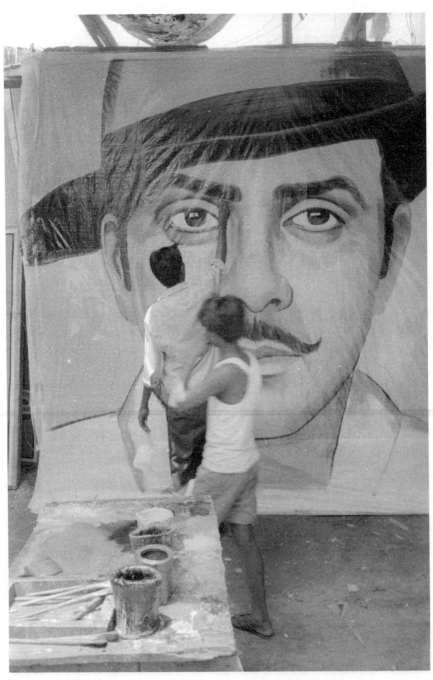

BHAGAT SINGH, Abbas Hoarding Studio, Delhi, 2001

IV
METAPHORS OF THE NATION

Bharat Mata, 1957
Film Poster
Coll. National Film Archives, Pune

Geeti Sen

Iconising The Nation: political agendas[1]

True womanliness is regarded in our country as the saintliness of love. It is not merely praised there, but literally worshipped; and she who is gifted with it is called Devi, as one revealing in herself Woman the Divine.[2]

Rabindranath Tagore.

Mother India (1957) can be argued to be the great classic of all Indian cinema, remembered by successive generations as their favourite film. Its appeal has much to do with an ideological mindset in this country: of identifying the woman with nature, with the soil of India—building upon a powerful equation between a biological mother and the primeval earth mother. On the other hand, for millions of viewers in the erstwhile Soviet Union and countries of the middle east, India then came to be projected, identified and recognised through the film *Mother India*.

Conceived in the definitive phase of Bollywood in the 1950s when screen heroines Madhubala, Meena Kumari, Nargis and Waheeda Rahman created their mystique, this film offers the least glamorous of all roles: of a peasant woman identified with land and her village; and equally in her biological role: surviving alone to bring up her four children. In an interview Nargis mentions it as her most challenging performance; after which, at 25 years of age, she virtually retired from the industry.[3] No other director perhaps other than Mehboob Khan, of village stock from Gujarat and a man who understood both poverty and peasantry, could have brought such value to the country as *earth*.[4] The struggle for survival against natural calamities invests his film with an unparalleled grandeur—

transforming the narrative into an epic scale of events. In this narrative a woman is awarded the ultimate role of heroism—she who in every sense embodies the feminine principle, the power (*shakti*) to control her own destiny and that of the village.

Consider certain scenes of pastoral romance: the devoted couple ploughing, singing and harvesting in open fields—drawing from a Pudokovian vision of land and labour.[5] But there are others: that critical moment when the rains fail, and Radha prevails upon the farmers fleeing the village not to desert their fields, their land. At that moment the camera pulls back to another perspective—to reveal not the village but the entire country! There is another moment of the floods washing away her child—when Radha is ready to yield to the lecherous demands of the Lala with the words, "I cannot sacrifice (*balidaan*) my children". At that dramatic moment when she turns to divine help with the words, "*Shakti de*", a miracle intervenes in the form of lightning bringing down the Lala's house.[6]

Significantly, these are the two moments represented in film posters by depicting Radha's two roles: as a biological mother, and as the earth mother with the plough on her shoulder, wedded to the land. These references are understood by an Indian audience—not in portraying 'reality' but by reinforcing their own beliefs. Popular Hindi films operate at a level of contemporising mythic prototypes, insisting upon a magical fusion of myth and reality. Such narratives are "cognitive attempts to make symbolic sense out of ordinary experience".[7] *Mother India* is just such a film: relying upon this combination, elevating Radha into a symbol of triumph to nourish the beliefs of generations to come.

As we know, in 1939 Mehboob had already made *Aurat* as his first major debut. Eighteen years later in post-Independent India, he returns to the identical story in *Mother India*—in the seductive new medium of technicolour and by casting star Nargis as Radha. Do changes take place influenced by the Nehruvian social ideology of the '50s? True, the film opens with the new symbol of progress, a dam, but following this is the unchanging India- —slowed down by bullock carts, impoverished by famine, flood and drought, exploited by the greed of the moneylender. Mehboob's remark is significant:

> Now that times have changed and life is different, I thought of remaking Aurat in the context of the changing world. But the main character has not changed: the Indian woman is one with the land she works on.[8]

The title of course, does signify a change in perception, whereby *Mehboob now identifies the woman not only as 'Woman' and a biological mother but in her role as Mother of the country*. To endorse my point we might recall that last unforgettable sequence in the film, where Radha makes her ultimate sacrifice as a mother. When Birju turns renegade, threatens and then abducts Sukhilala's daughter, as he rides into the distance she raises the rifle to her shoulder and shoots down her own favourite son. With this gesture she transcends her personal role to become defender of the honour of 'a daughter of the village'—identified with the land, and through inference, the country.

This is a political statement of the 'new' Independent India, where Radha in some senses transgresses (or violates) her role as a traditional mother. Later films from the '70s and '80s would introduce the mother icon as an essential ingredient, a mother who remains passive, suffering, a symbol of family unity—it is for her sake that the son with ferocious masculinity (Amitabh Bachchan) takes revenge.[9] Radha's character goes against tradition, as it were, in her heroic stance and her demand for justice. In this contemporary myth of modern India, she is conceived to represent social order and authority—that is, within the orbit of a secular Nehruvian ideology. Let me also note here the fact that Mehboob, Nargis and Naushad were all Muslim, engaged in constructing the 'metaphor of the nation'.

Cinema in India becomes an effective endorsement of role models—as much as it also reflects the social ethos of a time. Let us compare *Mother India* (1957) with a significant film which preceded it and others which followed. Just two years earlier Satyajit Ray had completed his first classic in the Apu trilogy: *Pather Panchali* (1955), portraying with authenticity the social mores of rural Bengal, honoured at the Cannes Film Festival by being declared as the "best human document".[10] Unlike Mehboob's creation of a patriotic vision, no epic-like miracles intervene in this narrative; nature here is not nourishing and bountiful but vindictive. The monsoon rages with torrential rain; and unlike Radha whose honour is saved by lightning, little Durga succumbs to fever. After her death her impoverished Brahmin family takes a major decision: *to leave the village and change their way of life*. This is a more realistic story of a family who relinquish their attachment to village and land.

But the miraculous persists in Indian cinema! Another story line in *Jai Santoshi Ma* (1973) invents the Cinderella tale of a hapless, exploited woman/wife who is empowered by her Goddess to work miracles. She struggles hard, but not as a resolute woman relying on strength within her. Solutions come by way of divine interventions at regular intervals, with even a little drama of jealousy amongst the Goddesses vying for attention. This film broke all box office records, raising the status of a regional deity into a pan-India cult with the audience prostrating themselves before the celluloid goddess.[11]

Since the '80s there have been more daring exponents in this genre of the miraculous, fortified by the growing religious temper of our times. That concept of latent power/ energy within the woman hinted in Mehboob's *Mother India* has now given way to spectacular melodramas and television serials titled *Shakti*—not to speak of brand names for cement and toothpaste. *That* combination of an earthy/epic/ mythic woman has experienced a metamorphosis. *Shakti* is now regular fare for daily consumption.

Of more recent persuasion is the 'global' film *Shakti* discussed in Deshpande's essay in this volume, which features an NRI heroine and a very different projection of village life. I am tempted to quote three sentences to suggest the journey traversed over forty years in Indian cinema.

> In a depiction that would put Kipling to shame, the Indian villagers are cruel, barbaric, bloodthirsty, while the NRI is civilised, decent, gentle. As the woman is on the run from her father-in-law, she meets a small-time bootlegger (a delightful cameo by Shah Rukh Khan) who helps her only after she offers him cash (dollars, not rupees)... The native then is moved to heroic deeds, but only after contact with higher civilisation—which comes in the garb of foreign exchange of course.. [12]

II

Perhaps it is now evident as to why I choose to begin my essay with *Mother India*—as one of the most persuasive films in its time to influence public opinion, both in India and outside. *And the time of its production in the Nehruvian decade immediately after Independence was crucial to its particular ethos, its representation of the nation as a woman from the village.* It can also be argued that such a film could not have been made without the political context and reference to the already established concept of **Bharat Mata**—whereby the woman was perceived from the late 19th century not as *real* but as metaphor: a site for the nation, and invested with divine power.

To be more precise, she was originally created as the embodiment of a country aspiring to free itself of colonial suppression. How else and how best could the forces of national identity be represented but through creating an icon of the Motherland? In his discourse on nationalism Hobsbawm cites cases of the Virgin of Guadalupe in Mexico and the Virgin of Montserrat in Catalonia as "holy icons" used to forge a sense of unity.[13] Now, *Bharat Mata* is engendered precisely as such a `holy icon'—as she appears first in *Anandamath* (1882), the novel where the *santans* are willing to give up their lives for the Motherland. This novel earned Bankimchandra Chattopadhyay both name and fame and, later, criticism And certainly, there had been earlier intimations in Bengal of the motherland: a play titled *Bharat Mata* was performed at the Hindu *mela* in Calcutta on 19th February 1879.[14] Possibly, there may also have been popular visual representations.

The worship of land as sacred was not new to Indian belief, or for that matter, visual iconography. The earth goddess is the most primeval of images in terracotta—continuing to be worshipped over three millenium and in villages until today. Powerful evocations of Prithvi rescued by Lord Vishnu (as Varaha) are found in Puranic texts and also cut into rocks as early as Udaigiri and Mamallapuram. *But now in the new climate of opinion there was a political purpose to be served: by re-inventing the earth mother as the Motherland.* As studies by Sumathi Ramaswamy suggest, the popular Puranic legend transforms in prints from the Ravi Varma Press (1915) where the bodyscape of Prithvi is replaced by the globe—the globe being perceived as a western/colonial symbol of progress and the 'modern' signifier of territorial power.[15]

Equally, I would assert, the creation of *Bharat Mata* owes greatly to Bengal's cultural legacy and the Shakta tradition of worshipping the goddess in her infinite variations—as Chandi, Durga, Kali, Jagadhhatri, Manasa… Bankimchandra's writing here is not polemical as are his political tracts, but to serve a defined purpose. His novel builds up to prepare his readers for the vision of the Motherland, which comes after the description of Jagaddhatri (Goddess of the primeval world) and of Kali (Goddess of the present world—robbed of all her riches and thus naked). Then, as *Bharat Mata* in *Anandamath* is 'revealed' to the protagonist, she appears as a ten-armed icon (*pratima*) in a marble temple, wondrous to behold, a bewitching enchantress (*Mohinimurti*). The hermit bows to her and says to Mahendra, "This is what our Mother will become".[16]

That of course was a prophecy, awaiting fulfilment! Two decades later, as the patriotic fervour of the *swadeshi* movement swept through the country, Bankimchandra's song of *Bande Mataram* describing the Mother became, as reported in the *Dawn*, "a battle cry and a divine inspiration" as a slogan chanted in street processions.[17] And in this charged atmosphere of a country awakening to its identity, it is believed, the first visual representation of **Bharat Mata** (1905) was painted by Abanindranath Tagore.

In *Gharoa*, his personal memoirs published many years later in 1941, the artist casually remarks that his painting was enlarged by a Japanese artist into a banner (*pataka*) and then taken around in processions of the *swadeshi* movement.[18] Even in it's own time, it was praised by an impassioned Sister Nivedita as "the first masterpiece in which the Indian artist has actually succeeded in disengaging, as it were, the spirit of the motherland…"[19] Inevitably then, in the discourse on power and nationalism, the image by Abanindranath has been appropriated by political and cultural historians as a 'national' icon, and thus dismissed in one or two paragraphs or perhaps a page.[20] I suggest that this icon deserves closer attention.

Never is it the end of the story, in completing an icon or text! Time moves on in political history… An image as much as a poem or a song changes in interpretation—in the manner in which it is *received*. The patriotic verses of *Bande Mataram* which were first sung by Rabindranath Tagore at the National Congress in 1896, uttered as a 'mantra' in the historic Town Hall in Calcutta and in taking the vow to boycott foreign goods in 1905, led to riots in 1908 and eventually a raging controversy between the National Congress and the Muslim League. In Nehru's correspondence with Jinnah, one of the points under consideration is that "The *Bande Mataram* song should be given up".[21] In 1937 Nehru wrote to Subhas Chandra Bose, "Certainly as suggested by you I shall discuss the *Bande Mataram* song with Dr. Tagore".[22] The poet laureate confirmed that the second stanza describing the goddess enshrined in temples was inimical to Islamic tenets against the worship of icons. And after considerable debate, in the wisdom of things as they had changed, *Bande Mataram* was not chosen as the national anthem.

The hermeneutics of art, as much as of politics, casts a different face today to Abanindranath's painting of **Bharat Mata**. I would like to suggest that this luminous icon is unique in his body of work, a painting of singular inspiration, both personal and universal. And yes, let me assert this also: viewed in retrospect this picture becomes almost an uncanny prophecy of what was yet to transpire for the future of/for the Motherland.

In the redefined purpose of art, Abanindranath casts her in the emblematic role of representing the nation. Yet already, the artist has imbued her with a certain ambivalence, the contradictions implicit in her birth. And how does one embody the "spirit of the motherland"? Does the authority invested in *Bharat Mata* derive from religion or from the state ? Is she divine or is she human? Is she to be viewed as goddess or as woman? These questions dog her transformation through decades as she transforms from 'high' to 'low' art, from terrorist to Congress posters in the 1920s and '30s (both prohibited), from official photographs to film posters in the 1940s, from one temple in 1936 to the other in 1983. These images contribute to that essential paradox of her existence, and the dual responsibility/role which from inception has been invested in her.

III

A detailed study of this fascinating metamorphosis of the Motherland has been attempted elsewhere, in my book. Yet, let us for a moment examine this little painting, worked delicately in water colour and the wash technique—in the 'indigenous' technique to which the artist had reverted deliberately, in all his pictures—to reawaken what he considered was an indigenous (*'desi'*) sensibility.[23] (And does that make Abanindranath's painting more 'national' ?)

Contradictions are implicit in his image of *Bharat Mata*. As a sign of her special status she is endowed with four arms, holding not weapons but the four promised symbols for a reconstructed India: *anna* (food), *vastra* (clothing), *siksha* (education) and *diksha* (spiritual salvation). Her head is ringed with a halo and she is placed on the curving green of a globe, with lotuses below her feet.. Yet her head is covered with her eyes averted, and her forehead anointed with *sindhur* as appropriate for a married woman. She seems demure and comely— without that fierce mesmerising look emanating from icons like Kali or Durga. She wears a saffron robe and remains asexual, raising questions about her identity: is she a virgin or married or a renunciate? Is she goddess or woman?

Bharat Mata, 1905
Gouache and wash on paper by Abanindranath Tagore
Coll. Rabindra Bharati, Kolkata

Kali, 1908
Chromolithograph by Calcutta Art Studio
Coll. Royal Anthropological Institute Photographs collection

These nuances were not lost on Nivedita when she describes the icon in the same journal *Prabasi* (1906) with the comment, " in every detail, of *shankha* bracelet, and close-veiling garment, of bare feet and open sincere expression, *is she not after all, our very own... at once mother and daughter of the Indian land...?"* And yet, it is Nivedita herself who offers us, and the terrorists with whom she was then closely associated, an alternative vision for the Motherland:

> Religions called by whatever name, has been ever the love of death. But today the flame of renunciation shall be lighted in My lands and consume men with a passion beyond control of thought. Then shall My people thirst for self-sacrifice as others for enjoyment. Then shall labour and suffering and service be counted sweet instead of bitter. For this age is great in time and I, even I Kali, *am the Mother of the nation* . [24]

Let us concede this point. **Bharat Mata** lacks that anger and revolutionary zeal required of an icon to inspire a nation-to revolt—as could be found in popular images of Kali from contemporary Battala prints in Calcutta; or in the imaging of *La France* by Delacroix. In contrast, our icon belongs to the *bhadralok*—she is domesticated and too civilised—she cannot fulfil the aspirations of an impassioned Bimala who declares in Tagore's novel, *Ghare Baire*:

> I am only human... I would be angry for my country's sake.. fascination must be supplied to me in bodily shape by my country. She must have some visible symbol casting its spell upon my mind. I would make my country a Person and call her Mother, Goddess, Durga—for whom I would *redden the earth with sacrificial offerings*. I am human, not divine. [25]

There is every reason why Abanindranath could have imbibed this spirit of fury in his engendering of the new icon. She is unlike that bewitching goddess beckoning us in *Anandamath* (1882); unlike bazaar prints of an avenging Kali in his own time; unlike Nivedita's interpretation of the Mother; and unlike Aurobindo's evocation of Bhawani, Mother of Strength (1906). Instead, Abanindranath's conception of **Bharat Mata** enchants us by the equanimity of her presence, by her gentle aura. She does not respond wholly to the political climate in which she was conceived. Were there reasons for this?

Twenty years had passed since Bankim introduced the Motherland in his novel—*to impart to the people a sense of identity.* Now she responds to a *nation in the making*—where the growing cult of **Bharat Mata** was leading to violence and anarchy. As is known the terrorist groups took their secret vows before Kali; and in later terrorist posters *Bharat Mata* assumes the iconography of this goddess as she holds a *trishula* and is offered the sacrifice of human lives.[26] Thus with perfect irony the martyred Bhagat Singh (who had written the pamphlet "Why I am an Atheist") is shown offering his head on a platter dripping with blood to the Mother, now Goddess. Curiously, posters and calendars continue to portray patriotism through the martyrdom of Bhagat Singh—from 1931 through into the early 1960s.

But let us return to Bengal in 1905—split by Government ordinance and followed by the *swadeshi* movement sweeping the country, with the quieter protests turning into anarchy. From 1908 the essays of Rabindranath change in tone, he takes a different position from other patriots—as is also quoted by Uma Dasgupta elsewhere in this volume. In his novel *Ghare Baire* published in 1916 and through the rational voice of Nikhil, Rabindranath Tagore expresses his deep misgivings about the growing cult of *Bharat Mata*—which was leading to communal riots. There rings a note of clear irony when Sandip the revolutionary declares in the novel:

> True patriotism will never be roused in our countrymen unless they can visualise the motherland—we must make a goddess of her! [27]

In his letters Abanindranath suggests that he was influenced and inspired by 'Rabi kaka'. An understanding of the artist, his writings and aesthetic predilections would suggest that he was concerned essentially in retrieving an *Indian* sensibility—not in engaging in the *nationalist* compulsions of the day. *He offers us then, an alternative imaging of the Motherland—one that is opposed to the aggression of a rising nationalism. By small subtle changes he transforms her iconography from a goddess into that of the mother of the country— thus transforming her from a religious into a secular icon. In my opinion this becomes the real significance of this painting, and why it needs our attention, in retrospect—after almost a century.*

IV

We discover that the icon of the nation is imbued with several, conflicting interpretations. The fascinating and paradoxical history of her transformation relates directly to the political climate of the country as it changed. As *Bharat Mata* evolves over a

Bharat Mata Mandir, 1936
Varanasi, interior
Photo Courtesy: Sumathi Ramaswamy

hundred years, she comes to signify the aspirations of each decade, to suit different political agendas. At the end, the question remains: what is her power and her constituency today?

Is she woman or goddess? Does she belong to the state or to religion? It is significant that only two temples of note have been built in her name where she is enshrined in marble. What is fascinating and of importance is that these temples are conceived with different forms of the Motherland, different objectives and opposing ideologies.

The first temple to **Bharat Mata** was built in Benares, a *tirthasthana* and the most hallowed of all cities in India for its temples. Yet this temple was quite unique—an endeavour of the country aspiring to become a nation rather than being created for/by religious sanctions. In October 1936 this temple was opened by Mahatma Gandhi amidst a great congregation of over 25000 people from all over the country. His speech at the inauguration is significant, voicing as it does the secular ideals with which this temple was conceived.

> The temple contains no image of any god or goddess. It has only a relief map of India made of marble stone in it. I hope this temple, which will serve as a cosmopolitan platform for people of all religions, castes and creeds including Harijans, will go a great way in promoting religious unity, peace and love in the country.[28]

Why, after all these fifty years of 'enchantment' with the feminised image of **Bharat Mata,** of representing her as a woman/goddess, was she replaced by the geophysical landscape? Let us recall these were those critical years when communal sentiments were rife in the country, when Nehru consulted Tagore about the singing of *Bande Mataram*, when letters between Nehru and Jinnah assumed an acrimonious tone, when the Congress was just going to the electoral polls in 1937. This 'resolution' of introducing the topographical map was surely in part political: as a means of inventing an apposite symbol which would unite rather than divide different communities—a symbol to which they would and could pay due homage.

Benedict Anderson has argued on the power of the modern map as *logo*: the purest sign of the country, any country, in its outline—so easily reproduced for utilitarian purposes, a constant reminder in popular posters, official seals, stamps, hotel walls et al...[29] When applied to India, we remind ourselves that there had always existed the predilection to worship through sign/symbol in place of iconic representation. Recall some of these: the *Bodhi* tree, the *dharma chakra* and the *stupa* to represent the Buddha; calligraphy as the noblest medium to invoke the name of Allah; the *Guru Granth Sahib* to invoke the Sikh Gurus; the *tulsi* plant for Vishnu, the *linga* as the purest of all 'signs' to represent Shiva, and the *Shri yantra* to invoke the Devi. And in certain senses (although it is most unlikely that the founding patriarchs 'saw' it this way), was the map not a *yantra* to invoke and represent the Motherland ?

But there was another reason for the map, a growing anxiety deep within the political psyche. This anxiety is built into current imagery; it is found equally in film posters as in official photographs of political 'stage sets'. In these critical decades of the 1930s and '40s, it is not the persona of **Bharat Mata** which matters so much as her physical boundaries: an obsession with mapping the country. Implicit is the notion of property, of sovereignty over land—and especially when land is rendered sacred as it is in India.

After the Congress victory at the polls in 1937, the Muslim League was not given its due share. In the 1940s Jinnah did not participate in the Quit India movement, and made clear the demand for a different 'homeland'. As the impending *crisis of Independence* draw nearer, another rationale is built into the map of Mother India. She appears now as the backdrop to the podium where the Mahatma, Nehru and Patel huddle together—in a mood of anguish, or is it resignation at the Congress Session in Bombay, 1946 …She is still in shackles, with the word *Ghulami* for her enslavement inscribed (in English!) along the western contours of the peninsula. *The mapping of the nation as the rightful reclaiming of sacred territory now assumes prophetic undertones— of a promise which may not be fulfilled.*

Yet the map could not fulfil the religious aspirations and political ambitions for the Motherland! Let us recall the return of V.D. Savarkar, President and guiding spirit of the Hindu Mahasabha from 1937, on his release from 28 years in jail. In his speeches he opposed the National Congress, characterising their approach as based on 'territorial nationalism'. As against abstract entity of the Motherland, Savarkar introduced the persuasive notion of *cultural nationalism*. A non-believer himself, he conceived Hindutva—not as a religion but as a concept whereby the generic religions and root languages born of the soil in India possess greater claim to the nation. He defined the cultural boundaries of India, including some but excluding *other* communities who had lived for centuries in this country.[30]

This new formulation of a cultural agenda grew over decades to acquire momentum from the 1980s. The last two decades are witness to an ardent return of nationalist consciousness, and not only in India. In the reinvention of political ideologies religion plays a crucial role—in claiming the legitimacy of one major religion. Space does not permit discussion of this remarkable convergence of purpose in nationhood, except to note that this has affected the resurgence of *Bharat Mata.* In 1983 she is resurrected in the temple now founded in her name, in the pilgrimage town of Hardwar.

One hundred years since her inception, *Bharat Mata* is enshrined as a marble icon in this second temple built in her name—as had indeed been promised by Bankimchandra! But there is none of that fatal enchantment about her as described in *Anandamath,* none of that fierce iconic power as with images and prints of Kali, no spiritual aura emanating from her... Like the goddesses of agriculture, she stands stiffly with merely two arms holding "an urn of milk and a sheaf of corn"– with the geographical contours of the country spreading across the floor to bring home her identity. There are no specific times for her *darshan,* no ritual offerings. Like a hostess, she greets visitors on the ground floor as they arrive... Then they rush up to the remaining floors to visit other icons included in the new pantheon.

This eight-storied temple to the goddess of the nation was built at an estimated cost of one crore. The remaining floors present images behind glass and labeled, as though you were visiting a museum. On the first floor the *Shoor Mandir* valorises heroes Chatrapati Shivaji, Maharana Pratap, Bhagat Singh, Veer Savarkar, Guru Gobind Singh, Rani of Jansi and others—*all espousing militant nationalism* with the notable exception of Mahatma Gandhi. The next floor is reserved for the *Matri Mandir,* (earlier called Sati Mandir) an essential component to glorify Sati Padmini (consumed by flames) and Sati Urmila, Anadal, Maitri, Savitri, Gargi, Urmila, with Annie Besant finding strange company among these mystics and saints. In the *Sant Mandir* are images of Gautam Buddha, Mahavir Swami, Tulsidas, Chaitanya Mahaprabhu, Vallabhacharya, Guru Nanak, Shri Shirdi Sai Baba, Swami Dayanand Saraswati and others. The top floor enshrines a tableau of Lord Shiva seated on Mount Kailash. *Darshan* is now completed, moving from earth to mountain and sky.

The claims to nationhood are thus defined by those represented here: assembling Buddhist, Jain, Sikh and Hindu saints and heroes—as would be appropriate.to the doctine of Hindutva. *It is not Bharat Mata who is paid homage in this temple built in her name, but the history*

Bharat Mata, 1997
Poster by E. Jesudass, Published by SPP Delhi
Coll. J.S. and Patricia Uberoi Photo Courtesy : Patricia Uberoi

and culture of India—as defined in Savarkar's book, The Essentials of Hindutva. This purpose is clearly stated in the guidebook to the temple:

> May this beautiful, yet powerful symbol of Mother India entice the hitherto uncommitted passerby, who happens to be a chance visitor, to the glory of Bharat Mata in her manifold facets, to the vastness of her resources and power, to get a glimpse of her history, culture, traditions and hopefully, be rejuvenated...[31]

For our purposes, we might note that the campaign by the Vishwa Hindu Parishad to restore and build temples *began with this ritual enshrinement of **Bharat Mata**.* The consecration was followed by a six month procession across the country, when crowds were given the opportunity to worship her and listen to religious leaders and public figures.[32] In the Souvenir Volume for this *ekatmata yajna* (and quite unlike her image in the temple), *Bharat Mata* is restored to her position of being the Goddess. Like the Goddess Durga she is seated on the lion, with a flaming aureole rising from her shoulders as she raises her hand in *abhaya mudra.* All three 'signs' including the gesture are appropriate to the iconography of Hindu Goddesses.

This iconography has now become the norm in countless postcards, calendar pictures and wall paintings across the country. On a walk along the *ghats* of Benares I discovered a wall painting of **Bharat Mata,** painted on Women's Day 2000. She is gorgeously bejeweled, superimposed against the map in a seductive pose that would put screen goddesses to shame. However, the unique aspect to this icon is to be carefully noted. Both in the Souvenir Volume of Hardwar and in the wall painting in Benares, she holds not the tricolour flag of the Indian nation but instead the bifurcated saffron flag of the Sangh Parivar. This most important of all 'signs' in her new iconography indicates that she now represents one political party. We might then legitimately ask ourselves the critical question: in this situation and reinvention of **Bharat Mata**, does she remain the icon for the dreams, aspirations and sacrifice of the entire nation?

V

For twelve decades **Bharat Mata** has continued to influence the rhetoric of India's leaders, to inspire her writers, artists, activists, populists and film makers. Through the 20th century *Mother India* has been represented in paintings, prohibited posters, calendars

Bharat Mata Mandir, 1983
Hardwar Ground floor with Image and map
Photo Courtesy: Sheba Chhachhi

and film. But where is the goddess of the nation today? Returning to the question in the last section, and as compared with her apotheosis in the early 20th century, her constituency has shrunk. At Hardwar she becomes the pretext for instituting the worship of a wider pantheon; she forms part of an ambitious cultural agenda that is both 'national' and religious in purpose. The temple aims to provide its visitors with an emotional experience of *religious and national unity*. The text explicates:

> Religion and nationhood should be complementary to each other. Religion motivates culture while nationhood evokes sacrifice for one's religious unity.[33]

Thus, nationhood, culture and religion have become part of a package deal. At her inception in 1882, *Bharat Mata* was invoked by Bankimchandra as a 'holy icon'—invented as Goddess to effect *national unity*. The reverse takes place in 1983, where nationhood is invoked to effect *religious unity*. This is subtle but a critically important difference. And today, patriotism is to accept the refashioning of our religious/cultural/national identity—carved out in the form of specific images with a prescribed iconography and a cultural program.

The enchantment with the goddess however, persists—with " "the deified feminised body of *Bharat Mata*" replacing the "disenchanted state-space of colonial cartography"[34]. Within the span of a hundred and twenty years *Bharat Mata* has continued to transform, adapting to differing political agendas. No doubt she will continue to evolve and there will be engendered new constructs for the nation…

Within this transformation there have been two instances when she has been brought 'down to earth'—transformed from goddess into woman: with Abanindranath's luminous image of 1905, persuading us against a rising militant nationalism; and Mehboob's memorable film of a village woman/matriarch in 1957. We need only to recall Jawaharlal Nehru's own vision of the country (quoted in Section One to this volume) to realise the `secularised' Mother of the Nation after Independence—as indeed *was* realised in Mehboob's film *Mother India*. Our attention returns to these—where *Bharat Mata* assumes the power not of goddess but of *shakti* invested in a woman. As such, she remains human, accessible to all—an icon conceived and constructed by the state rather than by religious ideologies. Both these remain 'prophecies' which are yet to be realised.

References and Notes

1. This paper derives substantially in its approach, ideas and phraseology from my research under auspices of the Jawaharlal Nehru Fellowship, and the first chapter of my book, *Feminine Fables; Imaging the Indian Woman, in Painting Photography and Cinema* 2002: Mapin Publishing, Ahmedabad. However, the arguments have been developed further here—as critical issues on cultural nationalism.
2. Rabindranath Tagore, *Creative Unity*, reprinted in *The English Writings of Rabindranath Tagore*, 1996: Sahitya Akademi, New Delhi, Vol. Two, p.554.
3. Interview with Nargis in *Indian Cinema Superbazaar*, eds. Aruna Vasudev and Phillipe Langlet, 1983: Vikas Publishing House, Delhi, p.258.
4. See the brief biography of Mehboob in Gautam Kaul, *Cinema and the Indian Freedom Struggle*, 1988: Sterling Publications, Delhi, pp.60–61.
5. In the 1950's film makers in India were encouraged by the visit to India of the Russian cineaste Pudokov, who advised them: "What you want to make are films of ordinary people in their natural life, not just film stars in an artificial story. Follow your own vision, your own people, your own landscape." Quoted by B.D. Garga, *So Many Cinemas, The Motion Picture in India*, 1996: Eminence Design, Mumbai, p.152.
6. Shakti is ambivalent in meaning. It can refer to the Goddess as the female embodiment of divine energy, or it can simply be interpreted as "energy/strength."
7. Pradip Krishen, "Cinema and Society: A Search for Meaning in a New Genre", in *Indian Popular Cinema*, 1981: *India International Centre Quarterly*, p.57.
8. Mehboob quoted in *Filmfare*, August 16, 1957.
9. For a discussion of roles of the new screen hero of "ferocious masculinity" and the passive mother, see Chidananda Dasgupta, "The Iconic Mother" in *The Painted Face, Studies in India's Popular Cinema*, 1991: Roli Books, New Delhi, pp.108–9.
10. Baswati Chakravarty "A Bridge Too Far: Culture and the Left in West Bengal" in *Art of Bengal, a vision defined 1955–1975*, CIMA Gallery, Kolkata, p.19.
11. Dasgupta, *op.cit.*p.199.
12. See the essay by Sudhanva Deshpande published in this volume titled "What's so Great about Lagaan?".
13. E.J. Hobsbawm, *Nation and Nationalism since 1870, Programme, myth, reality*, 1990: Cambridge University Press, Cambridge, p.68.
14. See Christopher Pinney's findings and his essay "A secret of their own country: or How Indian nationalism made itself irrefutable" in *Contributions to Indian Sociology*, special issue: *Beyond Appearances? Visual practices and Ideologies in Modern India*, ed. Sumathi Ramaswamy, Jan–August 2002, p.125 and following.
15. Sumathi Ramaswamy, "Visualising India's geo-body: Globes, maps, bodyscapes", *op.cit.*, p.162. Ramaswamy's essay (p.152) explores the hypothesis that "the modern map enables the citizen-subject to take `visual and conceptual possession' of the nation-space he inhabits".
16. Bankimchandra Chattopadhyay, *Anandamath*, 1882, consulted in the original Bengali in *Bankim Rachnabali, Upanyashe Samagraha*, pp.676–677. This text is also rendered in *extenso* with insightful comments by Sudipta Kaviraj, *The Unhappy Consciousness, Bankimchandra Chattopadhya and the Formation of Nationalist Discourse in India*, 1995: Oxford University Press, pp.152 ff.
17. Satish Chandra Mukherjee in the *Dawn*, 1906, quoted in *Bande Mataram and Indian Nationalism (1906–1908)*, 1957: Firma K.L. Mukhopadhyay, Calcutta, p.12.

18. Abanindranath Tagore, as told to Rani Chanda, *Gharoa, Intimate Memoirs*, originally published in Bengali, 1941: Sahitya Akademi, p.22.

19. Nivedita, "Abanindranath Tagore; Bharat Mata" originally published in *Prabasi*, June 1906, reprinted in *Works III*, p.57.

20. See especially Sumit Sarkar, *Swadeshi Movement in Bengal 1903–08*, 1978: Peoples Publishing House, New Delhi, p.500; Partha Mitter, *Art and Nationalism in Colonial India 1850–1922*, 1994: Cambridge University Press, p.272 and Tapati Guha Thakurta, *The Making of a New Indian Art, Aesthetics and Nationalism in Bengal c.1850–1920*, 1992: Cambridge University Press, Cambridge.

21. See Nehru's correspondence with M.A. Jinnah quoted in S. Gopal ed., *Selected Works of Jawaharlal Nehru*, 1976: Orient Longman Ltd., Vol. Eight, pp.232–33, Letter dated April 6, 1938.

22. Quoted in S. Gopal, ed., *op.cit.* Vol. Eight, p.186.

23. Abanindranath Tagore, *Shadanga or the Six Limbs of Painting*, reprinted in the JI5OA Jubilee Volume titled *Abanindranath*, ed. Pulinbari Sen,1961: Calcutta.

24. Nivedita, *Kali the Mother*, first published in 1909: London, reprinted in 1950: Advaita Ashram, Pithoragarh, Himalayas, p.35.

25. Rabindranath Tagore, *Ghare Baire* or *The Home and the World*, 1919, Macmillan and Co., London.

26. These posters are now in the collection of the British Library, and are reproduced with permission in my book *op.cit*, p.32 as also one by Pinney *op.cit*, p.137. See Sarkar, *op.cit* for mention of the vows to Kali by 'terrorists' at their initiation.

27. Rabindranath Tagore, *op.cit*, p.154.

28. M.K. Gandhi, *Collected Works of Mahatma Gandhi*, XIII, 1976: Ahmedabad, pp.388–89, cited from *The Bombay Chronicle*.

29. Benedict Anderson, *Imagined Communities*, cited by David McCrone, *The Sociology of Nationalism: Tomorrow's ancestors*, 1998; Routledge, London, pp.55–56.

30. V.D. Savarkar, *The Essentials of Hindutva*, also quoted by B.R. Purohit, *Hindu Revivalism and Nationalism*, 1968: Sathi Prakashan, Sagar University, p.138.

31. Booklet on the *Bharat Mata Mandir: A Candid Appraisal*, 1986: Samanaya Seva Trust, Hardwar, U.P., p.13.

32. See Lise Mckean's detailed study of this temple in her essay, "Bharat Mata, Mother India and Her Militant Matriots" in *Devi, Goddesses of India*, eds. J.S. Hawley and D.M. Wulff, 1998: Motilal Banarsidas in arrangement with University of California Press, p.257. Surprisingly, this temple has received none or little attention from Indian scholars. For this reason, after my visit to Hardwar, four pages in my book focus on this temple—conceived and built as a critical step in the rise of cultural nationalism.

33. *Booklet on the Bharat Mata Mandir, op.cit.*

34. See Sumathi Ramaswamy, *op.cit.* p. 174 and following.

Kavita Singh

The Museum is National

The Idea of a National Museum

Along with the national anthem, the national emblem, the national festival, a nation needs its national library, its national archive, and its national museum. Poor indeed is the country that cannot lay claim to enough history to fill an archive, enough scholarship to fill a library, and enough artefacts to fill a museum! Thus, shortly after Independence, the project of a National Museum for India was begun. Housed in an imposing building at the ceremonial heart of New Delhi, this Museum was filled with art treasures that traced the nation's history from earliest times. As the new museum of a new nation, the National Museum was to celebrate the ancient culture of the young state.

Like all new nations, India modelled the accoutrements of its nationhood on those of the colonial master states. Here, as in most Asian, African and Latin American nations, the erection of a grand national museum became an act of great symbolic importance after independence.[1] It was seen as a means of retrieving one's own past. The new nation would collect, protect and assign value to its own heritage—independent of the scrutiny and judgements of its erstwhile masters. And it would share its masterpieces with its citizens in a symbolic affirmation of their rights. These gestures were sufficiently urgent to overcome the conditions of financial stringency of the difficult early years. For to make a national museum of one's own was to establish equivalence with Spain, France or Britain whose grand national museums of Madrid, Paris and London had held and shared the nation's patrimony with its citizens for one, two, or three hundred years.

But while the desire to have a national museum was inspired by examples of museums in the European metropolises, what the museums of new states needed to do was markedly different from what had been done in Europe. The old European 'national' museums related a supra- or trans-national tale of the history of Western civilisation. Claiming as their own heritage the art of ancient Egypt, progressing to ancient Greece and Rome, and then directly to Renaissance Europe, the great European museums developed a 'universal survey'[2] of the history of art, incorporating all that it admired into its own past.[3] (Adjunct galleries might house artefacts from other world cultures which had no place in this evolutionary sequence, but they served to expand the territory of connaissance.)

Transcending nationality, the narrative retold by the museums in Europe was one of world dominance. Among the new nations, the purpose was different: national museums were required as shrines to the *national* culture, confining their scope to artefacts produced through the ages but within the boundaries of the modern state. This was the project desired and assiduously developed by the newly decolonised and non-western nations.

The Garden of Sculpture

In its formulation and celebration of Indian national culture, the National Museum had two tasks: it had to show that India was eternal, and it had to show that India was great.

Primordialism is useful in the self-fashioning of nations; it demonstrates that the nation has always existed, at least in a spiritual sense. The periods when the land was not a nation, was divided, or subjected, can then be presented as interruptions in the nation's natural destiny.

That the nation is and always was great is demonstrated through its possession of a high culture over a long period. In formulating a high national culture, one strand or a few interrelated strands are chosen as the dominant, representative or mainstream culture from among the proliferation of local cultures. Typical candidates for the 'mainstream' culture are associated with an ethnic group that is dominant in the present period (thus the past legitimates the present), is possessed of a textual tradition (which provides historical evidence as well as an expression of intentionality), is relatively widely diffused (so that it can claim to be proto-national), and offers in its history at least a few figures (patrons, artists) who can function as national heroes.

If the National Museum was to demonstrate that India had always been, and had always been great, it was inevitable that the main burden of the narrative would fall upon one category of objects: stone sculpture. They alone had survived plentifully through the centuries, and it was possible to trace a deep history through their evidence. However the value of stone sculpture lay not just in their antiquity but also in their resemblance—at least superficially—to the stone sculpture of Greek and Roman antiquity. By foregrounding the stone sculpture of India, the enthusiasts of Indian art could testify to a civilisation that in some respects rivalled European civilisation and which might also be considered its equivalent.[4]

What had to be depressed were the actual points of contact between Indian and European sculptural traditions. Early Western scholars had placed at the apogee of Indian art the Gandhara school whose 'Greco-Buddhist' sculptures, from the 1st - 2nd centuries AD, in the northwest of the subcontinent depicted Buddhist themes in a Hellenistic style. Nationalist writers spurned Gandhara art. They shifted Indian sculpture's highest point to the Gupta period (5th- 6th century) when a certain sophistication of form was achieved, and brahmanical forms proliferated along with Buddhist ones. Naturally, it was the nationalist history that is materialised for us in the galleries of the National Museum.

Today, as much as at inception, a visit to the National Museum is dominated by its sequence of sculpture galleries[5] which occupy almost the entire ground floor. As we shall see, this is the only set of galleries that is linked to form a coherent, chronological sequence.

The first gallery on the ground floor is devoted to the Harappan civilisation. Just as historical research has not been able to establish firm connections between this enigmatic civilisation and future history, the Museum too offers no bridge between this gallery and the next— which leaps across some 1500 years to pick up a narrative that will henceforth be continuous.

The proper evolutionary sequence of the Museum commences with a gallery of Maurya and Sunga art, with sculptures from the 3rd to 2nd centuries BC. The sculptures are all from Buddhist monuments, and are mostly railing pillars which depict Jataka stories, donors, tree spirits and guardians. At the threshold between this and the next room stands a Bodhisattva from Mathura. This figure inaugurates, as it were, the debate on the evolution of the Buddha image, a hotly contested issue in Indian art history in early decades of the 20th century. European scholars had asserted that the Buddha image developed due to impulses brought by Greek artists to the Gandharan school. Nationalists maintained that it developed indigenously from popular yaksha cults that commissioned icons of local guardian spirits that closely resembled this Bodhisattva. The presence of this Bodhisattva, located just before visitors encountered their first Gandhara Buddha, aligns the museum's narrative firmly with the nationalists.

The next room presents three schools of sculpture that flourished simultaneously in three different parts of the subcontinent, from the 2nd century BC—2nd century AD. These schools are represented through three rows of sculptures: one down the centre and one along each long wall. On the left we see sculptures from the Gandhara school, developed under Hellenistic influences in the Indo-Greek kingdoms; along the centre are the early images from the sculpture workshops in Mathura; and along the right wall are relief panels from Nagarjunikonda, belonging to the beautiful Roman-influenced school that produced the masterpieces of Amaravati. Although the museum possesses just a few sculptures from Mathura that are arranged along the spine of this room, there is no doubt that what is physically central here is also posited as the 'mainstream' tradition. For it is the art of Kushana period Mathura that develops into the calm and poised sculpture of the Gupta period, which was hailed by nationalist art historians as the 'classical' period of Indian art. Here, they said, Indian art arrived at a magical moment when balance, finesse, elegance and restraint all met—before skill turned to virtuosity, engendering the florid excess of medieval schools. And we come upon the sculptures of the Gupta period next, in a special gallery that houses a series of fine images of the Bodhisattva, Buddha, Vishnu and Shiva from the most important Gupta sites at Mathura, Sarnath and Gwalior. This shrinelike room is the only gallery exclusively dedicated to one period and school. Its special quality is all the more pronounced as, after the Gupta gallery, the chronological narrative breaks down and later medieval sculpture is shown in a vast jumble of places, periods and styles.

Buddha
Gandhara, 2nd century AD
Coll National Museum ACC. No. 87.1153

Bodhisattva Maitreya
Kushana, 2nd century AD
Coll National Museum ACC. No. 59.530/1

Bodhisattva
Gupta, 5th century AD, Sarnath
Coll National Museum ACC. No. 49.113

Vishnu
Gupta, 5th century AD, Mathura
Coll National Museum ACC. No. E.6

The history of Indian sculpture, as told by the Museum, is a history of progressive development in which naïve and eclectic styles struggle towards a sophisticated but 'pure' expression. From the 'foreign' influence in the Mauryan period (which was shrugged off), to the naïve and charming folkish art of the early Buddhist stupas, to the Indo-Greek byways and the earthy Kushana-Mathura and finally to the 'classic' phase of the Gupta period—it seemed as though Indian sculpture was striving for something that finally was achieved in the Gupta period. By this turn, Buddhist sculpture became also the prehistory of the authentic, Indian tradition of Hindu art, which came robustly into its own at this point.

If Indian sculpture had the unitary aim of evolving into Gupta sculpture, then Gupta sculpture had the unitary aim of perfecting a single theme: of the human and particularly the male body. Everywhere in Indian sculpture there is the inescapable presence of the full-bodied female form. But in the National Museum the achievements of the Gupta period are predicated upon the male body, seen again and again in the figure of the Buddha, the Bodhisattva, Vishnu, Rama or Shiva. Subtly rising and falling flesh beneath the ascetic's robes, the in-held breath of the yogic body, the eyes turned inward upon themselves—these became the corporeal signs of spiritual attainment. Not only does the yogic male body allow an escape from the embarrassing presence of the female form all too common in Indian sculpture, the single theme of the iconic male shifts attention away from the cultic differences between Brahmanical and Hindu, Vaisnava, and Saiva images—further unifying the purpose of Gupta sculpture. With the body of the divine male presented as the real theme of Gupta sculpture, the period became an icon of nationalism, integrating diverse people towards a common and spiritual goal.

After the Gupta gallery, the chronological narrative of the National Museum breaks down. The two 'medieval' rooms are jumbled, placing sculptures from different regions and periods side by side. The confusion of these rooms might be a reflection on the state of the field; for early studies of Indian sculpture had concentrated upon the ancient period, and later medieval monuments were not fully interiorised into the art historical narrative. But this means that the phase most prolific in the creation of Brahmanical monuments has been given little attention. Understandable in the colonial period or even at the time of Independence, this medieval medley which now persists within the National Museum is inexplicable, for in the intervening decades, these medieval sites and schools have been subject to intensive study.

Whatever may be the reason that the medieval sculpture galleries have remained undifferentiated, it has an interesting effect. Early developments in Indian stone sculpture are traced mostly in north and central India and could be placed within a single and unified process of development. The medieval and later medieval phases were times of tremendous regional achievements—enormous projects, distinctive styles, localised cults and iconographic innovations. But dealing with the particular qualities of north, south, east and west divides the river of Indian history into many distinct streams; regional identities become stressed over the national, and the strong centre is subjected to the forces of the centrifuge.

And the Weeds in the Path

Once the ancient sculpture is dealt with the Musem's historical narrative terminates and the rest of the museum is composed of specialised galleries for Manuscripts, Painting, Central Asia, Textiles, Carved Wood, Arms and Armour, Coins and Jewellery, and Anthropology and Ethnography. If downstairs the museum is arranged roughly chronologically with the intention of following the river of history, upstairs the museum turned into a series of still pools in which we might reflect upon the technical finesse of different kinds of artists and artisans as they work on metal, wood or cloth.

One consequence of the shift in this mode of display from 'chronology' to 'material'—whether it was intended or not—is that artefacts produced outside of the early Buddhist shrines and Hindu temples are placed outside the realm of history. When the Museum displays an object produced in an Islamic context, it is absorbed into a display not of a particular cultural or historical period, but of a particular material: textiles say, or metalwork. Thus the sword of a Mughal prince becomes an example of damascening; a sash worn by a nawab becomes an illustration of a block-printing technique. Even in the Painting Gallery there seems to have been a pronounced preference for 'indigenous' traditions over the Deccani or Mughal ones.[7] The result was and is that one can walk right through the

National Museum and be only dimly aware of the fact that the Mughals had been in India.

In the early fervour of Independence, the formulation of a national culture was undoubtedly powered by a desire to recover India's indigenous traditions, untainted by 'external' influences of the European or the Islamic world. Engaged in a project of recovery of the ancient past, scholars in the field may not have spared a thought for the more recent past which, it would have seemed at the time, had not suffered from the same degree of neglect as the 'much maligned monsters' in the further reaches of history. In today's context however, the National Museum's omissions are startling and its narrative, partisan.

Let us be aware that we should exercise some caution here. In critiquing the Museum's methods of classification and display, we should make a distinction between the way it appears to us today, and the intentions that probably guided it at its formation. If we see the National Museum in the context of its predecessor-museums it becomes possible to take a less than sinister view of the inclusions, exclusions, trajectories and deviations in the tale of the National Museum. Instead of reading a theory of conspiracy in the exclusion of India's late-medieval, and Islamic past from the Museum's historical narrative, one might see it instead as an unintended victim of the Museum's attempt to accommodate two colonial epistemologies within its walls. But for this one would need to glance backward at the early history of museums in India, the purposes for which they were established, and the kinds of order they imposed upon the collections in their charge.

A Concise Synopsis of India

The institution of the museum came to India as part of the vast knowledge-creating project of the Raj. The intention of early British museums that took India as their subject was to "present to the eye a typical collection of facts, illustrations and examples which... will give a concise synopsis of India—of the country and its material products—of the people and their moral condition."[8] The museum collections were to be a metonym for the land, presenting all the pertinent information about India through an inventory of her products, materials, and human resources. Moreover, objects in the museum would bear witness to the degree to which India had achieved or fallen short of civilisation, fixing the 'moral status' of the subject race.

Accordingly, the first museums that took India as their subject (whether in India or in Britain) were encyclopaedic in scope. Gathering[9] science and art under one roof, these museums included scientific, economic[10], industrial[11] and archaeological[12] collections. A satisfactory museum needed to possess sections for Natural History, Ethnology, Geology, Archaeology, and the Industrial Arts. The museum-as-microcosm was part of the imperial fantasy of being able to create a complete and comprehensive archive of the empire, in which a correctly classified and labelled array of samples could adequately represent the imperial domain.[13]

The two earliest museums dedicated to India were the India Museum in London, and the Indian Museum in Calcutta. The India Museum in London was established in 1801 by the East India Company to house the collections being brought to England by officers of the Company. No branch of knowledge was outside its purview: its collections included specimens of insects and molluscs, minerals and clays, and manuscripts and textiles, as well as jewels and arms taken from the treasuries of defeated Indian princes. This museum had a chequered history, reflecting the rises and falls of 'India' within the British public imagination. With the demise of the Company in 1858, the collections were transferred to the Crown, which dispersed the collections among various London institutions.[14]

While the fortunes of 'Indian' museums in Britain waxed and waned through the 19th century, the museum movement within India gathered strength as scholars explored the territory and gathered samples in the course of their researches. The Indian Museum in Calcutta, that other great encyclopaedic museum of India, began its life in 1814 as the museum of the Asiatic Society that housed collections made by its member-scholars. As the first museum instituted on Indian soil, it was, like the India Museum of London, dedicated to the study of 'art and nature in the East'. It included specimens of natural history, geology, zoology, and antiquities and currently available craft skills or 'industrial arts'. Both museums saw their mission as primarily scientific and their collections and the staff were dominated by scientists and natural historians.[15] In 1866, the Asiatic Society Museum in Calcutta was taken over by the Government and transmuted into the Indian Museum.[16] As the prime museum in the capital of British

India, it was nurtured as India's central, indeed as India's Imperial museum. It occupied pride of place among the evolving hierarchy of central, provincial and local museums; and for some time it was the official policy that all truly precious collections be centralised in this one museum, while museums in the provinces retain copies and duplicates.[17]

Today, the institutional form of the Indian Museum of Calcutta is as much a curiosity as any of its exhibits; it preserves for us a particular moment in the early history of museum-making. Even a mere twenty years further on into the Raj, specialist fields of knowledge had grown to such a point that the *encyclopedia indica* became too unwieldy for the one museum, one scholar or one government department to manage. The days of encyclopaedic museums were over, and museums that were set up henceforth limited themselves to a particular discipline or field of knowledge. Thus there were specialist museums for natural history, for medicine, for forestry, or for art. What today constitutes the field of 'art' was itself split into two categories, of antiquities—the monuments, sculptures, inscriptions, coins and relics that could yield information about India's historical past—and 'industrial arts': the living craft skills that were so admired in Europe, and which were seen to present economic opportunities for both India and Britain.

From 1851 onwards, the Government of India had begun vigorous participation in international exhibitions in which Indian materials, crops and products were displayed and advertised to an international market. These exhibitions were highly successful as a marketing device that expanded the demand for Indian products in many parts of the world. As trade in India's art-wares grew, the economic and industrial museums (which collected samples and information about raw materials, crops and craft skills) became increasingly useful to the Government's Revenue and Agriculture Department. Several Industrial Art museums were established all over the country, in which examples of native skills were gathered as a ready reference or as an exportable collection that could efficiently be sent to the next exhibition. The logical system of arrangement for the 'industrial art' museums was by 'industry': showing the many different processes and skills available within India for say, textiles, or woodworking, or metalsmithy.

Meanwhile growing numbers of antiquarians were pressing for governmental care for monuments decaying all over the country. In response to their pleas, the Archaeological Survey was established in 1861. The task of archaeological museums was to collect, decipher and date antiquities. These museums collected sculptures and fragments of monuments, coins, inscriptions in various media and other remains from the distant past. The field of early archaeology , however, remained dominated by an antiquarian attitude, which valued the most ancient over the medieval.[18] By and large, when archaeological collections were displayed they were arranged in a broadly chronological order, keeping together groups of objects from the one site or with a shared iconography.

In recognition of the divergent interests that occupied the field of 'art,' in 1882 the Government of India split the field between two government departments. Henceforth, archaeology and fine arts would remain with the Home Department which would arrange for the excavation, survey and protection of antiquities—a moral duty for the government that offered no financial returns. Practical Arts, exhibitions, and museums would go to the Department of Revenue and Agriculture, which would link art schools and museums for the furtherance of industry. The official who oversaw this division of labour observed

> 'The main object of the exhibition of Indian products is not the gratification of occidental curiosity, or the satisfaction of aesthetic longings among foreign nations, but the development of a trade in these products, whether raw or manufactured, rough or artistic.'[19]

It should be clear by now that the two typologies of display seen within the National Museum bring together the intentionalities of the two principal kinds of colonial museums. Downstairs, the National Museum is an archaeological museum. Upstairs it becomes an industrial museum. These two taxonomic systems which were united in the earliest, encyclopaedic museums of the colonial period, and then split apart in the face of growing specialist knowledge, were once again brought together to fill the halls of the new National Museum. Why? It would seem that in the desire to create an institution vast enough and grand enough to be the National Museum, the founders could only think to aggregate the different kinds of museum that then existed.

There is surely a failure of imagination here, in the inability to give shape to a new form of a museum, and to make new values and *new meanings* for the art within. In the face of a new task in a new era, the creators of the National Museum, instead of creating a new epistemology, fell back on one that was more that 150 years old.[20] If there is any consolation, it lies only in the concession that we may now make, that perhaps later-medieval and Islamic art are excluded from the Museum's national narrative unintentionally, in an unthinking application of two incompatible systems of taxonomy.

Three Quadrants Full

I f the National Museum is stalked by the ghosts of the colonial museum, it is perhaps because it lives in a haunted house. The history of the National Museum reveals that it is not just the Museum's sense of order that derives from epistemology of the colonial period. The idea of this Museum, its very location, and the exercise of research and collecting on which it was founded, all derive from colonial projects. Even the Museum's presence in the ceremonial centre of New Delhi is not so much the assertion of a new national confidence as much as the completion of an old colonial design.

When the decision was taken in 1911 to shift the capital of British India from Calcutta to Delhi, there were plans for the erection of suitably imposing structures to house the great archives of colonial knowledge. The original plan for New Delhi had always envisaged the intersection of Kingsway and Queensway (today renamed Rajpath and Janpath) as the nucleus of four important institutions. This intersection was at the halfway mark of the grand processional pathway stretching between the Viceregal Palace and the Memorial Arch. Four large lots were blocked out here: on the northwest, for the Records Office and the War Museum; on the northeast for the Medical Museum; on the southwest for the Ethnological Museum; and on the southeast for the Imperial Museum. Mirroring each other across the broad avenues would be the museums dedicated to the sciences of war and peace, death and life, as it were; and of the arts of forest and city, the tribal of today and the civilisation of yesteryears. Around this hub would be concentrated the sum of knowledge and understanding of India that had been gathered in the past century and a half.

The grand set of museums never were erected. This project was presumably overtaken by other, larger events. The first world war ocurred; and when it was over and most of New Delhi was built, the conditions within India were sufficiently unsettled to discourage investment in such triumphal gestures. There was even less sense in taking up the project after the second world war, when the loss of the Indian colony was apparent to all.

While Lutyens' plan for this hub was never completed, some structures did come to occupy three of the four quadrants. The Records Office was built according to plan, and is now the National Archives of India. In the space for the the Imperial Museum, the Archaeological Survey gained its offices and added a small structure to house Sir Aurel Stein's collection of Central Asian artefacts. In the place for the Medical Museum, however, temporary military barracks were built. This plot was given over to the Indira Gandhi National Centre for the Arts in the 1980's. The fourth quadrant, intended for the ethnological museum, remains empty to this day. Our honourable Defence Minister has long wished to see a War Museum built here. If he succeeds, the quadrant will be filled and will very nearly discharge Lutyens' original plans.

Of all these plans for the quadrant, the only grand project to be taken up in the early years of Independence was the building of the Imperial Museum, now recast as the National Museum. What were the circumstances in which the project of an Imperial Museum was revived after Independence? And in what way was the project transformed, allowing the Imperial Museum to turn 'national'?

Delhi-London-Delhi

To trace the history of Delhi's centrepiece, we must turn our attention now to an event that occurred in London. A scant three months after India's Independence, the Royal Academy in London had mounted an ambitious exhibition titled 'The Arts of India and Pakistan.' Remembered in Indian art history as a significant moment for Indian art, the show has been spoken of as a timely gesture on the part of the British, a gracious celebration of the independence of India and the creation of Pakistan very soon after the fact. That it was housed in the Royal Academy, a conservative and Eurocentric institution, has been construed as an ultimate acknowledgement on the part of the imperial masters of the deep level of civilisation, and indeed of the nation-worthiness of the ancient land. In truth this was the first time that the British art establishment was treating Indian artefacts as fine art, speaking of its carved stone as 'sculpture' rather than as 'antiquities' that were distinguished merely for their age.

It was inevitable that the Royal Academy exhibition would acquire political piquancy, coming, as it did, just three months after Indian independence. As it happens, the exhibition's exquisitely appropriate timing—and therefore, the inclusion of a number of politically correct gestures—was in fact an accident. In the late '20's the Academy had launched a series of very successful exhibitions of art from other cultures; and a group of Indian art scholars and collectors had advocated a similar show for Indian art as early as 1931. The 'International Exhibition of Greater Indian Art' had been scheduled for January 1940, when World War II intervened, scotching all plans for major exhibitions. After the end of the War the project was revived; but by this time the political situation was utterly altered. At the eve of India's independence and the creation of Pakistan, the exhibition was politically sensitive. Well done, it could 'make a great contribution in linking up (Britain) and India', [21] but poorly done, it could worsen relations between the two countries. In order to regulate the content of this important exhibition, the official art establishment had to take control of its planning and management. Thus the private initiative of a group of scholars was taken over and turned into an official performance.

The fact that the exhibition occurred with full support of the government machinery in both Britain and the Indian subcontinent had great effect on its curatorial scope. With the help of vast infrastructure, sufficient funds and the authority of two governments, the exhibition was able to gather over two hundred artefacts from British, European and Indian collections. Especially important was the inclusion of many colossal and ancient sculptures that travelled out of India for the first time. The exhibition attempted to be as comprehensive as it was extensive. Its sections on sculpture, painting, textiles and decorative arts included large numbers of rare objects of very fine quality.

Despite the best efforts of institutions and scholars, the exhibition failed to attract crowds in London and met with only mild approval from the critics. British interest in India was waning; perhaps there was even a note of bitterness and resentment in the response to the show.

The exhibition may have had only moderate success in London; but it was destined to have a far more significant afterlife in Delhi. When the objects loaned from Indian museums and private collections were returned to India, they were put on display in an exhibition of 'Masterpieces of Indian Art' in the Durbar Hall of the Rashtrapati Bhawan (the erstwhile Viceregal palace) for the Indian public at Delhi.[22] The exhibition in New Delhi was thronged with visitors. Its compression of five thousand years of Indian art was seen as a valuable mirror to the national self. The show was visited by high dignitaries. Even the prime minister felt that it would be a pity if the collection was dispersed. Accordingly, the Ministry of Education chose to retain this exhibition and make it the core of a new National Museum. Letters of 'request' were sent to the lenders to allow their objects to stay in Delhi and form the nucleus of the National Museum. Its inauguration was achieved by a simple act of renaming: the temporary exhibition in the Rashtrapati Bhavan had now become the National Museum of India!

Now that the Museum had been conjured into existence, it sought its own appointed place. When the monsoon of 1949 approached, sculptures displayed outdoors on the Rashtrapati Bhavan lawns needed to be housed. The new Director General of the National Museum—also the Superintendent of Archaeology—sought to take over the Museum's 'own' plot of land, but the plot earmarked for the Museum was already occupied by the Museum of Central Asian Antiquities. It was agreed that if the National Museum could demolish the pre-exisiting building and construct a suitable structure of its own, it would undertake to house Central Asian collection in its own future building. Thus, fortuitously—or perhaps superfluously—the ambit of the National Museum was expanded beyond the strictly national. But there is no doubting the priorities that the institution had set itself.

These then are the circumstances in which India gained its National Museum: its location determined by the plans for the Imperial capital, its epistemology the conflation of two complexes of colonial knowledge, its core collection determined by the committee of curators of an exhibition in London. By such accidents are institutions made. And the Museum reveals the accidents which gave it shape. This is most visible in its adherence to the dual and outmoded taxonomies of 'archaeology' and 'industry,' which allow so many areas of Indian history to remain underrepresented. It is visible also in the Museum's poverty in the precise areas of collection that it foregrounds: the National Museum's collection of ancient sculpture is not of the best. The great collections were already made in Calcutta, in Mathura, in Chennai or in Lucknow, fifty or a hundred years before the National Museum was established.

With its past coloured in colonial history, we must ask: is the Museum National? As we have seen, 'nationalism' is on display in the sculpture galleries which adhere to the nationalist narrative of art history. But little else in the Museum seems informed by the desire to be 'national,' to reflect a philosophy for the nation that it represents. I would contend, however, that the museum would have been received as 'national' regardless of its narrative or its display. It is not what the museum does, but the fact that it exists that makes the museum national. The National Museum acquires symbolic depth through the very shallowness of its history: that it was a new museum made by a new nation; that it would house Indian artefacts, and that it would judge them as aesthetic objects and display them as masterpieces. By the simple fact of its establishment in its particular place, in its particular place in time, the National Museum's symbolic meaning was strong enough to serve as an assertion of India as a sovereign land.

References and Notes

1. In many instances, a pre-existing colonial museum is made 'national' through a change in its emphases and interpretation. G. Wright (ed) *The Formation of National Collections of Art and Archaeology*, National Gallery of Art, Washington DC: 1996 and Flora E.S. Kaplan (ed) *Museums and the Making of "Ourselves": The Role of Objects in National Identity*, Leicester University Press, 1994 discuss several such cases.
2. Carol Duncan and Allan Wallach coined the term and pointed out pervasive patterns in art history survey books and museums in their classic essay, 'The Universal Survey Museum,' *Art History* 3, December 1980.
3. See Gwendolyn Wright, *The Formation of National Collections*, cited above.
4. I discuss in some detail the process by which a canon of 'fine art' was constructed for India in the first half of the 20th century in 'Museums and the Making of an Indian Art Historical Canon' in *Towards a New Art History: Studies in Indian Art*, (ed) Shivaji K.Panikkar, Parul Dave Mukherji, Deeptha Achar; D.K. Printworld, New Delhi
5. The next several paragraphs analyse the display of the National Museum, based on a description of the galleries published in Grace Morely, *A Brief Guide to the*

National Museum, National Museum, Delhi, 1962. Comparing Morely's description with the sculpture galleries today, it seems they have suffered little change
in the past 47 years.

6. Gupta sculptures from Mathura and Sarnath are highly skilled and refined, but
    their exaltation as the finest moment in the history of Indian plastic art was to
    some degree motivated by a desire to locate one, suitably early period as 'clas-
    sical' in which a purely 'Indian' aesthetic is achieved. As Romila Thapar has
    shown, the Guptas became the centrepiece of Indian history (not just art his-
    tory) because they provided a desirable ancestor for the modern Indian nation.
    The Gupta empire was prosperous and extensive, but it was also the period in
    which Buddhism declined and Brahmanism gained ground. See her *The Past
    and Prejudice*, National Book Trust, Delhi, 1975.

7. I quote here without comment Morley's passage on the History of Indian Paint-
    ings Gallery: 'To be noted are the early examples of painting in the west of India
    from which the long indigenous tradition of Rajasthani painting appears to de-
    rive; the Deccani and Mughal schools which drew on Persian styles and tech-
    niques (of which a few examples are shown for reference); early Malwa paint-
    ings from Central India; Rajasthani works from various Rajput courts; the Pahari
    (Hill State) schools up to the 19th century; the Company School (late 18th and
    early 19th century) in which Indian artists, especially of Lucknow and Patna,
    chose subjects appealing to European interest and taste; the painting of the south
    which had a late flowering in the early 19th century Tanjore paintings as a de-
    velopment of temple painting.' Morley, op.cit., p 23.

8. Thus Monier-Williams describes the encyclopaedic Indian museum that he at-
    tempted but failed to establish in Oxford. Quoted in 'History of the Indian Col-
    lections,' p x, in Indian Art in the Ashmolean Museum, J.C. Harle and Andrew
    Topsfield, Ashmolean Museum, Oxford 1987

9. Scientific collections dealt primarily with natural history and geology.

10. Economic collections dispayed raw materials that could obtained in India,
    whether these were crops that could be grown or minerals that could be mined.

11. Industrial collections demonstrated the craft skills that were available in India
    for the making of exportable produce.

12. Archaeological collections included antiquities of various kinds – sculptures,
    architectural fragments, stone or copper plate inscriptions, coins, relics, pot-
    sherds and other archaeological finds. As none of these objects was infused
    with the aura of 'art' reproductions mingled freely with the originals, and cop-
    ies of paintings, or plaster casts of sculpture or architecture were greatly valued
    parts of such collections.

13. See Tapati Guha-Thakurta, 'The museumised relic: Archaeology and the first
    museum of colonial India,' The Indian Economic and Social History Review, 34,
    1, 1977: pp 21 – 51. Guha Thakurta prefaces her discussion of the Indian Muse-
    um's Archaeological galleries with a succinct overview of colonial museum-
    making.

14. The early history of this museum is well known; it is the subject of *The India
    Museum, 1801-1879* by Ray Desmond, HMSO, London 1982. The dispersed col-
    lections of this museum form the kernel of the Indian collections in the British
    Museum (which derived its great Amaravati sculptures and Pala stelae from
    this source), the Victoria and Albert Museum, the Natural History Museum and
    the Kew Gardens. The subsequent history of the Indian collections in the V&A
    is the subject of a forthcoming book by the author, tentatively titled *The Jewel
    and the Crown: Showing India at the V&A.*

15. The keepership at the India Museum in London was held by a succession of naturalists; and one can judge the situation at the Indian Museum in Calcutta by the fact that even after the museum had acquired the Bharhut stupa railings and quantities of Gandharan, Kushana-Mathura and Gupta period sculptures, the handbook of the museum's archeological collections was prepared by a zoologist. This was John Anderson, Superintendent of the Indian Museum and author of its *Catalogue and Handbook of the Archaeological Collections in the Indian Museum*, Calcutta, 1883. See Guha-Thakurta, op.cit.

16. See Guha-Thakurta, ibid.

17. In a note dated 18/10/1882, E.C. Buck, Secretary to the Government of India, Home Department writes: "Local governments may be asked to use their influence to concentrate all archaeological collections in the Indian Musuem unless there are special reasons for preferring to deposit them at a Provincial Museum. Small local museums...simply interfere without any adequate object with the completeness of the archaeological series at the Imperial Museum..." NAI, Home Deptt. Archaeology A Dec. 1882 nos 3-7.

18. For instance, colonial-period archaeology showed a marked preference for Buddhist over Hindu art; it held that Indian art had been in decline since about the 2nd century AD. For discussions, see Pramod Chandra, 'Sculpture,' in *On the Study of Indian Art*, Harvard University Press, Cambridge Mass., 1983. Also, Tapati Guha-Thakurta, *The Making of A New 'Indian' Art*, Cambridge University Press, Cambridge UK, 1992: p. 178-9

19. 'Note on Arrangements for Exhibitions,' by A Mackenzie, Secretary (Home Dept) to the GO, in National Archive of India 1882: Home Department Public Branch 'A' File No 157 July 1882,.

20. The National Museum does limit itself to the category of 'art' and does not try to become an encyclopedic museum for all branches of knowledge. By this time, 'art' has come to be valued as the embodiment of the spiritual and intellectual qualities of the people. As such, it was a special category of objects and could no longer be ranked with commercial products.

21. VIA Registry: SF 47-45/1420: Indian Section General, part file Exhibitions—UK. Undated note (1946) by Leigh Asthenia, director of the VIA

22. Tapati Guha Thakurta has discussed the exhibition in the Rashtrapati Bhavan in her 'Marking Independence: the Ritual of a National Art Exhibition,' in T. Guha-Thakurta (ed.), Sites of Art History: Canons and Expositions, *Journal of Arts and Ideas*, special issue, December 1997.

Patricia Uberoi

Chicks, Kids and Couples: the nation in calendar art

As is well known, the history of modern Indian art is intrinsically connected with the history of Indian nationalism.[1] There was, first of all, the nationalist ambition to master the techniques and technologies of the colonial ruler; and there was the simultaneous quest for authentic subject matter and artistic styles to express the cultural genius of the Indian people. In both these respects, and in the tension that unites them, 'calendar art' (so-called) shares an intimate interface with art history proper. At the same time, calendar art prints have actively *worked* to create the nation as an 'imagined community' of fellow citizens, including some and excluding others in the process.[2] This was so from the very early days of colour lithography over a century ago, and it remains the case even today.

Expressly political calendars—called 'leaders' or '*rashtriya*' types in trade parlance—have always featured quite prominently in the repertoire of Indian calendar art, and have played a significant role in the mobilisation of patriotic and anti-colonial sentiment through the last century. The chief focus of patriotic fervour has been the figure of Mother India,[3] sometimes queen (Boadicea / Britannia), sometimes Goddess (Durga / Kali / Parvati / Lakshmi), sometimes Mother (nurturing / protective); sometimes the iconic Indian woman (haplessly enchained, awaiting the dawn of Freedom). Numerous, too, are portraits of patriots who have fought against foreign invasion and occupation (especially the Sikh Gurus, Rana Pratap, Shivaji, Rani Lakshmibai, Bhagat Singh, Chandrashekhar Azad); leaders of the Freedom Movement, in various permutations and combinations; and contemporary political figures, according to persuasion.

Characteristically, these portraits are associated with other symbols of nationhood: the sacralised map of India, the national flag, or nationalist slogans such as *Vande Mataram* or *Jai Hind*. Nowadays, such calendars are mostly confined to the classroom or to public and political party offices, and to the intermittent context of electioneering, only to reappear in profusion with notable events such as the Kargil operation (1999) or the release of a pair of Bhagat Singh Bollywood movies (2002). Keen observers and purveyors of poster art read this as evidence that the domain of politics has lost its charisma in contemporary India. Indeed, at the national level, there has been no *iconographically* worthwhile leader since Mrs. Indira Gandhi, though regional politics presents a more vibrant picture, as do particular constituencies of the political public (for instance, in the context of Dalit or backward caste mobilisation).[4]

'Leaders' apart, postcolonial nationalist iconography (especially of the first two decades after Independence) has sought to articulate in a visual idiom the developmental, modernising and nation-building agenda of the post-colonial state. Typically, it has done so in what one might call—following Claude Lévi-Strauss—a *mythic* idiom, that is, through the attempted (visual) reconciliation of fundamental contradictions in the state's developmental agenda by bringing opposites into a productive and symbiotic conjunction. There is thus no contradiction of choice between the development of agriculture and the development of industry; between enhancing agrarian productivity and national defense; between the purity and innocence of 'rurality' and the lure of the city; between Indian tradition and westernised modernity: all are in productive service to the nation-state. Similarly, the Indian people—North, South, East and West; rich and poor; peasant, soldier, priest and merchant; man and woman; brahmin, vaishya and kshatriya—are joyful co-participants in the regeneration of nation, state and society. And the communal divide that had ruptured the national body politic at the very moment of Freedom is erased: Hindu, Muslim, Sikh, Christian, Buddhist, Jain – *'Ham sab ek hain'*! ('We are all one'). Again, keen observers complain that the nation's secular agenda is often compromised by the visual appropriation of all communities within the overarching embrace of the Hindu goddess; and in any case that it is now 'drained of meaning'[5] and reduced to mere tokenism. Merchants of calendar art confirm this dour observation. Nowadays, secularism doesn't 'sell', they say.

Hindu religious icons dominate the output of calendar art and have frequently provided the idiom for the allegorical expression of nationalist sentiment.[6] The Goddess Kali atop the prone body of a pallid Lord Shiva can be read as awakened Bengal dominating Britain;[7] Shiva protecting the sage Markandeya from the Lord of Death (the Sage desperately clinging on to the *Shivlingam*) transforms into Gandhi protecting Mother India (similarly clutching the *Shivlingam*) from demonic British power;[8] Shahid Bhagat Singh offers his bloody severed head in tribute to the Mother / the Motherland / the Goddess Durga in the context of the 1965 War with Pakistan;[9] and Indira Gandhi herself takes on the role of the Goddess in the 1971 Bangladesh War.[10]

In recent years, commentators on the visual culture of the public sphere have read a number of developments in calendar art iconography as both witness to and incitement of an aggressive and exclusivist Hindu chauvinism. There is, first of all, the vigorous circulation of images of Mother India, now holding aloft the saffron standard of Hindu revival. There is the image of a militant Ram, defiantly straddling the (still un-built) Ayodhya temple.[11] There is a humanoid Hanuman, more muscle-builder than monkey.[12] There is an armed and upright Ganesh, neither hybrid–child of Shiva and Parvati nor the auspicious patron of new enterprises, but a warrior on the warpath.[13] And there is the Mother Cow, the whole pantheon of Hindu deities inscribed on her bovine body, whose potential for inciting communal passions is undiminished after a century and a quarter.[14] These phenomena have all been well-documented, first by the British colonial authorities, sensitive to the potential of such prints for provoking anti-British sentiment or inflaming communal passions, and latterly by scholars dismayed over the continued communalisation of public space.

In this pictorial essay, I seek to draw attention to certain *other* visual idioms for representing the nation: idioms which are more overtly secular, but which nonetheless in many cases bear the imprint of sacred iconography. Drawing on a personal archive of calendars of the last half-century,[15] I look at three different categories of prints: pin-ups (called 'beauties', or latterly 'ladies', in trade shorthand); the range of 'baby' iconography, a type that is so ubiquitous (and seemingly innocuous) that it has scarcely merited critical notice; and representations of the conjugal couple (or the nuclear family unit), a theme that seems to have been occluded or displaced in contemporary nationalist iconography, for reasons on which we can only speculate.

535 — VILLAGE BEAUTY

Village Beauty
Artist: Raja
Publisher: National Glass House, Ludhiana, 1969.

Chicks

Pin-up pictures of beautiful women, many of them photographic prints of film-stars in enticing poses and scanty costumes, are conspicuous in calendar art, in India as elsewhere. Designed to attract the male gaze, these provocative pin-ups also, in many cases, speak to the theme of national modernity. They do so, on the one hand, in the idiom of 'genre' painting (quasi-ethnographic portraits of peasant and tribal women, of fisherwomen, of women at work, and the like), or in the style of commercial advertising, where comely women are posed alongside desirable market products. In either case, the women subjects tend to assume the attributes of Lakshmi, Goddess of wealth and fertility, who bestows prosperity on industry and agriculture alike and thus presides over the nation's progress. Indeed, this conflation of religious and secular iconography is occasionally made quite explicit.[16]

The 'Village Beauty' of Figure 1 epitomises the pin-up style. The foreground of this striking 1969 print presents a winsome village belle/ fertility goddess, bearing on her hip a basket brim-full of garden produce. The soft curves of her body, barely contained by the tightly-knotted blouse, suggest both fecundity and sensuality. In the fields behind her we see some neat village houses (of no recognisable regional pedigree), while the low mountain range further back delineates a sacred territory that stretches from the Himalayas in the north, to Kanya Kumari in the south.[17] Prominently displayed are the twin insignia of the Green Revolution—the tractor and the tube-well—enhancing, not disfiguring, the attractions of the rural countryside. Poverty, gruelling labour and rural backwardness are nowhere acknowledged.

Not only the peasant woman, but also the dusky fisher-girl in her skimpy, leg-revealing sari, the agricultural worker, sickle in hand, the woman labourer wielding her hammer, the woman scientist peering eagerly through her microscope—all contribute to the building of the new India, even as their shapeliness provides ample feast for the eyes. For instance, we see a sturdy tribal woman joyfully at work on the construction of a huge dam, her efforts complemented by myriad other workers surging up giant ramps, and by the mechanical labour of a monstrous phallic crane.[18]

Modernity's other face is the city-scape, visualised as the satisfying site of consumption of the glamorous products of the market

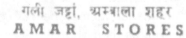

Two Girls with Bicycles
Artist: Swarup
Publisher: Amar Stores, Ambala, 1976.

place. Just as Swami Vivekanand could comfortably inhabit the sky-scraper filled landscape of Chicago,[19] bringing India into a global community, so, in reverse, the Indian pin-up can domesticate the urban environment. In Figure 3, for instance, a specimen of the sub-genre known as 'cycle-wali', two shapely college girls in short pleated skirts, clinging jumpers and neat bobby-socks, pose with their bicycles in a modern city-scape. Perhaps one is envying the other her latest-model moped. Their dress and hair-styles mark the girls out as 'modern' misses, as does the 'Bombay' background of towering apartments and luxurious pent-houses, set along a seaside boulevard. Also glimpsed in the background are other privileged signs of modern times—a double-decker bus, a flash car, (possibly) a suburban train and a giant petrol pump. This is not the urbanism of 'dark satanic mills', of unplanned growth, of filth, disorder, disease and despair, of the homeless underclass—but an optimistic scene of bourgeois orderliness and cleanliness, a sphere of pleasure and a playground for the leisure class.

Kids

Women are the most visible signs of agricultural prosperity, evoking one of the standard iconographic forms of the Goddess Lakshmi. But the same role can be performed by the child,[20] and by the conjugal couple as well. Sometimes, though rarely, we see the Green Revolution evoked through the figure of the male farmer plying his tractor,[21] particularly so, as in the truck and tractor art of present-day Punjab, when the productive farmer is linked with the patriotic soldier—'Jai jawan, Jai kisan' ('Hail the soldier, hail the farmer').

The sacredness of the earth is illustrated in the Farmer Baby image of Figure 4. A young boy in farmer's dhoti and turban sits in worship of the creative energy of a decorated *shivlingam*, fashioned from straw. Beside him we see ripened grain, ready for harvest, and the emblematic sickle implanted in the earth. Similarly, the little soldier-boy in the high Himalayas worships a flower-strewn snowy *lingam*, his rifle-bayonet standing upright in the snow beside him. The farmer and soldier, along with the priest, the sportsman and the doctor (see Figure 5), not to mention the engineer (whose precocious talent is revealed in his infantile fondness for gears, levers, and spanners[22]), are valued

Farmer Baby
Artist: Vijay Kumar.
Publisher: Kamal Calendar Company, Delhi, 1970.

Our Flag Flying High
Artist: M. Singh
Publisher: unknown, mid-1970s.

social roles, anticipated in the 'baby' icons, that are seen to contribute positively to the building of a strong nation-state.

'Our Flag Flying High' (Figure 6) provides an interesting take on the theme of infant patriotism. Notwithstanding his blond curls, the child is indubitably 'Hindustani'. Seated on a cushion whose colours map the Indian subcontinent, the child holds aloft the national flag against a tri-colour rising sun. Beside him are the signs of war-preparedness—a tank, an aeroplane (again, in the national colours), pistol, rifle, bugle and drum. Though signs of patriotic allegiance, these are also—in the form of toys—the insignia of play and of leisured life-styles. In this form they constitute products of consumerist desire, and of global modernity, and indeed, other calendars of the era have transformed these war toys into more secular objects of desire and instruments of pedagogy and social advancement and bourgeois ambition: the swing and see-saw, hockey stick and ball, abacus, toy-truck, wrist-watch and gold chain, all complementing the film-set mansion in the background.[23]

Couples

The valorisation of the conjugal couple as the core element of the 'modern' family began perhaps a century or more ago with the Bengal Renaissance (and the photo-studio portrait), but it was probably the influence of Soviet Socialist Realist iconography in the 1950s and 1960s that produced a range of calendars celebrating the nuclear family and the conjugal couple as signs of the new India. Often, the figures appear to be sculpted in stone, like the giant outdoor monuments to Freedom, Progress, and founding fathers that occupy public space. Labeled 'Progressive India', for instance, a sturdy peasant couple and their child are pictured at the site of a huge dam, the map of India radiating light behind them; or a print entitled 'Heroic Family' shows a stern-faced father, battle-ready, adored by his heroic wife and child; or a bride rises from the flower-strewn bridal bed to present a rifle to her soldier-husband as he leaves for the Front.

The iconic peasant couple dominate the frame surrounded by many other signs of national progress. There is the gushing tube-well (once again), the domestic hand pump, the big dam, the loaded truck, the power house and power lines, a chuffing train, and the scientific laboratory that enables all these developments and guarantees the

Peasant Couple
Artist: V.G. Narkar
Publisher: unknown, late 1960s early 1970s.

productivity of the land. In a tiny inset, too, we see an amputated reminder of the state's family planning agenda: a small family is a happy one. Similarly, in the lovingly and realistically rendered Figure 6,[24] we see another tribute to the symbiotic combination of agriculture and industry in ensuring the nation's future. The print is rather unusual, actually, for the conjugal couple here are not merely, and dutifully, productive in the service of nation, state and society, but also a trifle romantic!

* * *

The calendars presented here are all witness to the development agenda of the Indian state through the first generation following Indian Independence. Nowadays, it seems that address to the tensions and dilemmas of development through the 'mythic' reconciliation of opposites is relatively muted, though it remains as a residual feature of the visual rhetoric of the Indian state and its agencies, and of public-minded corporations anxious to establish their progressive and secular credentials.[25] From the optimistic age of nation-building to turn-of-the-century ennui, the sheen of 'development' appears to have worn off, at least insofar as secular calendar inconography goes. Or rather, the celebration of productive labour has given way to unembarrassed affirmation of the glamour of consumption. This is the case across the three types of prints discussed here (pin-ups, 'babies', and couples), as the explosion of commercial advertising in the print and electronic media since the liberalised 1990s has taken on one of the erstwhile functions of the calendar print as index of national modernity via the enticing products of the market-place.

However, even as advertising has appropriated the couple and the nuclear unit as contemporary icons of middle-class desire and ambition, the romantic motif, which we briefly glimpsed appears to have become in calendar art the specialised property of the film-couple, block-buster movies reduced to photo-stills. Or else it is transmuted into the legendary idiom of tragic love (of Mumtaz and Shah Jahan, of Heer and Ranjha, of Sohini and Mahiwal, of Laila and Majnu). Somehow, for reasons on which sociologists may endlessly ruminate, the romantic idiom has not been nationalised / naturalised as legitimate patriotic pursuit.

Peasant Couple
Artist: Vijay Kumar
Publisher: Navyug Calendar Corp., Patiala, 1969.

References and Notes

1. See, for instance: Partha Mitter, *Art and Nationalism in Colonial India, 1850-1922: Occidental Orientations* (Cambridge: Cambridge University Press, 1994); Tapati Guha-Thakurta, *The Making of a 'New' Indian Art: Artists, Aesthetics and Nationalism in Bengal, c. 1850-1920* (Cambridge: Cambridge University Press, 1992); Special issues of the 'Journal of Arts and Ideas' for 1995 (nos. 27–28) and 1997 (nos. 30–31).

2. Much of the writing on this theme has followed the lead of Benedict Anderson in his influential *Imagined Communities* (London: Verso, 1983). See also Christopher Pinney, 'The Nation (Un)pictured? Chromolithography and "Popular" Politics in India, 1879–1995', *Critical Inquiry* 23: 834–67; and '"A Secret of One's Own Country": Or, How Indian Nationalism made itself Irrefutable', *Contributions to Indian Sociology* 36, 1 & 2: 113–50; Sandria B. Freitag, 'Visions of the Nation: Theorising the Nexus between Creation, Consumption and Participation in the Public Sphere', in Rachel Dwyer and Christopher Pinney, eds, *Pleasure and the Nation: The History, Politics and Consumption of Popular Culture in India* (Delhi, Oxford University Press, 1999), pp. 35–75; Sumathi Ramaswamy, 'Visualising India's Geobody: Globes, Maps, Bodyscapes', *Contributions to Indian Sociology* 36, 1 & 2: 151–89; and, ed., *Beyond Appearances? Visual Practices and Ideologies in Modern India* (New Delhi: Sage Publications, 2003); Patricia Uberoi, '"Unity in Diversity"? Dilemmas of Nationhood in Indian Calendar Art', *Contributions to Indian Sociology* 36, 1 & 2: 191–232.

3. On the visual and literary depiction of Mother India / Bharat Mata, see e.g., Lise McKean, 'Bharat Mata: Mother India and her Militant Matriots', in John Stratton Hawley and Donna Marie Wulff, eds., *Devi: Goddesses of India* (Berkeley: University of California Press); Sumathi Ramaswamy,'Maps and Mother Goddesses in Modern India', *Imago Mundi* 53: 97–114; Geeti Sen, this volume; Tanika Sarkar, *Hindu Wife, Hindu Nation: Community, Religion and Cultural Nationalism* (New Delhi: Permanent Black), Chapter 8; and Amrit and Rabindra K.D. Kaur Singh, *Images of Freedom* (New Delhi: Indialog, 2003).

4. See Christopher Pinney, 'The Image in Indian Culture', in Veena Das (ed.), *The Oxford India Companion to Sociology and Social Anthropology* (New Delhi: Oxford University Press, 2003), pp. 625–53.

5. See Shahid Amin, 'Remembering the Musalman', in Hiroyuki Kotani *et al.* eds., *Fusing Modernity: Appropriation of History and Political Mobilisation in South Asia* (Osaka: National Museum of Ethnology, 2000), pp. 75–101; also Uberoi, '"Unity in Variety"?'.

6. See Singh and Singh, *Images of Freedom*.

7. See Mitter, *Art and Nationalism*, plate XII.

8. Singh and Singh, *Images of Freedom*, pp. 52–53.

9. See Fukuoka Asian Art Museum (FAAM), *From Goddess to Pin–up: Icons of Femininity in Indian Calendar Art* (Fukuoka: Fukuoka Asian Art Museum, 2000), Plate 4.9; and Geeti Sen, this volume.

10. See FAAM, *From Goddess to Pin–up*, Plate 4.13.

11. See especially Anuradha Kapur, 'Deity to Crusader: The Changing Iconography of Ram', in Gyanendra Pandey, ed., *Hindus and Others* (New Delhi: Viking, 1993), pp. 74–107; and Pinney, 'The Nation (Un)Pictured?'.

12. Philip Lutgendorf,'Evolving a Monkey: Hanuman, Poster Art and Postcolonial Anxieties', *Contributions to Indian Sociology* 36, 1 & 2: 71–112.

13. However, for a long term perspective, see Raminder Kaur, 'Martial Imagery in Western India: The Changing Face of Ganapati since the 1890s', *South Asia* n.s. 25, 1: 69–96.
14. See Gyanendra Pandey, 'Rallying with the Cow: Sectarian Strife in the Bhojpuri Region, c. 1888–1917', in Ranajit Guha, ed., *Subaltern Studies II* (Delhi: Oxford University Press), pp. 60–129; and *The Construction of Communalism in Colonial North India* (Delhi: Oxford University Press, 1990), esp. Chapter 3; Sandria Freitag, 'Contesting in Public: Colonial Legacies and Contemporary Communities', in David Ludden, ed., *Making India Hindu: Religion, Community and the Politics of Democracy in India* (Delhi: Oxford University Press), esp. pp. 215–34; Pinney,'"The Nation" (Un)pictured'; and Uberoi '"Unity in Diversity"?', esp. pp. 201–18.
15. Collection J.P.S. and Patricia Uberoi, Delhi.
16. A particularly striking calendar of the late 1960s shows the icon of the Goddess Lakshmi seated on a bed of harvested grain, with oil rigs and huge factories behind her.
17. For discussion of another such example, see FAAM, *From Goddess to Pin-up*, pp. 10–11.
18. See the print in FAAM, *From Goddess to Pin-up*, Plate 2.9.
19. For a typical image, see Singh and Singh, *Images of Freedom*, pp.42–43.
20. See Patricia Uberoi, "Baby" Iconography: Constructing Childhood in Indian Calendar Art', in Sujata Patel, Jasodhara Bagchi and Krishna Raj, ed., *Thinking Social Science in India: Essays in Honour of Alice Thorner* (New Delhi: Sage Publications, 2002), pp.264–81.
21. As an example, see Singh and Singh, *Images of Freedom*, pp.42–43.
22. An image executed with finesse by the renowned calendar artist, Yogendra Rastogi, whose fondness for gear levers as signs of modernity was evidenced in many prints.
23. See the print entitled `Kaka' (Kiddie) in Uberoi, "Baby" Iconography', Plate 17.6. The plump child's crawling posture mimics that of the child Krishna (substituting fruit pieces for *ladhus* and butter balls). A nearly identical print in the collection of Erwin Neumayer and Christine Schelberger (Vienna), dating from the mid-1930s, is expressly labeled `Bal-Krishna'. See Erwin Neumayer and Christine Schelberger, *The Oleographed Gods of India* (Vienna, Private Circulation), Plate 41.
24. The artist has also executed a charming image of the cycle-wali genre, a shapely woman in *salwar-kameez* posed with her bicycle against a modern city-scape whose architectural style, along with the background mountains, suggests the new planned city of Chandigarh, See FAAM, *From Goddess to Pin-up*, Plate 8.8.
25. See, for instance, Srirupa Roy, `Moving Pictures: The Postcolonial State and Visual Representations of India', *Contributions to Indian Sociology*, 36, 1 & 2 (2002): 233–63.

Rashmi Doraiswamy

Image And Imagination: reconstructing the nation in cinema[1]

Communities are to be distinguished, not by their falsity / genuineness, but by the style in which they are imagined....The nation is imagined as limited because even the largest of them, encompassing perhaps a billion living human beings, has finite, if elastic, boundaries, beyond which lie other nations. No nation imagines itself coterminous with mankind....It is imagined as sovereign because the concept was born in an age in which Enlightenment and Revolution were destroying the legitimacy of the divinely-ordained, hierarchical dynastic realm.... Finally, it's imagined as a community, because, regardless of the actual inequality and exploitation that may prevail in each, the nation is always conceived as a deep, horizontal comradeship.[2]

—Benedict Anderson

Modern nationalisms involve communities of citizens in the territorially defined nation-state who share the collective experience, not of face-to-face contact or subordination to a royal person, but of reading books, pamphlets, newspapers, maps, and other modern texts together. In and through these collective experiences of what Benedict Andersen calls 'print capitalism', and others increasingly see as 'electronic capitalism' such as television and cinema citizens *imagine* themselves to belong to a national society. The modern state in this view, grows less out of natural facts—such as language, blood, soil and race—but is a quintessential cultural product, a product of cultural imagination.[3]

—Arjun Appadurai

I

Mutations of the Nation

Popular cultural texts, in their narratives, more often than not express their imaginings of the nation. This is true of what is probably the most *popular* and *mass* of popular cultural texts in India, the Bollywood film. It is often thought that these films are formulaic and repetitive; but, embedded in the formulae are conceptions of the nation that change under the pressure of history.

In countries that have undergone the historical processes of colonisation, the nationalist fight for independence, the subsequent setting up of independent nations freed from the yoke of colonialism and imperialism; and, thereafter, faced with internal socio-economic inequalities and hierarchies, this imagining of the community mutates through several phases. More often than not, it gets fractured into the imaginings of smaller communities. The community 'imagined' during the struggle for national independence would thus be far more inclusive than in later decades, when the independent nation-state is established and continues to define itself through processes of fracturing and exclusion.

In India, the complex inequities of caste, class, religion, dominant/marginal states and the traumatic transition from a feudal-agrarian society into an industrial one, have lain at the root of this fracturing. Thus the imaginings of the nation in the commercial cinema has gone through several distinct mutations[4]. Add to this the fact that the imaginings of the nation are not always as urbane as the Andersonian definition cited above may make it out to be. Culture as a terrain of the struggle of ideological tendencies, as the great Russian thinkers Voloshinov/Bakhtin envisaged it, results in hierarchies and power-equations within and between groups. Stretching the Anderson, Voloshinov/Bakhtin arguments further, I would say that in creating discourses of the nation, dominant groups often impose *their* imaginings of other groups as an intrinsic feature of the identity of their own community.

Globalisation has engendered new narratives in the '90s in the Hindi cinema, in which the nation and its imaginings exhibit what—to borrow a term from Arjun Appadurai—can be called a 'deterritorialised' character. The transnational flow of finance, people, ideologies and images, according to him, now lead to imaginings that lie beyond the boundaries of the nation-state.

Thus from nationalism to the postcolonial situation, to the context of globalisation, the imaginings of what constitutes the nation in the popular cinema, has undergone many changes. We can delineate three corresponding moments in the post-independence history of the Hindi film[5:]

1. The aspiration towards a just social order: the period from the 40s to the 60s
2. Fractured identities: the '70s, and the '80s
3. The cusp of the local with the global moment: The 90s end on...

While this periodisation does not account for the diversity of the Hindi film, it does provide a framework to view the way in which narratives have changed in the decades after India achieved Independence. This article focuses on the changing ways in which the nation has been imagined vis-à-vis the 'outside' in key texts from the film industry.

II

The Unforgettable Story of Dr Kotnis

Shantaram's **Dr Kotnis ki Amar Kahani** (1946) is a crucial text from pre-Independence India in its imaging of nationalist ideals. Dr Kotnis returns to his native Sholapur, having got his medical degree. He meets his parents only to inform them that he has decided to go to China to treat the people affected by the war with Japan. The father is dismayed, but accepts that the call of the nationalist leaders to help in the war effort is of greater import. Dr Kotnis travels with a group of doctors to China, serves the people there, marries a Chinese nurse and dies experimenting with a vaccine on himself.

The film sets up a 'deep and horizontal comradeship' between India and China, beyond which is the common enemy, Japan. Into this bonding is woven a theme which is in actuality an 'imagined' one, but which serves the nationalist project of the director: the theme of scientific progress and the technological 'savviness' of the Indian nation as compared to China. The clinic which Kotnis' doting father has set up for him is a modern one, replete with an operating table and swivel chair. The medicine boxes that the Indians are taking for the Chinese, the record-player that plays the song Pardesi re to chase away the longing for home that the Indian doctors are experiencing...

this mise-en-scene carefully complements the theme of modernity and 'modern-ness'. The record player, in fact, is found in one of the medicine-boxes and is referred to by one of the doctors as 'the medicine for homesickness'.

As the doctors listen boisterously to the song, the ancient link between India and China is established: one of the doctors is holding a sculpted image of Buddha in his hands, a theme reiterated later. "Centuries ago you sent us Buddha, now you have come to help us", says Kaka Wong to Dr Kotnis, when he saves people caught in a fire. The civilisational link is thus established, and Kotnis is linked to Lord Buddha. In fact, the nation is constructed through metonymic tropes of this kind as a shift of significances from the individual to the national/civilisational. The father, for instance, gives Dr Kotnis a ring with a map of the still undivided India on it before his departure for China; this father, who is now bereft of support in his old age, but a dutiful son of India. That this is not in a colonial encounter, but a morally and ethically pure mission—of helping our neighbour in need—is also stressed through this link with Buddha.

Later images of medical aid dispensed, of surgery, of Dr Kotnis experimenting on himself with a vaccine ... all build up the theme of the Indian being superior in his scientific knowledge; the 'natives' are seen in an intellectually subordinate but emotionally grateful position. The mission is one of enlightenment, of integration (Kotnis marries a Chinese girl), and martyrdom (he dies on alien soil trying to test a vaccine on himself). India is the 'giver' and China the 'receiver' from time immemorial. As Anderson points out, the imagination of nations is to be judged not according to their genuineness/falsity, but according to the style in which they are imagined. The story of the real Dr Kotnis provided the grist to represent nationalist ideals. (The historical fact of a few Indians helping the Chinese in an act of Indian-Chinese brotherhood and good neighbourliness cannot render tenable the interwoven narration in the film of Indian superiority over Chinese abjectness). Made in the context of the nationalist movement that was then at its peak, the film is the classic plural text, having made the British, the nationalists and the Communists who are in fierce political confrontation with each other, happy. For the British and the Communists on the one hand, the film stood as an effort in the war against fascism; and for the nationalists and the Communists on the other, it created a self-image of a modern, enlightened community with progressive ideals, where the individual thinks nothing of sacrificing himself for a greater cause.

III

Fractured Identities

Manoj Kumar's *Purab aur Paschim* (1970) looks West. In more ways than one, we witness the reversal in this film of many of the premises of *Dr Kotnis ki Amar Kahani*. The immediate context of the film is 'brain drain' and the West turning to the East in the postcolonial period, for its spiritual values. The narrative, however, casts its net over a wider historical period and harks back to the time of the movement for Independence and those who went abroad to the land of the coloniser, as renegades to the nationalist cause. This film is about the second generation: the progeny of those who fought for and built the nation, and the progeny of those NRIs who left when the country needed them. Villainy and 'loss of Indian roots and values', it seems, is thus genetically passed on, as much as nationalist fervour is! Bharat, the protagonist, goes to England to study. He wants to visit Shakespeare's house, whereas his co-generationists are only interested in wild parties. The young Indians 'there' are thus cut off from the culture of the land they have adopted, as well as of the land their parents have left behind, discovering it at best through western hippie or *Hare Rama Hare Krishna* movements.

The axis of tension here is around similar sounding words with the same root—*'gyan/vigyan'* (wisdom/scientific knowledge). The protagonist insists on the fact that while the West has scientific knowledge, Indians are superior because of their ancient wisdom. In a crucial sequence, Pran the renegade loudly accosts Bharat in a restaurant in London and says that while he was happy to be on the side of the nation that 'gave' materially, Bharat was defending a beggarly nation, one that was only happy in 'taking'. To this Bharat replies in song, *'Hai preet jahan ki reet sada'*, outlining all the pearls of wisdom India has given the world, including the concept of the 'zero', on which all scientific-mathematical calculations of the West are based (including those that send rockets to the moon). To underline the fact cinematically, Manoj Kumar uses circular movements of sections of the floor of the restaurant as well as of the camera. (It is interesting to note that at these high nationalistic moments of narrative, cinematographic wizardry often comes into play. In **Dr Kotnis**, V. Shantaram uses a pathbreaking, temporally long single shot when Kotnis recounts to his father the rousing call given by nationalist leaders to serve in China, and his enrolling to do so.)

The discourse of self-assured scientificity in Dr Kotnis has now been replaced by the discourse of 'the superiority of wisdom'. It has become very apparent, more than two decades after Independence, that India had a lot of catching up to do, to be progressive and modern in the western sense. The '60s are a turning point in our political history. The 1962 the Indo-China war threw a cloud over the ideology of non-alignment and the alternative pacifist movement of non-violence for which India had been known. The defeat led to a repositioning of India and her self-image vis-à-vis the world. **Purab aur Paschim** in fact contextualises this ideological debate of India and the world outside. As such, it is a break away from films of the '60s[6] in which India and the world outside are represented in the Hindi film within the problematic of tourism. This world 'outside' had become accessible to the middle-class because of its economic prosperity, among other reasons. This tourist display of 'other' exotic cities was also made possible by the decisive collective shift to filmmaking in colour.

Raj Kapoor's **Sangam** (1964) best encapsulates this 'tourist' encounter between India and the West. The narrative of the protagonist and his bride's honeymoon in Europe is a handy reference book, representating all the activities possible in such an encounter. Sightseeing, shopping and the nightlife, this sequence sums it all up. Discovery of the spouse in privacy and discovery of another space and culture are the double registers of 'honeymoon tourism'.

That a war-hero pilot of very modest means with no familial wealth to back him can afford such a honeymoon, is once again that principle of unreality on which the entire narrative segment of *Sangam* is based. Paris is an important stop in their itinerary. To begin with, they see the sights: Eiffel Tower. While seeing the 'other' culturally, they make manifest their own Indian-ness (they do not kiss in public); two western women tourists exclaim in delight at them for being Indians[7]. They then shop. They do not have enough money for both their desires: for his bagpipe and her purse. "We are tourists", says Raj Kapoor, as an explanation for why they have to economise. He gives in to her and tells her to buy the purse; and she 'sacrifices' her desire to buy him the bagpipe. Parisian nightlife is seen from the streets. Raj Kapoor dresses to go to a floor-show and refuses to take his wife, because decent women do not visit such places, he says. The wife protests and calls men useless and always short of money (**takiyanusi aur phatichar**). The husband protests further and says marriage is a jail. All this is done by both of them in a manner that makes it clear that they are putting up an act. This doubleness of intonation and acting is interesting for it internally distances the supposed radical intent of the wife's protest. This particular mode of dialogue continues in the scene to follow.

The husband, on opening the door that has just been slammed, is shocked to find his wife dressed up as a dancer, blowing the bagpipe[8]. This mock shock leads him to tell her that she must not behave like 'those' dancers whose job is to seduce men. A woman who does not know how to seduce her husband loses him, answers the wife and proceeds to sing the song '*Main kya karoon Ram mujhe buddha mil gaya*'[9], changing tantalisingly behind the cupboard door into improvised floor-show costumes. This sequence is interesting for the way in which tourism—the viewing of a city that puts itself on display finally collapses into the voyeurism, fetishism and commodification of the woman's body. The tourist project, therefore, and the encounter with another city becomes the site for a mock dialogue in which issues of women's desire and liberty are actually masking her objectification when she puts herself on display for her husband—much as the city was on display for them during the day.

Thus, the binary opposition set up earlier—our Indian values vs. Western values (on the issue of kissing in public, for instance) collapse in the privacy of the bedroom. Who needs to go out to see the nightlife in Paris, when the wife is performing at 'home'? This sequence is also symptomatic of the chameleon-like change of 'national' values (Indian-Western) that we can slip in and out of, literally and metaphorically like clothes (saree-clad in the morning / revealing tights in the evening). The honeymoon trip abroad can also be read as an indication of the new pressures on the woman, who had to remain Indian in her values while she indulged in 'western' modes of pleasure-giving. This entire sequence encapsulates, in a paradoxical way, the main theme of the film: the jealousy and suspicion of the husband regarding the fidelity of the wife. How can a woman who so spontaneously changes into Western flesh be trusted?

IV

The Local-global Cusp

The pull of the nation-state and the global impact left its trace on Bollywood films of the '90s.

The stories of Aditya Chopra's *Dilwale Dulhaniya Le Jaayenge,* Subash Ghai's *Pardes,* Farhan Akhtar's *Dil Chahta Hai...* are set partly in India and partly abroad, to answer the call of national identity in its encounter with the global. There is another kind of 'local-global' film which creates an India of the multinational, consumerist imagination, by fusing the two spaces together, thus doing away with the need for a journey. Yash Chopra's *Dil to Pagal Hai* and Karan Johar's *Kuch Kuch Hota Hai.* Suffice to mention here the cityscape seen beyond the window frames in *Dil to Pagal Hai.* It could be the Bombay skyline, or then again, it could be Manhattan.

Ashutosh Gowarikar's *Lagaan* (2001) and the *'Muqabla'* song from *Humse Hai Muqabla* point to other possibilities of imaging the nation: of creating fable-like chronotopes in which subalterns were included in the notion of the community (*Lagaan*); or of creating a deterritorialised body and space as an ode to the certain victory of the dispossessed.

Lagaan (2001) posits an imagined community that harks back to the problematics of the pre-Independence and the immediate period after Independence. The benign community that bridges differences of caste, class and religion is seen in the Hindi film after a long time as a positive, creative and constructive force. This resurrection of the benign community is all the more significant in the context of the fact that, since the '80s, villainy in films has come to be represented through characters belonging to minority religious, regional or caste groups. N. Chandra's *Tezaab* is a pivotal film for the negative imagings and imaginings possible of this new face of the dominant community vis-à-vis the others.[10]

The story of *Lagaan* is set at the end of the XIX century, as a fictional charting of an Indian village's first encounter with the game of cricket. This is also the native's encounter with colonialism in all its oppressive, as well as laughter-inducing and self-liberating aspects. There is a large gallery of characters as archetypes on both sides, with traitors to the cause on the Indian as well as British sides. Scenes of community life are captured as tableaux, each family unit and the family's occupation being represented. It is worth examining some of the song sequences for the way in which the community is represented.

The song sequences have unusually long takes, following this tableau principle. In the *'Ghanana ghanana'* rain song, for instance, where the entire village comes out to watch the clouds that have made an appearance on the horizon, the stanzas are picturised in lengthy takes—creating the feeling of oneness and bonding within the community, which are very different from the dominant rapid-cut mode of song picturisations prevalent today. The lengthy takes dovetail well into the theme of the community. The lateral movements are further supplemented by foregrounding and backgrounding of tableaux in the frame, creating a level of complexity rarely seen in the Hindi film today. The film's songs, too, have a nostalgic feel about them, underlining the theme of the community in the way in which community films of the 50s did[11]. The *'Chale chalo'* song, for instance, shifts the focus to the *community* of bodies.

The male body on display, seen often enough in Hindi films today, found one of its most potent expressions in the 'tandav' dance by Rithik Roshan in Khalid Mohammad's *Fiza* (2000). *'Mere Watan'* picturised on Roshan as he decides to wipe out communal politicians fuses cultural references from different registers: the dance of destruction of the Hindu god Shiva is woven into the Muslim ritual of self-whipping, martial art-forms, and the new codes in the Bollywood film of the self-display of a very well-toned, muscular, male body.

While the focus is on the hero in *Lagaan*, it is not centred exclusively on *his* body, and attention is diverted to other bodies of the community. These bodies are also of specific types, belonging to different religions and castes, and welded into one energetic and explosive community. *Lagaan* also gains in the polemical subtexts which it creates. A song like *'Radha kaise na jale'* which can be interpreted as a song that is, in an immediate sense, anti-woman. On the one hand, it is an ode to the power and fascination that Krishna wields, that belittles many women in order to praise one (*'gopiyan taare hain, chand hai Radha, phir kyon hai usko vishwas aadha?'* / *'gopiyan aani jaani hain, Radha to man ki rani hai'*).

However, in the larger context of communal and fanatic morality brigades and culture, the song takes on other, more progressive, significations—opening up ambivalent registers of morality. Bhuvan announces just before this song to the British Elisabeth who has fallen in love with him, that Krishna and Radha were married to other spouses and yet were in love with each other. It is also of importance that the topography of the community film, which of necessity has to include a temple to exude moral authority (a benign religious one), is here dedicated to Radha and Krishna and not any other god of the Hindu pantheon. The song being discussed is sung at the *janmashtami* of Krishna's birthday, with celebrations of the entire community in which everyone takes part as they do in the singing of the bhajan '*O palan hare*' in times of stress and trouble.

Produced and performed by Aamir Khan, with lyrics penned by Javed Akhtar, and music by A R Rehman, the songs are some of the best testaments to India's composite culture in the realm of popular culture. The use of the bare, fragile, *bhajan* cymbals as the prelude to the song '*Radha kaise na jale*', along with the flute (the instrument Krishna plays), lead to a crescendo when the drums roll in, as one of the best combinations of the mood of private religiosity followed by the robust energy of community dancing.

V

Deterritorialisation

Shankar's *Kaadalan* (1994) was originally made in Tamil and dubbed into Hindi and Telugu. The Hindi version was called *Humse Hai Muqabla*, with the chartbreaking song "Mukaala, Muqabla" in it[12]. The film can be classified as a 'college to world outside' film, if one goes by the bare essentials of storyline. The film however is not just 'storyline'. The college-to-world-outside genre can serve the interests of a hegemonic North-Indian Hindu centred view of the world (as in *Tezaab*) or a view that destabilises all such hegemonic notions (as in *Humse Hai Muqabla*). Both films are peculiar journey films; where *Tezaab* charts an aggressive journey from one region of the city to another, *Hum Se Hai Muqabla* creates a wondrous fable journey through spaces.

Hum se Hai Muqabla is a rich film in terms of symbolic, iconic and other associations. These themes get denser as the film progresses—to reach a pinnacle in the '*Mukaala, Muqabla*' song where space becomes abstract. The song follows a sequence where a disheveled, rebellious Shruti forces her father (who is governor of the state and a terrorist!) to give in to the demand of releasing the imprisoned, tortured Prabhudeva, her beloved. The song is an imagined fantasy of liberation. But it clearly takes off thematically from the previous scene because we have Shruti galloping in on a horse to save Prabhudeva who is about to be hanged, just as she had done in 'reality' in the preceding sequence. The hero and heroine are, in this song sequence, not their 'real' selves but their metaphorical selves.

The song begins with a sign saying 'Colorado'. We are in a space that evokes the Western. This then turns into a *sarai*/inn-like space. But this is make-believe land where all oppositions mentioned above coalesce into one abstract opposition of the oppressed against the oppresser: the coloured (black, mulatto) against the whites, the colonised against the colonisers, and by extension in the Indian context, the lower castes against the higher . ..

The song and its stunning choreography create another space of tension: of a challenging gesture of the south Indian cinema to the Bombay industry—not just in terms of the creation of a unique song-and-dance picturisation, but in terms of the innovative use of technology and the creation of such celebratory icons. The words of the song use a spectrum of references from folk myths (Laila of Laila Majnu fame) to modern icons (Picasso, jazz music, cowboy, playboy ...) They also veer towards nonsense-verse in places (*strawberry aankhen*).

These references are not dense; they lack depth. They are playful and their significance lies precisely in stating that they can quote signs of the world with such nonchalance. Towards the end of the song, the white oppressors shoot the dancing Prabhudeva. His head, wrists and ankles disappear but the hat, shoes and clothes continue to dance frenetically. He then spits at the colonisers and shoots them. The clothes of the colonisers turn around and try to walk away in an act of equal bravado but collapse and fall to the ground. Shankar uses opticals to show that the spirit cannot be subjugated, and will continue to be possessed of energy even when effaced. The spirit is of *this* world. Despite being wiped off, it has a material presence (the dancing clothes are not 'empty' but are marked and filled out by an unseen body unlike the clothes of the oppressors which collapse) and from which can emanate a material saliva and spit. Despite effacement, Prabhudeva is given *a real presence*: we know that those dancing shoes can only be animated by *his* feet. In this engagement with technology there is a moment of philosophical subversion as well[13]: spirit can be material and this-worldly. The power of the image emanates not only from the seen, but also the unseen. This effect is achieved through the very specific body-presence of Prabhudeva. His is a weightless presence— physically (he is slim, unlike the weighty presence of a Nagarjuna or Chiranjeevi) and metaphorically (he is not into histrionics, he presents his own self).

This 'weightlessness' finds its ultimate realisation in the *"Muqabla"* song. One cannot imagine another actor, however well he might dance, disappear so effortlessly and leave his 'spiritual' imprint on the image! The *"Muqabla"* song is thus far richer in associations than MTV images can ever be[14]. Its editing pattern, too, has nothing to do with the MTV mode which cuts quickly and staggers its images.

According to Madan Gopal Singh:

> The point is that in his very body and rhythmic movements he incorporates the principles of editing making the oft-made comparison with Michael Jackson unsustainable because Jackson's image above all, is an electronically induced image, an assembled image, whereas Prabhudeva's is primarily a material image which teases and challenges the electronic mode and also complements it. Michael Jackson's image is rarely ever in a continuous mode unlike Prabhudeva's.

Prabhudeva's dance portions are in lengthy shots, unedited, or without too many cuts. Part of the reason is Prabhudeva's mastery over dance, and the ability to give long shots without cuts. But the director chooses to keep him in the frame as a whole body presence, and does not cut up his dance into visual segments. This is an instance where significations (of the East and West, the local and global among others) swing like a door on a hinge.

Journeys, whether on a good-samaritan mission, a quest for knowledge and education or a tourist enterprise, return us to roots. They are meaning-making experiences. In the films discussed above they are constructing notions of the nation. It is only in the '90s that the global coalesces with the local—in images that shrink distances, nullifying the need for journeys. These condensed images where the world is contained within one's own space and body, can, however, be merely consumerist or belong to the realm of celebratory destabilisation.

References and Notes

1. This is an expanded and slightly different version of 'Image and Imagination: Stories of the Nation', presented at the seminar 'Bollywood on the Bondi', Sydney, 11 October, 2002.
2. Benedict Anderson, *Imagined Communities: Reflections on the Origins and Spread of Nationalism*, Verso, London, 1991 p. 7.
3. Arjun Appadurai, *Patriotism and its Futures*, Public Culture, Vol. 5, No.3, Spring 1993, p. 414.
4. I have dealt with several of these new 'fractured' images in the representation of the imagined notion of the protagonist vis-à-vis actual regional and religious communities in my article 'Hindi Commercial Cinema: Changing Narrative Strategies' in (ed. Aruna Vasudev) *Frames of Mind: Reflections on Indian Cinema*, UBS Publication, New Delhi, 1995.
5. This periodisation is based on the premises of Madan Gopal Singh's article 'If Music Be the Food of Love' in *Cinemaya* 39-40, Jan-June, 1998.
6. Films like Shakti Samanta's *An Evening in Paris* (1967), Pramod Chakravarty's *Love in Tokyo* (1966)...
7. I have a personal reading of this particular scene. Raj Kapoor was very famous and widely loved in the Soviet Union. Given the close Indo-Soviet ties, Russians would recognise Indians positively and, more often than not, quote Raj Kapoor's *Awaara*. It is difficult to believe that the more restrained and cosmopolitan French would make such a show of delight at seeing Indians. I feel it is a case of transposition of Kapoor's Russian experience onto a western city scape, in this case, Paris. It is also interesting that for all his love of Russia and Russians' love for him, Raj Kapoor gives Russia the miss on this honeymoon trip in the film (which also includes the Swiss Alps and a song with the 'I love you' refrain in German, French and Russian thrown in—'Ich liebe dich').
8. The bagpipe is the shifting signifier par excellence: Kapoor has earlier referred to it as the only other beautiful thing in the world apart from a woman's body. His hand gestures when he refers to it in the scene make it indistinguishable whether it is a woman's body he is referring to or the bagpipe.
   The bagpipe has other associations as well. Vyjantimala, the lead actress of this film, was very famous for her snake dance in a hit film called *Nagin* (1954) where she gyrates to the *'been'*, the Indian snake-charmer's musical instrument, which in its own way resembles a bagpipe. The western floor-show gyrations here thus quote the gyrations of the Indian snake dance!
9. The words posit a village belle (the *ka* and not *kya* of the opening line, the address to god Ram), humourously bemoaning her fate for being stuck with an old man..
10. Refer to Madan Gopal Singh's interview on the film in Mediastorm's series on the Bombay commercial cinema.
11. One of the posters for the film with Aamir Khan and Gracy Singh, looking up towards the sky remind me of *Naya Daur* frames, with their rhetoric of looking ahead with optimism and hope.
12. This song had at least two more plagiarised versions in Hindi films of that time but these were not as popular or excitingly picturised as the original was.
13. Clothes without body, riding away on a cycle, is used as early as in Bunuel's *Un Chien Andalou* (1929). But in *Humse Hai Muqabla*, this image takes on many subversive meanings as well.
14. Refer to "The sequence itself (i.e. the "Muqabla" song) is a strip of narrative very much in the MTV genre...." (p. 5) or in 'Kaadalan and the Politics of Signification: Fashion, Violence and the Body' by Vivek Dhareshwar and Tejaswini Niranjana in *Journal of Arts and Ideas*, No 29, 1996.

Sheba Chhachhi

The Householder, the Ascetic and the Politician: women sadhus at the Kumbh Mela

So free am I, so gloriously free
Free from the three petty things-
From mortar, pestle and my twisted lord
Freed from rebirth and death am I
And all that has held me down
Is hurled away.

— Mutta, from the *Therigatha*
(Songs of the Nuns) 6th century B.C.

Translated from Pali by Uma Chakravarthy and Kumkum Roy,
Women Writing in India Vol. I, Eds. Tharu & Lalitha

I

Mutta may or may not have recognised the thousands of women sadhus gathered at the first Kumbh Mela of the new millenium, in Allahabad, January 2002.

Like her, these women have stepped out of the narrow confines of the domestic. Whether moved by a profound devotion, answering a spiritual call, simply attracted to the chastity and simplicity of a mendicant's life, or, obversely, cast out by family, society or circumstance, the woman ascetic surrenders the pleasures, burdens and markers of ordinary female existence. Unlike Mutta, they are bound into a complex parallel social order, structured by ritual, patriarchal hierarchies and increasingly, the politics of power.

The woman seeking initiation is systematically stripped of her secular identity. Shorn of hair, clothes, name, kith and kin, the elaborate ritual culminates in her performing her own death rites. Reborn a *sadhvi*, (more commonly called a *mai*) committed to a rigorous code of conduct and personal spiritual practice, she is formally presented to the rest of the *akhada* to which she now owes allegiance. In return she receives spiritual guidance from her guru, tenuous legitimacy, protection, occasional material support and the possibility of refuge. In essence, though, these are women on their own—autonomous, highly mobile, and curiously trans-gender, they negotiate these structures within the narratives of their particular lives.

In the grand spectacle of the Kumbh, power is constructed by and through performance. Performance has always been an integral part of the culture of religion in India. But today women are increasingly emerging as significant protagonists in this arena, whether manifesting in the humble tent from which an ageing *mai* graciously accepts offerings for the display of her young disciple's swollen feet (a testimony to her vow of remaining standing for a year), or the attractive *mai* on the huge television screens sermonising in mellifluous Sanskritised Hindi.

Many years ago, Shri Shri Mahant Mira Puri had shown me photographs of herself as a young initiate: shaven, austere, withdrawn into *sadhana*. Today that fragile androgyny has retreated behind the pomp and circumstance of mahanthood, the now long hair concealed beneath a large, assertive turban. Mahant Mira's *lila* is rich and varied. She moves seamlessly from the warm, caring mother with the new initiates, to the playful 'master' with her closest disciples, to the powerful meditator with awestruck visitors.

The inward drawn gaze of the yogi has always attracted the curious, almost envious eyes of the lay person. In fact, the performance of the trans-social self (nakedness, 'mad' behavior, and severe ascetic practice, for example) serves to underline the ascetic's freedom from ordinary social mores, eliciting both reverence and revenue. The assertion/enactment of aberration, paradoxically, becomes a bridge between the world of the householder and that of the ascetic. However, even though obedient daughters-in-law make offerings to chillum smoking naga sadhus, the Dharma Shastras forbid interaction between the 'good wife' and women ascetics!

II

Mahant Mira is unusual as one of only three women mahants of the oldest, most respected *akhada*, the *juna akhada*, but her position is by no means a sinecure. The *maivada* is thronged by hundreds of *mais* from all over the country. Only briefly a sorority, they congregate at the Kumbh for sacred purposes as well as pragmatic ones. They may need help from the Mahant to secure, for instance, the much sought after sadhu identity card, but after that they will return to independent lives, linked through a huge network of ashrams, sacred sites and events.

Could this community of women be moulded into a constituency? The Mahant's aspirations meet with a curious form of recognition— she is invited to share the dais with Sadhvi Rithambara at the first ever Vishva Sadhvi Sammelan. A mixture of coercion and cajoling is needed to persuade the women of the *maivada* to attend. Here the *mais* are individually garlanded, welcomed as *sadhvis*, a term they do not use themselves. Indeed, the vituperative rant against the loss of cultural values, the dangers of westernisation and the need to prevent cow slaughter seem to have little connection with the largely rural, non-literate Shaivite *mais* that finally fill the space. However, when issues closer to their lives, such as domestic violence and alcoholism are addressed, heads nod, hands go up and when women's *shakti* is invoked, there is an enthusiastic response.

Her customary flamboyance cloaked behind a mask of sobriety, is this just another of the many roles that I have seen Mahant Mira play? Or will I have to bear witness to the transformation of the gentle *mais* into *sadhvis* of the ilk of Rithambara—her triumphant face engraved upon the nation's consciousness as she revelled in the destruction of the Babri Masjid? Will the long lineage of the *bairagan*, her expanded heart detached from both anger and desire, 'free from all that has held her down' vanish from sight in order to survive?

These images are excerpted from an ongoing photographic project on women ascetics.

MAI/MAHANT
Kumbh Mela 2002
PHOTO ESSAY by SHEBA CHHACHHI

Shri Shri Mahant Mira Puri

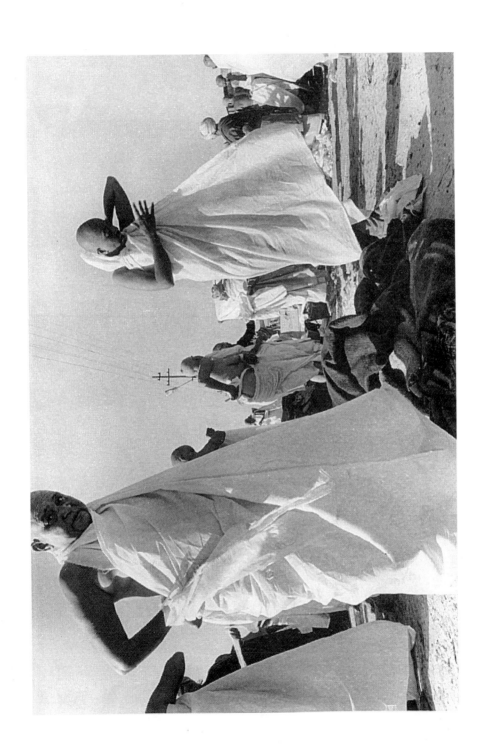

V
VISTAS: THE GLOBAL CUSP

Lagaan, 2001
Aamir Khan Production
Nominated for the Oscar Award for best foreign film

Sudhanva Deshpande

What's so Great about Lagaan?

T he first time I saw *Lagaan* a couple of weeks after it was released in June 2001, I was mesmerised by its sheer exuberance! It has great music, a tight screenplay and excellent performances. I also loved its audacity—an unlikely plot, but narrated so wonderfully well. The triumph of the underdog overcoming all handicaps is always compelling, in sports as much as in fiction. And when the handicaps include race and colonialism, caste and religion, the mix becomes headier still. Yet, what is great about *Lagaan* is more than all this. *Lagaan* imagines an India fairly different from the India we have become used to seeing in commercial Hindi cinema for a long time now. To see this more clearly, we need to look at *Lagaan* in the context of a large number of films that have appeared in the last 15 years or so. In particular, we will look first at films with the Muslim villain; and then briefly, films about the new globalised hero.

Let us go back to 1988, as the campaign for the temple at Ayodhya was heating up. This was the year of N. Chandra's *Tezaab*, with that sizzling Madhuri Dixit number, *Ek Do Teen*. We could make three points about the villain in this film. One, Lotiya Khan was a Muslim; he created and inhabited a space that was distinct from the space inhabited by the rest of the characters. This is nothing new; many films create for the villain a distinct space with laws of its own. In *Tezaab*, however, the villain's space is not outlandish and strange. It is, on the contrary, actually just a vast and teeming urban slum, a ghetto. In other words, the Muslim villain rules over the ghetto.

Two, the villain is Muslim but he is a Pathan. In Bombay, in an earlier day and age and as the working class was coming into being, the Pathan was a familiar character. He was the moneylender and also often the thug who worked at the behest of the factory owners to 'discipline' recalcitrant workers. In both these roles, he was a hated figure. So the film refers back to that historic memory of the urban poor. Now this is a point open to debate, but my feeling is that except at moments of heightened communal tension, the Pathan could not, and did not, stand for Muslims as a whole. And three, while the villain wears a Muslim identity, the hero does not project himself with a very self-conscious Hindu identity. To my mind, while *Tezaab* is significant for depicting the Muslim as villain, the film almost slips in this fact—hoping that we won't quite notice.

Tezaab is quite different from a film like Rajkumar Santoshi's **Ghatak**. Here we have the hero, played by Sunny Deol, who is a brahman from Varanasi and is appropriately named Kashi. He takes on a gang of villains, the land mafia in this case, and cleanses the city of them. Now, this gang is actually a gang of some nine brothers, led by the eldest, played by Danny. Their names as well as their getups are outlandish—the leader appears in a fur cap and overcoat through the film, and keeps a pet leopard. Yet, they are unmistakably Muslim. In the fight sequences, we see their thugs sporting the typically Muslim chequered lungi. Other stereotypes also come into play: Muslims increase their numbers exponentially; they are dirty; they don't eat, they hog; they enjoy bloodletting; and so on.

On the side of the hero, we see a young brahman boy always dressed in saffron dhoti, with tonsured head and that unmistakable marker of caste identity, the 'sacred' thread, across the chest. When the entire *basti* trembles at the mere appearance of the villains and their gang of thugs, this small brahman boy takes them on. In *Ghatak* then, the communal identity is explicit, and the triumph of good over evil is the triumph of Hindu over Muslim. A similar case is that of **Shool**, where the good guys are from the thakur-brahman alliance, and they overcome the bad guys who are from the Muslim-OBC alliance. The film is set in small-town Bihar.

In this context a rather unusual film is Priyadarshan's **Virasat**, with Anil Kapoor, Tabu and Milind Gunaji in the lead. This film has not received the sort of attention it probably should have. The story revolves around the NRI son of a landlord, who comes home for a holiday with his girlfriend. Circumstances compel him to assume leadership of the family after his father's death, and he has to marry a village girl. He finds himself embroiled in a dispute with his own cousin—a dispute that partitions the village into half—and after all efforts fail to make the evil cousin see reason, he kills the cousin with a giant axe in a final, dreamlike, apocalyptic sequence in front of the mother goddess.

Told this way, the story is fairly standard run-of-the-mill stuff. What I find interesting, however, is that for a film entirely located in a village, we never see a Muslim character. This is quite remarkable, and it is useful to ponder over this. I would argue that the family of the cousin is depicted in a manner that conforms to virtually every communal stereotype of the Muslim. They are bigamous; they are dirty; they eat greedily; they are not amenable to reason; they are violent; they are deformed. The conflict between the families, moreover, centres around a temple. Both claim they have a right over it, a right sanctioned by tradition and history. There is an uneasy truce over the issue, and the temple remains locked up. The conflict escalates after the hero opens the lock of the temple. In the film he appears to do it very reasonably, but the essence of his argument is: the temple belongs to us, why are we prevented from going into it? We are simply expected to believe and accede to the hero's natural right. Now, this is *exactly* the argument of the Hindutva brigade vis-à-vis Ayodhya.

Now, I don't know Priyadarshan and I don't know what he had in mind. I am quite willing to accept that I am reading into the film more than Priyadarshan had intended. I would much prefer though, that the filmmaker deliberately made those choices. Because if not, then it only shows how deep the Hindutva argument has penetrated—that it shows up in a film without the maker being even aware of it. Thank you very much, I think I prefer the conspiracy theory.

II

Then there are the spate of films on war/terrorism: *Roja, Border, Sarfarosh, Pukar, Maa Tujhe Salaam, Indian*. Much has been written on some of these films, and we do not have the space to look at them separately. We may, however, note three points here. These films feed on the reality of Pakistan's role in fomenting trouble in Kashmir, as well as the intrusion it engineered in Kargil leading to the war. By this logic, as in all war films, the enemy country is forever the aggressor and the motherland forever the victim. Yet, and this is the first point, there is now a new aggressiveness in these films; and this aggressiveness feeds on the fantasy that India's comprehensive military superiority over Pakistan will result in the latter's annihilation.

In this fantasy, a new and macho India preens over and flexes its nuclear muscle. Recall a film like *Pukar*. Released immediately after the Kandahar hijacking drama, the army officer hero says to the terrorist: "Do not gloat over the fact that you have managed to run away with three. If we decide to cross the LOC, we will wipe out your entire country in three minutes." This film by Raj Kumar Santoshi won for Anil Kapoor a National Award. The jury that year included the editor of the RSS mouthpiece.

The second point to be made is the obvious one: the identification of terrorism with Islam, depicted in several of these films. The most striking is in *Roja*, where the hero hurls himself to save a burning India flag as we see the Islamic terrorist villain unmoved, deep in prayer, while a patriotic number is belted out on the soundtrack. Earlier in the film, we see images of things being blown apart juxtaposed to those of terrorists in prayer. At one stroke, Islam becomes anti-India. To be sure, some of these films do show a patriotic Indian Muslim character. But this character is a token one, put in the film precisely to ward off criticism of the film being communal, as well as to appeal to the large minority of Indian Muslims. And the terms on which this character appears in the film are often very problematic. Recall *Sarfarosh*, where we have a Hindu (Rajput) police officer hero battling and eventually defeating a bunch of terrorists. The hero has a Muslim subordinate though, and this subordinate earlier in the film refuses to fight for India, saying that the country has given them (Muslims) nothing. Eventually of course the man proves every bit as patriotic as the hero, but not before he is told by the hero in a crucial scene: "I don't need the help of any Salim to save my country."

A number of these films have started mouthing the rhetoric of the RSS. They are no longer just influenced by vaguely Hindu majoritarian sentiment, but they espouse the RSS line quite explicitly. We mentioned *Pukar*. The Sunny Deol-starrer *Maa Tujhe Salaam* goes a step further. It coins a slogan, which has been picked up by the Hindutva brigade since: *Doodh mangoge to kheer denge, Kashmir mangoge to cheer denge*. (Ask us for milk, and we will give you *kheer*, but we will dismember you if you ask for Kashmir). A slogan like this in a mainstream Hindi film would have been hard to imagine some fifteen years ago. The road from *Tezaab* leads to *Maa Tujhe Salaam*—but there is still a long distance that separates the two. Chillingly, this distance has been traversed in very short time.

And then, of course, there is *Gadar*. There is just no running away from the fact that it is the biggest hit of recent times. It is possible today for a film to be declared a hit without too many people actually watching it in film halls. You can sell music rights, overseas rights, satellite channel rights, merchandising rights, and so on, and make a killing. Karan Johar's *Kabhi Khushi Kabhi Gham* had started earning profits even before a single shot had been canned. *Gadar* however is not one of those films. It did well abroad, but after it had started doing well within India. Its music became popular, but unlike some Rahman films it had not started topping the charts before the film was released. *Gadar* is one of those old-fashioned hits which earns money because millions of people queue up at the box office for a ticket, and having seen the film once, go back a second or third time.

Gadar says some very nasty things about Muslims, about the Partition, about the India-Pakistan relationship, about the Hindu-Sikh relationship. Consider the infamous sequence where the hero Tara Singh converts to Islam in a desperate attempt to get back his wife. He is told by his father-in-law, as part of the conversion ritual, to say, 'Islam zindabad' (Long live Islam). The hero does so. He is then asked to say, 'Pakistan zindabad'. This is a bitter pill to swallow, but the hero does so. He is then ordered to say 'Hindustan murdabad' (Death to India)—which of course the hero refuses to say. Islam equals Pakistan equals hatred of India. Simple and uncomplicated.

One can list more such sequences. But I wish to make here only two points. One, *Gadar* is no flash in the pan; several preceding films paved the way for it. A film like *Gadar* could not have been made without the ground being prepared for it over the last 15 years or so, slowly, insidiously. Two million of our countrymen and women have seen and liked *Gadar*. There is a very large constituency lapping up this stuff. Profit making is the only logic that underpins the Bombay film industry, and there is profit in depicting communalism.

III

On the one hand, there are all these films with the Muslim villain. On the other hand, there is a different kind of film, with the globalised hero—*Dilwale Dulhaniya Le Jayenge, Kuchh Kuchh Hota Hai, Pardes* being some examples. This character first appeared as the chocolate faced hero in teeny bopper romances of the mid-1990s, soon after the Indian state ushered in policies of economic liberalisation. Initially, his role was limited to romancing and winning the girl, though only by winning over her father and not, like in *Bobby* some two decades before, by eloping. In doing this, he had to extol the virtues of tradition, the joint family, 'Indianness', and so on. Sometimes, especially if he happened to be an NRI, he had to go to the length of applying Indian soil to the wounds of an injured pigeon—thereby curing, not killing it—to make the father look at him with new eyes.

It is almost as if to be NRI is to be really *Indian*. Recall how in *Kabhi Khushi Kabhi Gham* we hear the score of *Saare Jahan se Achha* on the soundtrack as the younger brother (Hrithik Roshan) reaches London. There is much that can be said about this hero, particularly about his proclivity to bigamy and the disappearance of memory from his life. Elsewhere I have written on some of this, placing it in the context of the new kind of economics that regulates filmmaking in Bombay.[1]

In some recent films, though, one notices a further edge to this character. No longer is this rich kid starry-eyed about India and Indians. Increasingly, he, and often she as well, displays a disdain and contempt for the poor. Think of the recent film, *Road*—a story of an eloping couple waylaid by a criminal. This criminal, after ousting the hero from the car, falls for the girl, with the hero in hot pursuit. Eventually, after the mandatory and final confrontation, the criminal is left to die in a desert. Now recall that sequence where the hero and heroine are exiting a roadside hotel. The receptionist asks them if they liked the room. They say yes. Did they like the service? Yes. Did they like the food? Yes. Is there anything they did not like? Yes, the hero replies. "You," he says to the receptionist.

This of course is a joke, and perhaps one should not read too much into it. But suppose one does. Suppose one reads this joke as being the attitude of the rich towards someone who is not their class. If read thus, the film throws up an interesting question: what distinguishes the hero from the villain? Indeed, this is precisely the question the criminal keeps asking the girl: suppose you had met me and him (the hero) in college, whom would you have chosen? Who indeed, I found myself asking, for what separates the two? Not their looks—Manoj Bajpai in the film looks no worse than Vivek Oberoi. Not their clothes. Not their obsession with the girl. Not their ethics— both have none. (Neither has the girl, by the way.) So what sets the two apart? Class, of course—one is rich, the other is not. And it is class that the hero and heroine flaunt as she climbs on to his hips and he carries her, in that coital position, into the sunset.

Even more striking is another recent film, *Shakti*. In this, a young woman (Karisma Kapoor) gets married in Canada to the son (Sanjay Kapoor) of a village potentate (played with characteristic brutishness by Nana Patekar). Visiting her husband's village, not only is she repelled by the dirty, smelly and uncouth villagers, but she loses her husband in a bloody internecine family feud. Subsequently, she has to fight with her life to rescue her young son from his own grandfather, who wants to bring the boy up 'like a tiger' to avenge his father's murder. In a depiction that would put Kipling to shame, the Indian villagers in *Shakti* are cruel, barbaric, bloodthirsty, while the NRI is civilised, decent, gentle. As the woman is on the run from her father-in-law, she meets a small-time bootlegger (a delightful cameo by Shah Rukh Khan) who helps her only after she offers him cash (dollars, not rupees). He eventually dies gazing longingly at the dollars, but not before ensuring that the woman has escaped her tormentors. The native then is moved to heroic deeds, but only after contact with higher civilisation—which comes in the garb of foreign exchange, of course.

IV

We can now begin to answer the question that is contained in the title of this paper. *Lagaan* is an audacious film. Not simply because of its unlikely plot, but because it actually manages to run counter to the dominant trends of the market—some of them, at any rate. The hero of the film and all his associates are peasants and other rural folk. They are poor, smelly, sweaty, and they work with their hands. This by itself is remarkable. I do not recall a major film with a peasant hero in the last 15 years.

Then there is Team Champaner. The composition of the team is quite obviously made to point at the social composition of India. So you have the Hindu-Muslim-Sikh triad; you have people from various occupations and social standings, and therefore, by inference, various castes; and you have a dalit in the team as well. The cricket match itself is carefully constructed, and all the members of the Champaner eleven—which actually numbers 13, including as it does the boy Tipu and the British coach Elizabeth, who provides the Christian component to the team—contribute to the win. But there are three performances that turn the match: the leg-spinner's hat trick which engineers a middle-order collapse of the rampaging British batsmen; the injured batsman's heroic innings; and the captain's century capped by the sixer scored with the last ball. These feats are performed by the handicapped dalit Kachra, the Muslim Ismail, and the peasant hero Bhuvan. This, I believe, is a deliberate political statement. And coming as it does in our times, it is quite a remarkable one.

To be sure, there has been some criticism of the portrayal of the dalit in the film. Essentially, this criticism is based on two points: that he is included in the team not for his ability but his disability; and that he is never asked if he wants to be in the team, so his subjectivity is erased. On the first, I would argue that Kachra's disability should be seen as the physical symbol of his social standing; or, put another way, Kachra suffers a double handicap, physical and social. The fact of his handicap only heightens the significance of his achievement. Kachra is in line with a whole range of characters in literature, drama and film, where the weakest of the weak overcome their social and physical handicaps to accomplish heroic deeds. The hunchback of Notre Dame, or the deaf-mute daughter in *Mother Courage* are instances.

The second point of criticism is more valid. My argument here would be that *Lagaan* is, in essence, a Gandhian film. There are three elements to this. One, that not only is the struggle against the colonial oppressor entirely non-violent, but even the possibility of a violent struggle is not considered. Two, the depiction of the *raja* as a closet nationalist is in line with Gandhi's insistence that the national movement should not extend to the Indian princely states. Three, there is insistence on unity across classes of the colonised against the coloniser, and the relegation of all internal contradictions to that forever future moment of true *swaraj*.

This political-ideological position is deeply contradictory, and necessarily involves erasures. In the film, these erasures are most evidently present around the character of the dalit and the raja. Thus, for instance, we never learn what Kachra thinks about the match and his participation in it, and the question of what happens to him after the match is over is never considered. Similarly, the raja's closet nationalism puts a cloak on the collaborationist role played by Indian princes under colonialism. My point is not that these erasures are not present, nor that they should not be critiqued; but that in spite of them, the film is actually quite remarkable in imagining a peasant-dalit-Muslim combine leading India to victory.

Yet of course, *Lagaan* is not a revolutionary film—any which way one looks at it, and whichever sort of revolution one desires, red, blue or green. It is a charming fantasy tale that constructs a Gandhian utopia. It is a measure of the hopelessness of our times that, in opposition to fascist fantasies, Gandhian utopia seems radical. We are clutching at straws.

References and Notess
1. *Himal*, August 2001, available online.

Ashis Nandy

Ethnic Cuisine: the significant 'other'

We can take the easy way out and answer Arjun Appadurai's question—why a pan-Indian cuisine did not emerge—by pointing out that even fifty years ago, to a non-urban Indian, no cuisines other than his own region's looked decisively foreign or, if you so prefer, ethnic. Most descriptions of inedible food that I have heard from Indians involve 'strange' Indian cuisines, not foreign ones. But that does not mean that there was no concept of other kinds of food; but to qualify as such they had to be the cuisine of one's significant `others'.

There always were ethnic cuisines, though nobody called them so. The cuisines of others were always a part of one's life—as markers of cultivation and class, as indicators of social status, or as esoteric rituals, meant for adventurers, travellers and, beginning in the nineteenth century, the anthropologists. French cuisine did traditionally perform an important function for the European élite. For a long time, it had a particular cultural role to play, for instance, in the English public life, despite widespread stereotypes of English insularity. English cuisine, in turn, had a place in colonised societies like India where, to spite the detractors of English food, many Indians accepted it as a marker of cultivation and others developed its more labour-intensive, spicier, tropical versions.

However, in the civilised world, the ethnic styles of cooking were mostly organised within a stable, hierarchical frame. Even in bland Scandinavia and in the gloomy, self-sure ambience of Victorian and Edwardian London, the cognoscenti, the learned and the beautiful people served French food or some domesticated version of it on formal occasions. It is true that some members of the gentry seemed committed to good old, healthy English food, but that was often a self-conscious gesture rather than a matter of preference. British Islanders in general, and not merely the English, have for centuries lived with feelings of inferiority as far as food and wines are concerned, and even their love for their own food is tinged with a certain ambivalence. This is best reflected in Somerset Maugham's well-known saying that one could eat very well in Britain if one decides to have breakfast morning, afternoon and night.

In the United States too, despite occasional paeans to the beauties of homegrown, wholesome American food, there has been a similar reverence towards French and, to a lesser extent, Italian and Viennese cuisines for a long time. On formal occasions, presidents, members of the cabinet, generals and university professors, have tended to serve French food or some 'Frenchified' version of domestic fare. Sometimes, as an elegant variation, it has been Italian food. Everyone sings the glories of the American mom and her exploits in the kitchen, but a formal, public banquet is another matter. There you stick to cuisines that are recognised as appropriate for such occasions.

Many societies have similar ideas of occasion when it comes to food. In my native Calcutta, Bengalis have always sung the glories of Bengali food but, when it comes to eating outside the home in a restaurant, they tend to choose some version of Mughal, North Indian or, less frequently, European food (by which they usually mean Indianised British food, given fancy French or Italian names). The famous clubs of Calcutta, true to their colonial heritage, also serve English food that, unfortunately, often tastes like English food. The city's first recognised Bengali restaurant was founded in the 1960s and it was a particularly modest affair, run by a women's cooperative. The city's first up-market Bengali restaurant opened in the 1990s. Kasturi in Dhaka, the capital of Bangladesh, is arguably the best Bengali restaurant in the world. At least one distinguished non-Bengali Indian editor, Dilip Padgaonkar, who is also a gourmet and a food theorist, has said so publicly. But it also is relatively new; my suspicion is that it began to function in the 1980s. There still persists the belief that you do not eat Bengali food in a restaurant; you eat it at home, or, on formal occasions like marriages and anniversaries, as long you do not organise them as events in restaurants. Bengali food is only now becoming restaurant food.

When it is not occasion, it is a combination of occasion and lifecycle. For a long time, Chinese food in the United States was meant for university students with meagre budgets, eating out on the weekends or playing host to their friends and teachers. It was different and it was cheap. For decades, Indian food has played a roughly similar role in London and other large cities of Britain. An entire generation of British women have been brought up, thanks to their boyfriends and classmates, with random but sustained exposure to an amalgam of Mughal and Punjabi curries, cooked mainly by Bengalis. Exactly as an entire generation of older Americans now lives with their memories of Chinese food consumed in their student days in the company of their dates.

Things have been changing gradually but radically during the last three decades or so. Ethnic food is now serious business. It has made deep inroads into the global metropolitan culture all over the world. It has become a marker of the width of one's cosmopolitan experience. You can now talk with erudition and sensitivity on ethnic food for hours, and the listeners are unlikely to be bored. Ethnic food as a public concern now occupies the same place that health food did three decades ago. The ability to discriminate among the different shades of a specific ethnic cuisine, and the ability to have an informed chat with the waiters before ordering food in a restaurant that serves lesser known fares like Ethiopian, Moroccan or West Asian food, have become signs of learning, elegance and sophistication. These abilities are now the contemporary analogues of the older status play that became popular during the Victorian period—the ability to address waiters by name in well-known restaurants. Ethnic food has become the measure of one's tolerance of cultural diversity. Only the philistines are supposed to grumble about any ethnic food served to them. You make a social and political statement if you dislike a particular ethnic cuisine, not if you like it.

Exogenous cuisines are now acquiring the status of African safaris and becoming the arena of a different kind of power play. No cuisine, however limited or flat, is considered inferior, except probably a few European ones; and certainly they cannot be called so in polite company. Though mainly tourists and the brave at heart are expected to frequent restaurants serving local fare in countries like Scandinavia, Netherlands or Scotland, if you find Argentinean, Philippino or sub-Saharan food uninteresting or not distinctive enough, you are supposed to keep your feelings to yourself.

Simultaneously, some of the old cast of suspects have acquired new stature and cultural meaning; they are basking in re-invented glory. Eating Chinese food in Chinatown is no longer a lowbrow or downmarket venture, nor eating Indian curry in an Indian restaurant in a university town like Oxford in the United Kingdom. However, you may convey something about the level of your cultivation and cosmopolitanism if, when your business partner or research collaborator asks what kind of food preferences you have, you blandly proclaim your love for Chinese or Indian food. You are expected to specify what version of Chinese or Indian food you like. Your host will have much more respect for you if you suggest a Hunanese or Szechwanese restaurant or if you specifically demand that he takes you to a Malayali joint for *appam* or even to a Gujarati fast-food stall for *bhelpuri* or *khandvi*. Indeed, ethnic fast foods are never stigmatised unless they get associated with multinational chains. They are not even called 'fast food'.

Because everyone is looking for newer, stranger and rarer kinds of ethnic eating-places, the variety of ethnic cuisine available in the global metropolitan culture has proliferated enormously in the last twenty years. So have the skills demanded from the guests in these restaurants! On the one hand, customers visiting a Sri Lankan or Thai restaurant are expected to order the more fiery versions of the curries, and not their domesticated editions that try to be kinder to one's palate and taste buds by avoiding an 'excess' of chillies. On the other hand, such restaurants have to distinguish or distance themselves from their more familiar neighbouring cuisines, so that their customers do not feel cheated. Nepali restaurants at Manhattan naturally try to avoid preparations that are close to or indistinguishable from some forms of Indian food, however central to Nepalese cuisines these preparations might be in real life. In a global metropolis, a Cambodian restaurant just cannot serve the same fare as the Laotian or Vietnamese restaurant next door. At the same time, the former must cleverly include a few familiar things from the neighbouring cuisines to give itself a wider range and a longer menu, perhaps even a touch of familiarity.

There are other subtle shades in the canvas that cannot be all listed here. However, a couple of examples should give the reader a flavour of how, in global cosmopolitanism, the expanding tradition of ethnic dining has become an institution and a billion-dollar enterprise. All visitors to ethnic restaurants in North America and Europe must have noticed the growing tendency to serve or demand country-specific beers with ethnic food. In general, you may choose your wines from all over the world, but you are supposed to drink Ethiopian beer with Ethiopian food and Japanese beer with Japanese. The demand is relaxed only in the case of American food; no one insists that one must only have American beer with it, though that also is coming, with more exclusive brands of American beers being identified. There may be some justification for this practice in the case of cuisines that use less spice and depend on flavours that are not overwhelming. But a good case can be made that in the case of cuisines that have 'overwhelming' tastes and flavours, the choice of beers becomes partly notional. Before you dip into a fiery Thai curry, you might legitimately claim to enjoy the subtleties of the Singha beer, which is after all a light ale, as the British call it. But once you start eating, nearly all beers should taste more or less the same. Perhaps a Guinness with its strong taste will survive the onslaught of chillies and spices better. At least, there is some chance that one's palate would be able to savour the stout's personality. But drinking a Guinness with a Thom Yam soup would be considered blasphemous in the present dining culture of global metropolitanism.

Likewise, for years, experts on food and gourmets have advised those eating Indian food to opt for beers, not wines, because the heavy spices used in such food drown the flavour of wines. But that is no longer considered acceptable in the new global food culture. It is seen as an insult to Indian food—and to the Indian civilisation—to say that it is not compatible with a sophisticated, expert choice of wines. A plethora of columnists on food and wine have begun to dole out a plethora of advisories on how to choose 'correct' wines for different kinds of Indian food, to the utter surprise of Indians, accustomed to drinking mainly plain water with their meals and having learnt, during the last two hundred years, that gallons of Scotch whisky of dubious quality and, in its absence, arrack—the poor man's Tequila—is the ultimate in dining pleasure.

One suspects that the culture of ethnic cuisine and ethnic dining has become more and more sophisticated and complex because it has become a major symbolic substitute for the cultures it is supposed to represent. This culture of food is paradoxically becoming more autonomous of the cultures from which the cuisines come and the civilisations or lifestyles they represent. And that is the way things should go, most people seem to believe. Ethnic cuisine is expected to survive the demands of culture and, as the contemporary world pushes more and more cultures into extinction, talking incessantly of multiculturalism and democratic tolerance, ethnic cuisine becomes more and more like a museum or a stage on which a culture writes its name or signs an attendance register for the sake of appeasing our moral conscience and declaring its survival.

The Los Angeles Museum of Holocaust displays some artefacts of Jewish culture, thoughtfully collected by the Nazis for a projected museum on an extinct race after the Final Solution. Those were not the days of ethnic cuisine. Otherwise the Nazis would have surely added a wing to their museum where one could include a well-appointed restaurant serving traditional Jewish fare from all over Europe.

Acknowledgement

Extracted from the keynote address at a conference on food organized by Rachel Dwyer at the School of Oriental Studies, University of London, 22 November 2002.

Cricket's Social Subtext

One inspiring image in the backdrop of insensate communal violence in Gujarat that stayed with the television viewers in 2002 was India's main strike bowler Zaheer Khan's bristling burst of pace targeting an opposition batsman. Young Zaheer, who has already established himself as the team's most dependable speedster by virtue of his sheer pace and penetration, happens to be from Baroda, an important city and cultural landmark of the afflicted state.

At a time when the gloomy landscape of strife made even the most incurable optimist wonder about the future of Indian pluralism, the beaming face of the new cricket star after hunting down yet another victim in the willow war, comes across as a reassuring symbol of hope. The red ball in hand, the left-arm bowler striding down the run-up in an upfront movement acquired an iconic dimension. When Gujarat was about to become a metaphor of anarchy, of a new schism, Zaheer appeared on the scene as an acre of comfort. A Muslim boy's heroics on the cricket ground negated the cynicism of those keen to see the collapse of the Indian experiment at every provocation. In equal measure he rebuffed the tendency to draw lines among the people labelling them with colours of divide. For the cricket loving Indian masses Zaheer is the only he-man handing down death orders to adversaries around the cricket playing world.

The unifying role of cricket in a country of both physical and psychic divides has not been adequately stressed. For reasons that have something to do with its geography and civilisation, India has not embraced uni-dimensional institutions nor has it encouraged a rigidly uniform viewpoint. As much politically as culturally the country has lived in circles within a circle and confronted rebellions inside revolution. The major outline of a defining military campaign has not been able to smudge out the little battles for local aspirations. The inexorable march of empire's juggernaut could not erase the tribal assertion of independence. Indeed, the collective memory of the Indian people is uniquely devoid of an all-embracing, cohesive construct. Our journey has been through an imaginary archipelago whose innumerable islands merge on the top but remain distant underneath.

Only in the second decade of the past century—to be precise, since Mahatma Gandhi's return from South Africa in 1915—a sense of nationalism began to cast a unifying influence on the people across the great Indian land mass. The political structure that was built at the euphoric onset of Independence had a unitary tendency, in a way reminiscent of the great empires of the past. Despite isolated areas of dissent, the monolithic political trend of conformity prevailed for just about two decades. In the first stunning reverses in its political fortunes the Congress in 1967 lost majority in eight states—Uttar Pradesh, Punjab, Rajasthan, Tamil Nadu, Kerala, West Bengal, Bihar and Orissa. After that blow it took exactly a decade for the primary party of power to face its first defeat in a general election. Since 1977 it has been a game of Russian roulette, of rise and fall of political fortunes, of power sharing and coalition politics.

The breakdown of the early political synthesis is reflected in the social tension and rising aspiration of those classes which have been out of the power structure for centuries. The politics of consensus has been replaced by identity politics. A new volatility is visible in the assertion by social groups from the bottom of the caste structure. India in the beginning of the 21st century is desperately in search of a unifying symbol, an abiding influence of social cohesion.

In cricket the country sees one such facilitator of integration. Nothing unites India more assuredly than the game of willows. With the phenomenal popularity of one-day cricket it is a bonfire of celebrations every time the team wins a crunch match. The live telecast of such an encounter brings the country on its edge. Cricket is to India what football has been to Latin America for long—a passionate obsession. In a society thwarted by bad governance, corruption and accumulating frustration, cricket takes the people to a make-believe world of fulfilment.   In the victory of the team a fan experiences a success that has always eluded him. He tends to identify himself with the heroes in flannel. In Sachin Tendulkar he discovers an idol who is infallible, endowed with enormous power which he himself does not possess. In the exploits of the cricket star he inhabits a comfort zone which is not otherwise available to him. The technical finesse of live telecasts with dollops of entertainment cleverly packaged by the sports channels has brought cricket closer to average Indian life.

In a significant way today's cricketer has taken over from yesterday's Bollywood hero. Compared with the real battle on the ground under the floodlight the tinsel actor's fight with the ludicrously bad villain seems phony, frivolous. His simulated rage and cardboard wars no longer interest today's youngster. In a nationwide poll some time back Tendulkar was voted as the young Indian's new icon. Perhaps the cricketer's star status has something to do with the shift of Hindi cinema to romance and family from the musty warehouses stacked with empty packing boxes where most of the battles have been fought. A glance at the personal life of the cricketers will only confirm their increasing sex appeal to women fans. Struck by such a god in the Indian colours, a young woman is even ready to wreck her marriage, embarrass her family. In her idol's scintillating performance on the field to the accompaniment of hyperbolic commentary by experts, she enjoys a sensual satisfaction. When his bat flashes or he draws blood with the ball, she experiences a sexual arousal. The sham heroics of a movie star she now finds boring.

With the redefinition of the cricketer as hero his every action packs up a lot of meaning, his gestures acquire much significance. He surely has a hold on the masses, otherwise why should there be such a craze for him to endorse so many products? It is a measure of his popularity that when a cricketer teams up with a film star in a commercial, the clear directorial thrust is to his superior status. The filmy man only mimics or pampers him. In the larger social context, therefore, a message from such a man is indeed powerful.

When Mohammad Azharuddin walked down the pavilion after the fall of the fourth Indian wicket in the first Test of the series against England at the Eden Gardens in 1993, he did not know that apart from achieving a personal milestone, he was actually going to write an important chapter in the social history of the game. After a devastating South African tour earlier, the Indian captain had an urge to regain his supremacy and silence his critics. But that was just cricket and almost every player before and after him felt such a need. What invested Azhar's outing that day at his favourite ground with immense social significance was the long trail of death and devastation since the razing of Babri Masjid on December 6, 1992. The country had been convulsed by an orgy of violence and a bloodbath. Communal riots erupted in many places. For the Muslims the demolition of the 400-year-old mosque was an act of infringement on their rights. The disquieting times in many ways were a throwback to the days before Partition.

The wristy batsman from Hyderabad played with his trademark composure. By the time he walked back to the Club House to join his teammates there was an awesome figure etched against his name on the scoreboard—182. "I have always believed in letting my bat do the talking," he later said replying to his critics who had already begun to look for his successor. As Indian captain it was the beginning of a dream run for Azhar. But more importantly, his innings had a magic effect on the frayed nerves and charged passions aroused by the events of the recent past. It helped cool down the rage, close the gap and forget hostility. The innings, rated by Azhar as one of his best, provided the much needed healing touch. It made the ordinary Indian celebrate cricket leaving the nightmare behind. Perhaps Azhar's limited ambition to play the impressive knock was only to recover from the ruins of the away series. Unknowingly his bat did more than talking, it preached peace. Social scientists researching the larger meaning of cricket have studied this innings like ancient hieroglyphics to understand its contribution in restoring sanity in a country that was on the verge of madness.

The role of cricket as an expression of social concerns has long engaged experts. The emergence of Brian Lara as a sensational Caribbean superstar long after the heyday of West Indies cricket was over, has been invested with similar significance. When literary magazine *Granta* advertised for photographs of celebrities with their unknown admirers and chance acquaintances, someone sent a picture of her son with Lara wondering if the Trinidad player still passed for one. Lara indeed shone as a star when his side had eclipsed. More importantly he performed a historic role with his batting brilliance much like Azharuddin. A year after the Indian cricketer's superb knock at Eden Gardens, Lara set a world record in Test cricket by scoring 375 against England. This is the highest individual score in international cricket. This innings came in the backdrop of a gnawing social debate among the Caribbean people about their cultural propensity caught as they are between America and Great Britain. Historically they have been closer to the English who brought cricket to the islands like many other things. But geographically they are closer to America. More than geography it makes sound economic sense for the islanders to have a stronger affinity to the mighty USA. In fact, the Caribbean coast has seen a kind of cultural invasion by America. At a time when the debate created uncertainties and tension, Lara came to embody the islands' old ties with England by a flash of his cricketing genius. West Indies will stay, his bat seemed to be saying, the way they have been.

Cricket speaks the same language everywhere. In India it bears an unmistakable stamp of the milieu that nurtures it. In the pre-Independence era, despite the domination of the elite, Indian cricket carried a subtext of nationalism. The runaway success of the Bollywood blockbuster *Lagaan* is a testimony to the strong approval of cricket's nationalist assertion. The evolution of cricket from the Maharaja's palace ground to the city backlanes is itself an engrossing story. The prerogative of the privileged has become the sport of the masses. Despite charges that the game has degenerated into an industry and become a cockpit for cola warfare, cricket has been intertwined with the life of India. An India-Pakistan match can raise the tension on the line of control.

Cricket has accommodated every social segment and reflected its hopes and ambition. It promoted together two close friends from the same school—one from a middle-class Brahmin family, the other a Dalit from Mumbai's Bhendi Bazaar. Both exploded into overnight fame and became folk-heroes. Tendulkar and Vinod Kambli captured the nation's imagination as two princes from a fairytale. In the beginning Kambli's story had a greater social relevance since in him one saw the child of the disinherited coming back with a flourish to ask for his due, reclaim for an entire generation of the disadvantaged their lost territory. In his mythic popularity were visible the syncretic tendencies of society. But the impulsive genius erred and started sliding down as fast as he had ascended.

An equally engrossing story is the fall and rise of Sourav Ganguly, the present Indian captain. After an unimpressive debut in a one-day match against the West Indies in Australia even when he was in his teens, the left-hander faded away from international cricket and waited for four years for a comeback. When that opportunity came on a tour of England in 1996, he made his signature in the most assured style—with two consecutive centuries. No opinion poll is required to prove that he is the most popular man in West Bengal now. In the state with a mature political culture politicians are nowhere near him in terms of popularity. For the ordinary Bengali, hard hit by the industrial slump and economic backwardness caused by an insulated Marxist regime with a flawed vision, his stunted hopes and dashed dreams find a fulfilment in the elegant southpaw's fluent strokeplay. He symbolises a success that has not happened to the people in the state. Like the disadvantaged in Brazil for whom football has long been a symbol of hope, their only identity, in the industrial wasteland of Bengal, a big hitting cricketer's flamboyance on the ground is a glimpse of an arrival that has not been part of an ordinary man's experience.

In a segmented society like ours cricket often appears like an extension of identity politics. Like the caste tag of a politician, the regional or social identity of a player takes precedence over his attributes. Protests, unseemly demonstrations occur in some places if a player of that region is suddenly dropped from the team. This interestingly happens in more economically deprived areas than in an affluent social segment. Mumbai or Bangalore, for instance, is unlikely to erupt in protest if a local hero's name is omitted from the list of the playing eleven. The same social factor explains why there is a possibility of the stands turning violent if Pakistan lose a match at Karachi and not at Lahore. Social stability and a sense of deprivation have much to do with the crowd volatility. The same reason holds good for the fact that while the English soccer fans have earned a notoriety all over Europe for their propensity to violence, the country's cricket spectators should be strong candidates for a good-conduct award. The class identity of a game determines its ambience as well. Soccer in Britain is the passion of the lower middle-class, underprivileged youths. Manchester United star Bekham, son of a brick-layer, is the rags-to-riches story that every unemployed young man wants to be. Cricket on the contrary has an appeal to the upper crust of society.

The mass appeal of a sport can trigger riots, it can contain mob violence as well. When the ghastly terrorist strike at the Akshardham temple took a heavy toll of innocent pilgrims, in a socially fractured Gujarat there was apprehension of an immediate revenge replay. The state was still hobbling back from bouts of communal violence. Surprisingly nothing happened. To understand the intriguing silence of the mob in the streets of Ahmedabad one should take a look at the date of the tragedy—September 24, 2002. The ICC Champions Trophy tournament was in progress in Sri Lanka and the Indian team on a roll. The next day when the elite commandos evacuated the temple complex, India played South Africa. In a nerve wrecking, heart stopping match India pulled off a thrilling 10-run win. Just when the mob should have been busy preparing for another round of incendiary acts, its members were probably busy watching the day-night match in progress under the floodlight. The feel-good factor triggered by the victory was cited as reason for the absence of reprisals.

During the Queen's visit to Australia years ago, the Prime Minister of the host country committed what was considered by the British as an act of abhorrence—he put an arm around the Queen. The televised image of that brief moment of impertinence sparked protests in England. While the hosts officially explained the matter as unintended, it was interpreted as Australia's insistence on its freedom from the burden of the past and the country's own identity as a Pacific country. In a cricket match between the two countries that followed England star Ian Botham played a dashing innings. Asked to comment on his knock later, Botham remarked, "I hope the Queen watched it."

The role of cricket as a purveyor of nationalist aspirations is nowhere better stressed than in the subcontinent. One wonders whether the game will evoke the same passion and retain its hold over the people's imagination if by some strange incredible feat the country one day really achieves a 10 per cent growth rate, makes good governance possible and the rupee becomes half as strong as the US dollar. Will the Indian fan be still looking forward to his icons in flannel to translate into reality his ambitions? What will be the role of cricket in a social situation marked by an economic boom? Can it still arouse the same level of passion as now?

Leaving aside the future possibilities an Indian fan can resort to an action replay of the magical moment of the NatWest trophy final at Lord's when a young, wiry Mohammad Kaif completed an impossible run chase with rugged determination. His partnership with the energetic Yuvraj Singh has remained an immaculate picture postcard of Hindu-Muslim camaraderie unspoiled by the most chilling nightmare in Gujarat.

T.K. Oommen

Demystifying the Nation and Nationalism

The entity designated as nation has undergone such devastating changes in its form and substance over the last few centuries that the enterprise called nation building can mean diametrically opposite things. In fact, the concept of nation has entered only recently in to the vocabulary of humankind. However, the idea of nation is such an electrifying one that people of one nation are willing to murder the people of other nations for self-preservation and/or prosperity. Soldiers and suicide bombers sacrifice their lives for their nations. Tracing the career of the concepts of nation and nationalism is a necessary first step in trying to demystify them.

I

The first reference to 'nationes' occurred at Leipzig University (founded in 1409) in the context of a religious and scholastic dispute at Prague involving Bohemian and non-Bohemian 'nationes'. The word *nationes* referred initially to associations of Leipzig professors, who were organized into four *nationes* to defend their common interests. Hence, the term had a restricted meaning and in the contemporary context referred to an interest group or union. In 1731 when John Innocent Micu, a bishop, demanded the right of the Walachian nation (Rumanian people) to be represented in the Transylvanian Parliament, his words met with the cry: "There is no Walachian nation, there is only a Walachian Plebs."[1] The idea of equating nation with elites or assuming that only some nations are privileged to have elites was prevalent at the time, although it is totally at variance with the contemporary impulse. The term nation is derived from the Latin *nasci*. In its original classical Latin sense *nasci* meant a tribal-ethnic group, a people born in the same place or territory and wherein the political dimension was not a necessary element. The term nation has been interpreted in five different ways, in the different phases of its history. Hence, nation has variously been seen to mean: (1) a group of foreigners, (2) a community of opinion, (3) an elite, (4) a sovereign people, and (5) a unique people.[2]

The nation as a community of citizens, that is a political entity, is the creation of the French Revolution. Nation has thus become at once a cultural entity (the original connotation of the term) as well as a political entity in Europe. Small wonder then, that a nation is defined as "a people, a folk, held together by some or all of such more or less immutable characteristics as common descent, territory, history, language, religion, way of life, or other attributes that members of a group have from birth onward"[3] as well as "a community of sentiment which would adequately manifest itself in a state of its own: hence a nation is a community which normally tends to produce a state of its own."[4] It thus came to be believed that it is not only natural for a nation to have a state but also necessary for a nation to have its own state, so that its cultural identity could be maintained and protected.

While in the above noted sense nation is a people of a country without distinction or rank, at least there are a few who use the term to denote class. Thus Disraeli[5] referred to:

> ...two nations between whom there is no intercourse and no sympathy; who are ignorant of each other's habits, thoughts and feelings, as if they were dwellers in different zones, or inhabitants of different planets; who are formed by different breeding, are fed by different food, are ordered by different manners and are not governed by the same laws, the rich and the poor.

Similarly, Marx refers to "the division of the French nation into two nations, the nation of owners and the nation of workers."[6] Responses to such descriptions have been made by many, as for example, by Gramsci, who equates the national with the popular so as to avoid the nation-people hiatus. However, one of the reasons why nation-based inequality and oppression are ignored in much of Western analyses seems to be that the empirical situation of the Western states did not warrant it, most Western states being uni-national. The issue of dominant nations oppressing and exploiting the weak and subordinate nations, however, is germane to all multi-national states in the East and West. Therefore, it is no accident that the expression 'internal colonialism' was first used in the case of Great Britain, implying that Scotland, Wales and Ireland were the colonies of England.[7]

In France, Abbe Barnel first used the word nationalism in 1798 but its usage was not very common even in the early nineteenth century. The 1836 Oxford English Dictionary provided a theological connotation to the word nationalism, which is referred to as a doctrine that certain nations are objects of divine dispensation.[8] Given the trajectory of Western history—which is replete with instances of advocacy of intense and terminal loyalty to one's nation, ranging from the call for 'one-nation, one-state,' to the Crusades, the World Wars, Nazi horrors and Colonialism—nationalism has come to be perceived both as a positive and negative force. These views are clearly articulated by J. S. Mill and Lord Acton. Mill[9] unambiguously endorsed the doctrine of national self-determination. He wrote:

> It is, in general, a necessary condition of free institutions that the boundaries of government should coincide in the main with those of nationality. Where the sentiment of nationality exists in any force, there is a *prima facie* case for uniting all the members of the nationality under the same government, and a government to themselves apart. This is merely saying that the question of government ought to be decided by the governed.

In contrast, in his essay on 'Nationality' Lord Acton[10] wrote: "Nationality does not aim at either liberty or prosperity, both of which it sacrifices to the imperative necessity of making the nation the mould and measure of the state. Its course will be marked with material as well as moral ruin...."

In the voluminous literature on nation and nationalism both the positive and negative connotations surface frequently. But it would be correct to say that these connotations change depending upon the historicity of context. Thus nationalism was viewed as a positive force in the ex-colonial countries in the context of the anti-imperialist struggles, but if any of the constituent units of the multi-national colony were to assert its separateness as a nation and mobilise its national sentiment after the attainment of freedom, the rest of the constituents, particularly the dominant nation, would invariably dispute the claim and instantly condemn the mobilisation as being 'anti-national'!

II

It is untenable therefore to follow the Latin sense of the term nation, which refers to a tribal-ethnic group, in the contemporary world. Before the French Revolution, the polities were either small (tribes, peasant villages, caste councils, city-states) or large (empires, federations, universal churches). Today the tendency is to establish viable polities. In fact, there are about 220 or 230 states in the contemporary world, while in Africa alone there are about 6,000 and in South Asia over 600 tribes. A large number of tribes may still be too small in size to constitute viable states; besides, they may not always have any cultural distinctiveness. Further, if the political dimension is taken into account many of the erstwhile tribes were either stateless societies and/or incorporated into larger polities. Therefore, Coleman's[11] definition, "The tribe is the largest social group defined primarily in terms of kinship, and is normally an aggregate of clans, intermediate to nationality," constitutes a limited viewpoint. Some large tribes with their own exclusive territory and language could be nations. That is, even if all tribes do not automatically qualify as nations, the possibility of some tribes being considered as nations should not be ruled out.

Some authors refer to tribes as ethnic groups. In this sense an ethnic group is relatively small, shares a common culture and traces descent to a common ancestor. But in today's world societies and groups are not insulated by descent and kinship, they are constantly exposed to alien influences through migration and colonisation as well as through the mass media. This changing context has also invested a new meaning on ethnicity. In Africa, a tribe in its homeland, that is, its original village, is not referred to as an ethnic group. It is a term used to refer to the uprooted, the migrant segment of the tribe in the urban settlements.

The terms ethnic and ethnicity are most favoured and popular in the USA, as they should be, because they aptly capture and convey the social situation there: the USA is a conglomeration of varieties of people uprooted from different nations. But the equivalent concepts, more suited to describe the over-all situation in Europe are nation and nationality given the strong attachment people have to their homelands. This is equally true of South Asia, although of course these terms are scarcely used. And this reluctance should be understood in terms of the prevailing situation in South Asian countries. Most

South Asian states encapsulate several nations and the process of state formation is not yet complete and stable largely because of their multi-national composition. Therefore, if a collectivity asserts its identity in national terms it spells danger to the state. The national identity is often de-legitimised to uphold the integrity of the state.[12] Further, identity assertions based on religion, language, region, tribe, etc., are viewed as 'communal', 'parochial' and even 'anti-national'.

If in Europe nations are essentially cultural entities, in the colonised parts of the world and in ex-colonial countries nations are viewed as political units. Further, most of the 'new states' are culturally plural. Thus African nation-states emerged through the incorporation of many tribes which spoke different languages/dialects and followed different religious faiths. While race is the most salient common feature, even this criterion is not universal in nation formation as exemplified in the case of South Africa which is a multi-racial state. In South Asia almost all states are multi-religious and multi-lingual. In the case of Latin America, the populations of particular nations have aliens and natives, who are multi-racial, multi-lingual, multi-religious, or all of these. In North America and Australia national populations are constituted predominantly by migrants from Europe who spoke different languages and who belonged to different Christian denominations. Understandably, the connotation of the term nation and the background of the national population vary vastly across the continents. In the case of Western Europe, the nation-states were conceived as culturally (that is, linguistically and even in religious terms) homogeneous but in most cases they gradually became culturally heterogeneous.

The point to be noted is that it is the historicity of context which invests meanings on concepts. The 'people' of the United States of America did not have a pre-existent 'nation' (in the European sense) to latch on to their nationalism and yet American nationalism led to the formation of a state. On the other hand, 'nations' may not always clamour for their sovereign states as borne out by the experience of India. In fact, available evidence suggests that it is usually the smaller nations located on inter-state borders or those nations which are vivisected across state boundaries which exhibit secessionist tendencies. The presumption that each nation would necessarily give expression to its common sentiment in nationalism, which in turn would normally give birth to a state, is not borne out by facts.

The nationalist movements of ex-colonial countries were explicitly political and oriented to state building. These movements were efforts to transform colonies into states and subjects into citizens. But at the height of the anti-imperialist tempo it was often forgotten that colonies were multi-national entities, because the primary objective of the anti-imperialist struggle was to liberate the colony from the foreign political yoke and establish self-government. Understandably, but unfortunately, nations and states came to be treated as synonymous entities in the ex-colonial countries, creating enormous conceptual confusion. In the case of Europe instead, the nation (a cultural entity) co-exists with state (a political entity) hence the viability of the hyphenated term nation-state. But even in Europe the term does not always convey the content of the entity referred to, as exemplified by the cases of Great Britain, Spain or Belgium.

While a nation may constitute itself into a state, the state covers an immense variety of political structures, viz., kingdoms, empires, city-states, principalities, republics, federations. A state implies establishing successful claim within a territory, with a monopoly on the legitimate use of force.[13] Keeping these considerations in mind, it would be helpful to list the varieties of situations represented by 'nation-states' in the world today:

1. One-nation, one-state. Although this is pursued as an ideal and a possibility there is hardly any case of such a pure type. However, Japan could be cited as an example.
2. Parts of different nations come to constitute a state for geo-political reasons (e.g. Switzerland).
3. One nation is divided into two (e.g. Germany until 1990; Korea) or more states (as in the case of the Arab nation).
4. Part of a nation is constituted into one sovereign state (e.g. Bangladesh or the Republic of Ireland) and the remaining part is incorporated into another sovereign state (e.g. West Bengal in India or Northern Ireland in the United Kingdom).
5. A nation may be divided between two sovereign states and constitute parts of them along with other nations (e.g. Indian Punjab and Pakistan Punjab; Azeris in Soviet Union and Iran).
6. A number of nations come to constitute a state (e.g. India, the United Kingdom, and the Soviet Union before the break up).
7. A set of migrants drawn from a multiplicity of nations constitute a state (e.g. the USA).

III

From the foregoing discussion it is clear that the meaning and content of the three crucial concepts—ethnicity, nation/ nationalism and state—have been transformed substantially over time and any insistence on applying their original connotations and meanings would render them incapable of capturing the essence of the evolving reality. Therefore, it is imperative to view these concepts in their processual relationship.

The content of the concept of nation was essentially cultural and it encapsulated a variety of attributes: nationhood was a product of the conjoint existence and interaction of these attributes. But as nations started to constitute themselves as states, as political entities, in Western Europe following the maxim 'one-nation, one state', a new socio-political formation emerged and the hyphenated term nation-state came into vogue as noted earlier. However, it is often forgotten that the nation-state implies a process and it is possible and historically true that the process can even be reversed. Not only can a nation be constituted into a state, a state can dismantle and destroy nations. Further, a state can create a new nation. It seems the eclipse of the nation as a cultural entity is almost complete and it has invariably come to mean a political entity.

It is clear however that the state and nation need not be conterminous. And the term nation connotes society in the sense in which sociologists use the term. But the difficulty arises when there is a multi-national state and one of its constituent units gets designated as a nation by the people concerned with the intention of establishing a sovereign state. The moment the term nation is used to refer to societies contained within a state considerable alarm is expressed because this implies a threat to the territorial integrity of that state, and change of citizenship status to a section of its population. And those who assign the label 'nation' to their 'society' invariably imply precisely this. Conversely, once a multi-national or poly-ethnic state emerges and consolidates, it becomes a reality-in-itself, and the co-existence and interaction of its different nations or ethnic groups produces certain emergent properties, which give a new meaning and a collective self-definition to the constituent units. That is, just as a state can dismantle or divide nations it can also weld and fuse together different nations.

Ethnicity as understood in contemporary social science emerged from the interaction between different peoples; it was a product of conquest, colonisation and immigration. Ethnicity implies dislocation from one's original country, region, or nation, which is homeland. In contrast, nation invariably alludes to a people belonging to a specific territory whose claim to political authority over it is perceived as legitimate. Ideally, the nation fuses three dimensions: territory, culture and citizenship. That a whole nation can be uprooted from its territory and rendered into an ethnie (a people without a common territory and citizenship) only points to the historical process and possibility of one category being transformed into another. Therefore it is the rupture between territory and culture, which creates ethnicity. What deserves our attention is the process through which a nation dissolves into an ethnic group and an ethnie crystallizes into a nation.

The attribute of homeland is crucial in the case of a nation. Even if all other attributes are present together a nation does not come into being unless it establishes legitimate moral claim over a territory which in turn provides it with the potential for state-formation. The *ethnification* of a nation takes place precisely when it does not have the resources for state formation, namely, a homeland and legitimate political authority over it. Therefore, ethnie, nation and state should be viewed in a processual relationship. When an ethnie acquires legitimate moral claim over a territory it becomes a nation and when a nation secures political jurisdiction in its homeland, it becomes a state. Pursuantly, to be an ethnic group is to operate *within* a specific nation-state or to be dispersed over several of them. By the same token to be an ethnic group is to be on the periphery and to be a nation is to be at the centre of the polity.

When a state has different nations within its territory that state will and should have multiple cultural centres.[14] It may be noted here that (a) cultural pluralism, that is, dignified co-existence of a plurality of cultural groups, *within* nation-states needs to be accepted as axiomatic, and (b) states in the contemporary world form a continuum, extending from extreme simplicity to great complexity. Let us take as an illustration the simplest of all the factors, namely size.

An analysis of demographic data relating to 177 nation-states shows that 25 per cent have a population of less than 1,000,000. In fact 46 per cent of the states have a population of 5,000,000 or less. On the other end of the continuum there are only eleven states with 100,000,000 or more population—China, India, Russia, USA, Indonesia,

Japan, Brazil, Bangladesh, Pakistan, Mexico and Nigeria. And it is not true that a bigger size necessarily implies greater cultural complexity. Thus China, with the largest population in the world, is culturally much less complex as compared with say Indonesia which has only one-eighth of its population.

Although a wide variety of factors provide the base for constituting states the most frequent ones are race, religion and language, often a combination of two or more of them. While races or physical types and geographical spaces were originally closely linked, conquests, colonisation and immigration have drastically changed the situation. Today a large number of states have a multi-racial population. Similarly, notwithstanding the fact that particular religions originated in specific parts of the world due to the process of conquest, proselytisation and immigration, the original association between religion and territory has become irrelevant except for symbolic purposes. But, generally speaking, there is a close association between language and territory. When groups migrate and settle down in a new linguistic region they have to learn the language of the new place whereas they need not change their religion and they cannot change their race. A common language is an imperative for communication. This however does not imply that each linguistic group (nation) should have an exclusive state for itself. One can visualize several substantial linguistic groups co-existing within a state as in the case of India. But this co-existence necessarily implies a viable and creative linguistic policy.

IV

I have already alluded to some of the specificities of the South Asian situation, but let us take the case of India. Broadly speaking there are seven ways in which the Indian 'nation' has been defined, that is, as: (1) an ancient civilisational entity; (2) a composite culture; (3) a multi-national polity; (4) a religious entity; (5) a geographical/territorial entity populated by a multiplicity of religious communities; (6) a collectivity of linguistic communities; and finally as (7) a unity of great and little nationalisms.[15]

Those who characterise the Indian nation as an ancient civilisational entity[16] invoke natural geography, ancient Hindu culture, economic self-sufficiency and the urge for political unification as its basis. However, if geography were the basis of constituting nations most of the continents would have been unified into single nations. The reference only to Hindu culture ignores the cultural contributions of other religious communities. Many nations were not and perhaps could not ever have been economically self-sufficient even when these authors wrote on the subject. The urge for political unification seems to have been motivated by colonialism. This would mean that in the absence of colonialism political unification would not have occurred. At any rate these writers are conflating civilisations and nations. Civilisations are much broader entities within which usually there are several nations.

The idea of composite culture[17] in India essentially refers to the fusion of Hindu and Muslim cultures; it ignores the pre-Aryan cultures and their contributions in the making of the culture of India. In retrospect, it would seem that the characterisation of Indian culture as a composite culture was a political project intended to mollify militant Hindus and Muslims so as to avert the partition of India. Instead of celebration of cultural diversity, which would have facilitated co-existence, the idea of compositeness wished away the distinctiveness of Hindu and Muslim cultures. The intentionality of the project apart, it failed and in the process an erroneous notion got wide currency: the 'two nation theory'.

Those who recognised the difficulty in characterising India as a composite culture conceptualised India as a multinational state.[18] And yet, the basis of nation formation was not clearly specified. While language, generally speaking, was accepted as the basis of nation by Marxists, the support extended to 'Muslim nationalities' of the north-west and north-east for self-determination, endorsed, although indirectly, religion also as a basis of nation formation. This was a fatal error in that religious communities were recognised as the carriers of nationalism wherever they were in majority.

If the religion of the majority community could be the basis of nation formation in a specific territory it is but logical that at least a section of the population in each of these territorial communities would try to form 'nations' which are advantageous to them. But in doing so the units they would invoke for this purpose would vary. Thus for Hindus keeping India as one unit was advantageous as they were the overwhelming majority.[19] But for the Muslims this was not an acceptable proposition, not only because they feared discrimination in the emerging nation but also because they were in a majority in certain parts of India.[20] The same logic was applicable in the case of Sikhs in the Punjab. Understandably but unfortunately nationalism and communalism became two sides of the same coin; a matter of perception based on a community's standing. If the majority community insists on its collective rights it is nationalism and if a minority community demands collective rights it is communalism!

To get out of this impasse and to discredit the two-nation theory several writers[21] conceptualised the Indian nation as a multi-religious entity. It needs to be underlined here that this conceptualisation was articulated in pre-Partition India and yet it was unable to contain the rising tide of Partition. Finally Partition occurred but the untenability of religion as a basis of nation formation was demonstrated by the subsequent division of Pakistan.

There was yet another conceptualisation of the Indian nation which shifted the focus from religion to language. In this rendition India was to be viewed as a collective of linguistic entities co-existing under one political roof.[22] This view had the potential of de-legitimising religious nationalism (or communalism, if you will) *and* chauvinism based on language. But given the obstinate persistence of constructing the Indian nation-state on the basis of the European model that had conceived nation as a territorial-linguistic homogeneous entity, the Hindi language had to be projected as the 'national' language which would presumably provide the cement for the diverse cultural elements. Indeed Hindi *was* adopted as the 'national' language after a virulent controversy. As Ambedkar noted "… there was no article which proved more controversial than article 115, which deals with the [Hindi] question. Hindi won its place as a national language by one vote."[23] Perhaps this provides the clue for the persistence of several 'national movements' in the post-colonial period.

If anti-colonialism was indeed nationalism there was no possibility of national movements crystallising in independent India. But the beginnings in this direction already started in 1921 when the Indian National Congress endorsed the idea of creating administrative units based on linguistic homogeneity. In 1928 the Nehru Report acknowledged the desirability of creating linguistic provinces. Prime Minister Nehru accepted the principle underlying linguistic provinces on 27 November 1947 in the course of the Constituent Assembly debates. However, the mobilisation by linguistic collectivities to form states with some level of political autonomy *within* the federal framework was perceived as a threat to the nation (read the Indian state) and was labeled as chauvinist, parochial and even anti-national. Some of the tribal communities too have started demanding separate provincial states. These were labelled 'sub-national' movements.[24]

Admittedly language and tribe became the bases of national movements in post-colonial India as against religion in colonial India. The two nation theory transformed itself into multi-nation theory. But the reluctance to recognise the demands of the linguistic and tribal communities for separate provincial states as 'national' reveals not only the persisting obstinacy in ineluctably linking sovereign states with nations, but also amounts to conflating state and nation.[25] Thus new conceptualisations were floated: the anti-colonial movement came to be designated as 'great nationalism' and flaunted as the ideology of the pan-Indian big bourgeoisie, in contrast to the `little nationalism' of the regional small bourgeoisie in free India.[26] Similarly the demands by tribal communities for separate sovereign states was labelled 'proto-national' and the demand for some level of political and cultural autonomy within the federal framework to cope with the issue of disparity in development was designated as 'sub-national'.[27] These new coinages unfold the widespread ambivalence prevailing in independent India: the tendency to designate India as a nation and to label the national urges of linguistic and tribal communities as less than national. This anxiety is understandable in the light of the artificial and unfortunate partition of India based on religion but unacceptable if nation is conceptualised as a territorially anchored linguistic community, wherein the political and cultural boundaries co-exist.

V

Independent India has witnessed two types of nationalism: state-centred and state-renouncing nationalisms. These may be called 'new nationalisms'.[28] State-centred nationalism conflates state and nation and views the sovereign state as the critical marker of the nation. In turn, there are two types of state-centred nationalism, one being state-seeking nationalism. Old nationalisms too were state-seeking. But there is an essential difference between the old and the new variety of state-seeking nationalism. If the old variety of state-seeking nationalism had consisted of a struggle to wrest a national state out of the external colonial power, the new state-seeking nationalism was a struggle against the 'internal coloniser'. The secessionist movements in independent India—the Tamil national movement in the 1960s, the Mizo National Front, the Naga National movement, the Khalistan movement, the Azad Kashmir movement and the like—are movements which aim to establish sovereign states. Secessionist nationalism is usually an extreme response to assimilationist nationalism and its project of cultural homogenisation.

The second variety of state-centred nationalism invariably needs an 'Other', an enemy, to sustain itself. If there is none, it is to be constructed and nurtured. The United States of America, a poly-ethnic state, created its 'nationhood' by constructing its Other in the 'totalitarian regime' led by the erstwhile Soviet Union. Today, for the USA the Other is constituted by a powerful state like China which is not yet democratic. But if the Other is anchored to concrete empirical bases such as religion, language, race etc., it will be more enduring. And if the Other is in the immediate neighbourhood with a disputed common border it will substantially intensify the state-centred nationalism of this variety. This is the situation in South Asia today, particularly in the case of India and Pakistan. It is no exaggeration to suggest that Pakistani 'nationalism' cannot be nurtured without the existence of the Indian enemy and vice versa. From nuclear explosion to cricket matches everything is neatly fitted into this syndrome; management of inter-state conflicts is confused with nationalism.

What I call state-renouncing nationalism is characterised by demands for cultural and fiscal autonomy *within* the federal polity. The mobilisations for the linguistic re-organisation of India, which had started in the 1920s, culminated in the appointment of the State Reorganisation Commission in 1954. Most of the linguistic and tribal movements which were demanding a separate province for themselves in post-colonial India were *not* secessionist (i.e. state seeking) but only autonomist, that is, demanding the preservation of their cultural identity and parity in economic development. They pursued state-renouncing nationalism in that they did not demand sovereign states. It may also be noted that through conceding an appropriate level of autonomy within the federal political framework state-seeking nationalism can be transformed into state-renouncing nationalism as exemplified by the cases of the Mizo, the Tamil and to a large extent the Khalistan movement. Demands for separate states and Union Territories have continued even after the linguistic re-organisation of India in the 1950s, and between 1960 and 2001, seventeen new states and Union Territories have been created. At present there are 12 mobilisations demanding the creation of new politico-administrative units.[29]

The second variety of state-renouncing nationalism in independent India manifests as identity-seeking ethnic movements. They are 'ethnic' in that they do not have a territorial base; they are products of dissociation of territory and culture. The most outstanding cases of this type in post-colonial India are Urdu and Sindhi mobilisations for collective rights.[30] The Sindhi speakers (little over two million), who migrated to India from Pakistan, are dispersed all over India. Similarly, the Urdu speakers who remained in India are reduced to a linguistic minority everywhere in the country although they constitute little over 5 per cent (counting 43.4 million) of India's population, according to the 1991 Census. The reference to this category of movements is necessary here because some writers refer to these as movements for Sindhi and Urdu nationalism; more appropriately they are ethnic demands for protection of collective cultural rights.

With the ongoing process of urban industrialisation and the consequent increased movement of populations across cultural regions the conflicts between nationals (insiders) and ethnies (outsiders) are likely to increase. The examples of anti-ethnic mobilisations by 'nationals' in independent India are the anti-Tamil mobilisation by the Shiv Sena in Mumbai, the anti-Bengali mobilisation by the Assamiyas, the anti-Bihari mobilisation in Jarkhand, and the like. While the 'nationals' are asserting their cultural identity and demanding better economic entitlements within their homeland vis-à-vis the ethnies, the tension between all-India single citizenship and multiple national identities is getting exacerbated.

VI

The trajectory of nation and the career of nationalism that I have traced in the pages above makes it amply clear that the metamorphosis that these two phenomena have undergone in the last five centuries or so is tremendous. In most parts of the world where state formation is firmed up, the conflation between state and nation is no more in vogue. All nations do not have, and may not ever have, their exclusive sovereign states. But one should not deny the label of 'nation' to them because of this as this would mean a double denial. The processes of modernisation and globalisation are accelerating the spatial movement of people everywhere. Thus an increasing proportion of people are living outside their ancestral homeland. They are different from their co-nationals, who continue to live in the country of their origin. Consequently, the distinction between nationals and ethnies is becoming more and more relevant. Therefore the three concepts of state, nation and ethnie are best viewed in their dynamic and processual relationship rather than insisting on their obsolete and old connotations.

References and Notes

1. See G. Zernatte, 'Nation: The History of a Word', *Review of Politics* Vol. 6, 1944, pp. 351-66.
2. L. Greenfeld, *Nationalism: Five Roads to Modernity*, Cambridge, Harvard University Press, 1992.
3. W. Petersen, 'On the Sub-nations of Western Europe', in N. Glazer and D. P. Moynihan (eds.), *Ethnicity: Theory and Experience,* Cambridge, Harvard University Press, 1975, p. 181.
4. See, H. Gerth, and C. W. Mills (eds.), *From Max Weber: Essays in Sociology,* Routledge and Kegan Paul, 1948, p. 176.
5. B. Disraeli, Sybil, London, John Lane, 1945.
6. K. Marx, *Collected Works*, Vol. 7, Moscow, Progress Publishers, 1977, p.144.
7. M. Hechter, *Internal Colonialism: The Celtic Fringe in British National Development 1536-1966*, London: Routledge and Kegan Paul, 1975.
8. See A. D. Smith, *Theories of Nationalism*, London, Duckworth, 1983 (second edition).
9. J. S. Mill, *Considerations on Representative Government,* London, George Routledge, 1872.
10. Lord Acton, *Essays in Freedom and Power*, Boston, The Beacon Press, 1949.
11. J. S. Coleman, *Nigeria: Background to Nationalism*, Berkeley and Los Angeles, University of California Press, 1958, p. 423.
12. See T. K. Oommen, 'Social Movements and Nation-State in India: Towards Relegitimization of Cultural Nationalism', *Journal of Social and Economic Studies*, Vol. 3(2), New Series, 1986, pp.107–29.
13. See H. Gerth and C. W. Mills, op.cit., 1948.
14. For elaboration, see T. K. Oommen, *Citizenship, Nationality and Ethnicity: Reconciling Competing Identities*, Cambridge, Polity Press, 1997.
15. For a detailed discussion, see T. K. Oommen, 'Conceptualising Nation and Nationality in South Asia', in S. L. Sharma and T. K. Oommen (eds.), *Nation and National Identity in South Asia*, New Delhi, Orient Longman, 2000, pp. 1–18.
16. For example, R. Mookerji, *The Fundamental Unity of India*, London, Macmillan, 1914; Beni Prasad, *The Hindu-Muslim Question*, Allahabad, Indian Press, 1941.
17. See, Beni Prasad, ibid.; H. Kabir, *The Indian Heritage*, Bombay, Asia Publishing House, 1955; Tarachand, *Influence of Islam on Indian Culture*, Allahabad, Indian Press, 1963.
18. See, A. R. Desai, *The Social Background of Indian Nationalism*, Bombay, Popular Prakashan, 1948; I. Habib, 'Emergence of Nationalities', *Social Scientist*, Vol. 4 (1).

19. See M. S. Golwalkar, *We or Our Nationhood Defined*, Nagpur, Bharat Prakashan, 1939.
20. M. A. Jinnah, *Speeches and Writings* Vol. 1 (edited by Jamiluddin Ahmed), Lahore, Shaik Muhammad Ashraf, 1960.
21. See M. M. Malaviya (1905) as referred to in G. Pandey, *The Construction of Communalism in Colonial North India*, Delhi, Oxford University Press, 1990, p. 212; Lala Lajpat Rai (1920) as referred to in P. Nagar, *Lala Lajpat Rai: The Man and His Ideas*, Delhi, Manohar, 1977, p.175; M. K. Gandhi, *Hind Swaraj*, Ahmedabad, Navjivan Publishers, 1938, p.49.
22. See especially, D. P. Mukerji, *Diversities*, New Delhi, People's Publishing House, 1958; Jawaharlal Nehru, *Discovery of India*, Bombay, Asia Publishing House, 1961.
23. B. R. Ambedkar, *Thoughts on Linguistic States*, Bombay, Ram Krishna Press, 1955, p.14.
24. N. K. Bose, 'The Hindu Method of Tribal Absorption', *Science and Culture*, 7 (2), 1941, pp.188–194.
25. For an explication see, T. K. Oommen. op. cit., 1997.
26. See A. Guha, 'Great Nationalism, Little Nationalism and Problems of Integration: A Tentative View', *Economic and Political Weekly (EPW)* 14 (7 & 8), 1979, pp. 455–58 and 'The Indian National Questions: A Conceptual Frame', *EPW*, 17(31), 1982, pp. 2–12.
27. See, B. K. Roy Burman, 'National Movements Among Tribes', *Social Democracy*, 4 (3 & 4), 1971, pp. 25–33.
28. See, T. K. Oommen 'New Nationalisms and Collective Rights: The Case of South Asia', (MS), Paper presented at the seminar, 'India and the European Union: Challenges and Opportunities', India International Centre, New Delhi, 2–3 December 1999.
29. For details see, T. K. Oommen, 'Linking Development, Governance and Culture: Completing the Unfinished Task of Reorganizing Indian States', keynote address to the national seminar on 'Development and Governance: Fresh Imperatives for Reorganizing Indian States, Initiative for Research, Analysis, Development and Action', New Delhi, 23 November 2001.
30. See, T. K. Oommen, op. cit, 1999.

Antara Dev Sen

News Watch: in search of a national culture

The news media? Everyone knows they have no sense of culture, those johnnies who spoil our mornings with price hikes and springing charred corpses on our television dinners. To them, culture would be potbellied politicians in ridiculous ethnic headgear grinning sheepishly with tribal dancers in fancy dress. Or the kind of pictures we need to hide from our children, those skinny women in skimpies. And you don't mean the page 3 stuff, do you? That wouldn't quite be *culture*, would it? True, some of the social circuit regulars happen to be from the world of culture... but would the pictures and the who-wore-what-while-airkissing-whom reports qualify? You need to look at cinema, at television soaps, at radio plays,—that may not be 'culture' as we like it, but still a certain kind of rather lowbrow, pop culture, wouldn't you say? You don't get proper culture these days, you know. Except the kind in the petri dish, that is.

The point of this article is to look at culture not as a given, static entity, but as a developing, constantly morphing set of values and symbols. In that sense, culture would be that dynamic system of thought that allows us to distinguish between and accept or reject situations or acts. We rely on our culture for the images and vocabulary that will help us respond to our social and individual environment. Importantly, mass media helps build that culture, besides reflecting it. Culture thus becomes a symbolic system within which all media producers and media users (like readers or viewers) work. So, instead of the obvious 'cultural media', I choose newsmedia here to see what kind of culture it portrays as national. This is particularly important at this time, since our dependence on media is much greater in an insecure or rapidly changing social environment —as is the case in India now—and we try to make sense of ambiguous situations through the cultural symbols and values that the media throws up.

Indian newsmedia, undoubtedly, has established itself as one of the best in the world. Traditionally, it has maintained an adversarial relation with authority. It has been hard-hitting, fearless, gentle and humane, exposing injustice, forcing constructive action. From sculpting patriotism at the time of the Vernacular Press Act through articulating the demand for food during the Bengal famine, and the enraged protest during the Emergency, to the lashing out against dubious arms agreements like the Bofors deal, the Indian press has been an effective weapon of people's power. Unfortunately, of late there have been worrying symptoms. Whether in 'hard news' or 'soft stories', the thrust is less on ideas and ideology, more on events and personality cults; more on immediacy, less on accountability. This seems to be the culture emerging through national newsmedia today.

Part of it is because all media has been affected by the global 'dumbing down' phenomenon, which has led to a significant trivialisation of journalism.[1] Selling dreams, always a good element of any business, has moved centrestage. So entertainment, which used to have a subsidiary role, has become the first priority, while drab, non-entertaining news is being slowly turfed out. (In its most startling *avatar*, this is called a 'city news supplement', but for reasons of sanity, we shall not discuss these.) To illustrate this paradigm shift in mainstream newsmedia, let's take just one example of a valid subject matter: women.

I Crave, Therefore I Am

She's there, wherever you look—in newspapers and magazines, on television. She is the dream woman, polished, pretty, dolled up in snazzy designer outfits and dazzling jewellery, who is empowered in every way which the average Indian woman is not. She has money, class, style, looks and come-hither eyes. Increasingly, she is becoming whiter, her eyes lighter, her looks and carriage more Anglo-Saxon than Merle Oberon. She rules over a make-believe world of endless choices and Eurocentric dreams. This is the aspirational Indian woman whom we see scattered exquisitely throughout magazines and newspaper supplements, striding effortlessly through the main newspaper, raising the standards of your morning tea with a flash of her gorgeous legs or a flutter of those extra-long eyelashes. She promises us eternal happiness in an aspirational land; she is the escape key to unknown bliss.[2]

Enamoured by the fantasy woman, the Indian media has been steadily turfing out the harassed Indian woman. Talking numbers, she is closer to the real woman in this developing country, one who makes up the appalling statistics in human development indices, malnourished, underfed, underpaid, overworked, subjected to childhood neglect, illiteracy, dowry demands, deprived of family fortunes, health care, individual choices and decision-making authority even within the home, which is supposedly the woman's world. She is violated in every way, from the womb (female foeticide is not uncommon) through childhood (she gets less food, less education, less health care, less leisure, far less parental attention, in short less of a childhood, than her male siblings) and adult life. She is not only subjugated totally to male members—a father, a husband, a brother and later a son—but is treated so much as property that raping a woman is still common currency in feudal power games between males, frequently seen in caste, class or sectarian conflicts. This is the Indian woman we see in single-column, single-inch news reports, if at all, who hardly ever makes an appearance in magazines or supplements. She is the woman who reminds us of our problems, who smells of poverty, of disease, of death.

Not surprisingly, clever media producers steer clear of this woman. The average reader of the English newspaper would not even relate to her, they explain; she couldn't possibly boost circulation, looking the way she does, dead or alive. We must be sensitive to the reader—he has problems of his own, he doesn't want a scruffy, illiterate, dying woman spoiling his day.

Except when she is gangraped, maybe. She is allowed to figure in stories of rape, incest, murder and curious sexual escapades, in stories that can be sensationalised, because scandal and sensationalism are an integral part of news as entertainment. Which triggers public emotion, but doesn't create reasoned opinion. And given the way we have been acting on our primal passions lately, I doubt that it is constructive.

So the national culture that emerges from all this doesn't quite warm your heart. It's an aspirational, Eurocentric, escapist culture that is being wrapped around the media user. A culture that is not alien to our traditions, but is not the most integral. It becomes objectionable primarily because it edges out other cultural considerations that have more to do with our daily realities in all segments of rural and urban life.

Let's try and list some factors that may have led to this curious state of news media.

1. *Commercial pressures:* these are the most obvious. With increasing competition, the rush for quick and easy bottomline enhancers has become particularly graceless. Even in the late eighties, I remember, we used this 'babe' trick, but in a limited way. Called the 'pretty face' in the company of elders and 'tit factor' behind their backs, it consisted of a couple of close-ups of pretty women, usually just the faces. That was also when we needed one lead story on sex every six weeks. In today's world, behaviour fit for a nunnery.

2. *A new promotional culture:* public relations professionals compete to exploit the power of the press. They thrust press releases into your fist, carry you on their shoulders to foreign lands for a junket, lure you to press conferences showering you with gifts and alcohol. Image managers and PR firms make the journalist's task easier and newsgathering less expensive for the press. In short, they buy tailormade coverage.

3. *Lazy journalism:* largely an effect of the above. As the pampered journalist, we have got lazier and 'legwork', once an integral part of the journalistic process, has become as rare as background research. Naturally, we don't seek out information on issues that no one promotes, and since stories on social/development concerns don't have image managers, they are getting less visible. Also, we rarely think while reporting or editing, so a bare description of an act/event/speech can go in as a full 'objective' story on its own, without furnishing a relevant background or possible consequences.

4. *Populism:* linked to commercial pressures, this limits news to what people may like. 'Infotainment' isn't eating up entertainment space, it is replacing dreary old information. We find this in both political and social segments. Quick, easy answers to quick easy concerns of you and me, more me than you. Or something with shock value. A scandal is yummy. Sex is best. Sex and politics? Thank you, God. And if it's not about that, just make it short,

light and crispy. Remember the reader's shrinking attention span—say it in 300 words.

5. *Cultural imperialism:* we give in to it. We look up to the western models of television, newspapers and magazines, take their design and their style, their language and their subject areas, even their pretty women. And we do not challenge their models, smug in our belief that we've nicked a winning formula and not paid for it. We will pay dearly for it in the coming decades, of course.

6. *The Sim-City syndrome:* we seem to be building imaginary lands, with imaginary rules and experiences. It has the target audience as its citizens and mostly excludes others, the non-consumers of the media product, who may get a guest appearance once in a while, but are strictly to be viewed as aliens and not worth too much bother. There is significant danger of that becoming a serious affliction.

Together, these help in creating this culture of escapism, a culture that applies only to certain segments of the people, and therefore cannot really be termed a national culture, even if it is reflected in most 'national' newspapers. Let's see what else these help to create.

Agendas, Prejudice and Our Own WMD

Contrary to popular belief, newsmedia has never been without an agenda. In any democratic country, its aim has generally been to inform and educate, to create reasoned public opinion and thus strengthen the democratic process. So agenda-setting has always been a part of journalism. Unhappily, the agenda changes according to the situation and the changing culture. What is important here is journalism's code of ethics. As in any country, in India too the news providers are mostly from privileged backgrounds—and the voices they project reflect that. Add to that the demands of the market and political and economic power groups, and you get a media that is largely exclusionary, elitist, aspirational and self-centred. As Noam Chomsky had pointed out years ago, "what appears, what doesn't appear, the way it is slanted, will reflect the interest of the buyers and sellers, the institutions and the power systems around them."

Chomsky had alerted us to the dangers of corporate conglomerates and monolithic media corporations, which pursue a narrow profit-driven agenda and stifle voices that are not important to them. In India, we had an added fear of The Foreign Hand. Terrified of it, we clung to a 1956 Cabinet decision barring the entry of foreign media, which we are only now— half a century later—taking steps to change. Personally, I believe it would be an insult to Indian democracy to assume that we cannot hold our own as The Foreign Hand tinkers with our mind. We are rather unlikely to lose our cultural integrity at the breakfast table, seduced by a wicked foreign media. The real danger is in losing ourselves to the demands of the market and the politics of the day. Smaller voices may die out, perspectives may be lost, sensitivities trampled to a pulp. We seem to be doing precisely that quite well by ourselves.

As mentioned before, media operates within a culture and uses its symbols. That includes prejudices and stereotypes. A media dominated by male, urban, middle class, Hindu media producers therefore largely reflects dominant social values and often perpetuates stereotypes that become the norm and may be followed unquestioningly by female, non-urban, non-middle class, non-Hindu media producers as well. Prevalent in every sphere of public life, prejudice has a devastating power over the lives—and deaths—of individuals. It could be about religion, like when after the recent carnage in Gujarat, the Police Commissioner was busy explaining on national television how policemen were human too, how as Hindus they were upset after the inhuman Godhra incident, and so did not contain the resultant sectarian violence. So the mob— that convenient, home-grown, low-cost weapon of mass destruction (WMD)—got away with murder. No significant follow-up on this comment was noticed, probably because it was part of a larger disbelief of and deep distrust in the administration and its motives.

It could be about caste, like when the police apparently failed to protect Dalits who were lynched in a police station near the country's capital around the same time by another specimen of that WMD, again a mob. Or it could be about women, like when the country's Defence Minister stood up in Parliament defending the atrocities on women during the sectarian violence in Gujarat. Was this the first time that women were being raped, slashed, slaughtered, that unborn children were being ripped from their bellies? Haven't we seen it all before? His indignant rhetoric was of course immediately attacked by women's groups and sections of the media. This was too graphic, too immediate, too televised to be ignored.

But not all justifications are this tangible. Especially when they work within the justice system. According to a 1997 study by an NGO reported by the Media Advocacy Group, 68 per cent of judges interviewed felt 'provocative' clothes were an invitation to sexual assault, 55 per cent believed the 'moral character' of a woman was relevant in sexual abuse cases, 49 per cent felt slapping your wife once or twice was not cruelty and 48 per cent felt that there were occasions where beating your wife was justified. Finally, 90 per cent of the judges said they would not opt for legal redress in a domestic violence case and 74 per cent believed that preserving family harmony should be the primary concern for women. Even when reported in the media, these prejudices are hardly ever addressed and therefore remain valid justifications.

In this context, the importance of images cannot be ignored. The meaning of an image, as the world after Roland Barthes is particularly aware, is constructed through relating the visual signs to a wider set of understandings, depending also on extra-textual cultural knowledge. This includes prejudices. Take for example film star Salman Khan's arrest last October, after his car ran over five people, killing one. In a swift makeover that would challenge any Bollywood choreographer, the media changed its image of Khan from the suave, muscle-flexing, idolised star brat to a hunted, caged Muslim. We saw a close-up of the detained actor's face, the emphasis on his prayer-cap. This was telling and particularly offensive in an atmosphere of confused, imagined fears of Muslims—a community being projected as terrorists, killers and worthy of being murdered. The media, which bays for Salman's blood given half a chance (apparently because he has little regard for the media), was till then busy giving us details of Salman's womanising, girlfriend-battering, blackbuck-killing evil ways. That helped, because you could toss in glam shots of the exquisite Aishwarya Rai, ex-girlfriend. Now, with the close up of the caged man in prayer cap, it moved the focus away from the alleged wrongs of the privileged class, to the assumed wrongs of a minority stereotype.

But stereotypes work because of the oldest trick in the media business: brand recognition. The reasons don't matter, brand recognition is an end in itself. As the Congress and other political parties practically vanish from the front pages of our newspapers and dwindle in visibility on other pages, the Sangh Parivar dominates the news with jargon, propaganda, assaults and stomach-churning accusations. This is over and above the regular space that the BJP gets while running the government of the day. So Narendra Modi, widely believed to be the architect of the Gujarat genocide, was made a superstar by the media. When he "decided to pardon" a young engineer who had apparently sent him hate-email, we frontpaged it with large photographs and worshipping headlines like "Look, he sent threat to kill, I have pardoned him" (Indian Express, page 1, 30 December 2002). The photograph showed a smug and seated benevolent Modi, patting a meek, submissive, grateful Razaq Kasim standing awkwardly beside him. Of course there are other young Muslims who threatened Modi, but we only get to see occasional one-liners about them in the inside pages declaring that they had been killed in 'an encounter'. Since the Gaurav Yatra, everything Modi did and said and breathed was reported, verbatim, with little or no perspective or comment. That would be 'editorialising'. News has to be objective and fair. We need to be even-handed about both the murderer and the murdered.

Thankfully, during the Gujarat carnage the English language media had largely cast aside such misconceptions about fair play and displayed exemplary courage and good sense. If it wasn't for the responsible and ethical coverage by these opinion makers, the 'riots' could have well spread to other parts of India. Unfortunately, that wasn't true of the Gujarati press. As is clear from the Editors Guild Fact Finding Mission's report, sections of the Gujarati press had helped inflame passions in the state. The difference between regional and national 'cultures' was never so stark.

But then, there is no such thing as bad publicity. The newsweekly *India Today* was dominated firmly by Modi, who had four cover stories lovingly dedicated to him over ten months, a rare achievement for any personality. The magazine also carried propaganda material for him marked out as an advertisement feature, along with a multimedia CD that stirred passions against Muslims. Modi, the new mascot of Hindutva, is a star today as much for political support as the media limelight, with or without intent. One cannot deny, of course, that *India Today* is a respectable magazine, especially now that its editor has been awarded the Padma Bhushan, the prestigious State award.

Fearless Nadir

T he one significant cultural trait that emerges from the
newsmedia is our lack of shame and accountability. We have
no fear, since we have nothing to lose but the depths of our
depravity. Drunk with success after the state polls, BJP chief Venkaiah
Naidu declared, "We shall replicate the Gujarat experience
everywhere... It was a mandate for the Hindutva ideology" (December
24, 2002). The same day there were two more significant news items,
both frontpaged. One was about Iftikar Geelani, the *Kashmir Times*
journalist, who had been detained for nearly seven months apparently
because he possessed "secret documents" that were a "threat to
national security." The Director General of Military Intelligence had
finally declared in court that the documents possessed by Geelani were
neither secret nor threatening. An opinion apparently given earlier,
but not presented in court. Maybe, the press justifiably implied,
because Geelani—son-in-law of Hurriyat leader Syed Ali Shah
Geelani—was being punished for the sins of his father-in-law.

The other story of importance was the acquittal of Congress leader
Sajjan Kumar in the 1984 Delhi riots that followed Indira Gandhi's
assassination. Most papers merely stated part of the verdict: "The total
evidence fails miserably to prove whether Sajjan Kumar (or the 12
other accused) were a part of unlawful assembly. The three witnesses
produced by the investigating agency had flaws in their testimony."
Nothing more, just the 'objective' report. *Hindustan Times* skirted the
issue of justice, and concentrated skilfully on the possibility of an
improvement in the Congress's electoral chances, now that their name
had been cleared in this mass murder. Interestingly, though, *Indian
Express* had an accompanying story on the front page headlined
"Bhagat free, now Sajjan: how politics bailed politicians out." It gave
the background of Congress leaders H.K.L. Bhagat and Jagdish Tytler
being earlier acquitted of similar charges. And the *Times of India* talked
of the enormous disappointment of the widows of the 1984 riots, who
had been waiting for justice for 18 years.

And there's more from where those came. Here's a low-profile
one. On January 13, 2003 suspected activists of the Rashtriya
Swayamsevak Sangh (RSS) in Kerala attacked American missionary
Joseph W. Cooper and his associates, including two children, on their
way back from a Bible convention. The missionary narrowly escaped
being killed. The Sangh Parivar promptly denied any RSS hand in the

incident. But significantly, three days after this, as Cooper lay fighting for life in hospital, the Vishwa Hindu Parishad demanded his arrest on grounds of proselytising. Chief Minister A.K. Antony—a Congressman and a Christian— meekly asked the evangelist to leave India, since preaching violated Indian visa rules. There weren't any noticeable protests from the Congress at the Centre either. Maybe because the leader of the Opposition, too, is a Christian? Maybe because the Congress too is hesitantly following the Hindu agenda? Maybe the same reason that Digvijay Singh, Congress chief minister of Madhya Pradesh, has lost interest in development indices and developed a passion for protecting cows and Hindu holy grounds? If we are so insecure about our own identities, and do not have the courage to protest gross violations of human rights, do we really have the right to aspire to rule this multi-ethnic, multi-religious, multicultural country?

Significantly, the attack against Cooper happened the same day that RSS leader K.S. Sudarshan gave an anti-conversion call in Kerala. It suddenly seems necessary to clamp anti-conversion bills on a people promised freedom of religion by the Constitution. Such a bill was passed in Tamil Nadu in October. Following the victory of Hindutva, the Gujarat government is preparing its own version. And the Sangh Parivar has asked for it in Kerala as well. The trend that started decades ago, with Congress governments passing the bill in states like Madhya Pradesh and Orissa, is back in fashion.

Then on January 28, there was this tiny news item: "The CBI on Monday told a court hearing the murder case of missionary Graham Staines that none of the arrested persons had any links with Bajrang Dal" (*Hindustan Times*, page 9) Single sentence, single column, single inch, singularly inadequate report tucked away deep inside the paper. Of course, we have difficulty believing this as the same newspapers, displaying similar disinterest and/or fatigue, had reported earlier how the mother of Dara Singh, the prime suspect in the murder of Staines and his two minor children, had been felicitated by the Sangh Parivar for unspecified reasons at a public function and rewarded Rs. 1 lakh. The verdict we are being readied for is that Staines was killed by a 'mob' in response to his 'conversions'.

Other acts of the 'mob' getting away with murder include the December 1992 Babri Masjid demolition and the Mumbai riots that followed. There has been no legal action after ten years, still no justice for the nearly 1,800 people killed in sectarian violence, more than four years after the Srikrishna Commissions's report on it. The leaders who were frontpaged looking happy as the Babri Masjid came down—L.K. Advani, Murli Manohar Joshi and Uma Bharati—are all respected Union ministers leading our country into a spotless twenty-first century.

Clearly, we don't need other weapons of mass destruction—we have the *Brahmastra*, the greatest WMD of all, The Mob. It comes with no strings attached, doesn't invoke the wrath of the superpowers, and can be, with some tailoring, fitted into our Hindutva ideology of protecting one's own.

So there is no reason to believe that the 'mob' that recently left almost 2,000 dead in Gujarat shall be brought to justice. Or that the media can help substantially in the process. It is a culture of irresponsibility. With no accountability at any level, might is indeed right. It makes the prime minister of the country justify the saffronisation of education with the argument: "Saffron is our colour. Do you expect (Minister Murli Manohar) Joshi to paint education green instead?" (January, 2003) The clash of colours—saffron for Hindutva and green for Islam/Pakistan— has never been so lurid. It makes one forget that green and saffron occupy the same dignity of space on the Indian national flag.

National Culture vs. Cultural Nationalism

Painting education saffron has its clear and vivid dangers. For a multicultural society to work, as the philosopher Charles Taylor had pointed out, various groups (racial, ethnic, religious or gender-determined) need to see themselves in what passes as the national culture, often reflected in the educational curriculum. Cultural pluralism is necessary in a heterogeneous culture, as much for political reasons as philosophical. It is necessary to understand the various value systems that weave different colours into our social fabric. Destroying pluralism by a political determination leads to a deep cultural loss that can only be fathomed decades later.

Through all this, the logic for cultural nationalism is unwittingly becoming more acceptable. Yet cultural nationalism is like reinventing the wheel that failed—when the whole world has discovered the advantages of the 'salad bowl' of distinct identities and cultures contained in one national space, we now want a 'melting pot' of a pre-determined, static, national culture and an even more scary cultural nationalism. The melting pot concept, which the US laboured under for years, has not worked in any society deeply divided by ethnicity or religion. Cultural diversities refuse to melt in the pot of nationalism. Besides, equating diversity with divisiveness goes against the grain of the Indian spirit and the Constitution. So do the implications of cultural nationalism.

Almost a hundred years ago, in the context of ethnic discrimination in the US, John Dewey had said, "The fact is, the genuine American, the typical American... is international and interracial in his make up." The typical Indian too is a mix of several races and religions through several centuries. However important the present religious identity of an individual may be, it cannot wipe out what Dewey termed "the past contributions of every strain in our composite make up." This is the pluralistic tradition that we carry in our genes and in our cultures, in our rituals, our lifestyles, our thoughts and languages.

And this is what we are busy destroying at the moment as we grope for a dead national culture to impose on a living society. Along with the killing of Muslims by that convenient mob in Gujarat in 2002, there was also desecration of the dead, like that of the tomb of the poet Wali Gujarati. The past, the present, the future all need to be attacked at once if one is to destroy the rich cultural synthesis that we have been privileged with for centuries.

If we do find a national culture reflected in the newsmedia, we have no reason to be proud. What emerged from the Gujarat experience, for example, was a culture of shameless violence, of lying, cheating, murdering and appropriating 'nationalism' in ways that would ordinarily have made us cringe. Our culture was Hindutva, we insisted, anything else was alien and suspect and a threat to our lives and society. Anyone who supported values that differed from this 'cultural nationalism' was a danger to Hindustan. They may be agents, in fact, of Pakistan, and of 'Mian Musharraf' ! Modi's entire poll campaign was based on this. He talked of the alien people who believed in *Hum paanch hamare pachees*, a clear reference to the baseless stereotype of the Indian Muslim: a man with four wives, innumerable children. Any available statistical data would prove this to be untrue, but who cares about facts when you can have rhetoric instead? Through the daily newsmedia, that was what we learnt of our culture: that it was intolerant, vicious, lying and suffocating. Mystifyingly, we also learnt through reported speeches of the same leaders that our cultural nationalism would be based on what Hindutva offered: a broad and tolerant culture, non-violent, tender, wise and loving.

And in keeping with standards of 'objective journalism'—which I have argued above is often based on laziness and ignorance—we perpetuate these myths, with or without intent. Take this example from *Indian Express* (29 January 2003, page 3). Headlined "RSS now takes on CPM over Vivekananda," it describes how in West Bengal, "RSS chief Sudarshan took potshots at Chief Minister Buddhadev Bhattacharya for saying the Sangh had no right to quote from the works of Swami Vivekananda. "The Marxists are out to destroy schools of Ramakrishna Mission. While they have all the right to take the name of Vivekanandji, we who have been following his path have no such right? Isn't it double standards?" Sudarshan said. It ended there. There was of course no need to go into the larger picture. Why let facts get in the way of a good quickie? It may embarrass some, for example, to be reminded that Vivekananda believed in the equality of religions and the brotherhood of man, that he had even gone to the extent of saying publicly while on his visit to the US in 1894, "We want missionaries of Christ. Let such come to India by the hundreds and thousands and bring Christ's life to us, and let it permeate the very core of society. Let him be preached in every village and corner of India."[3] No, such reminders wouldn't be polite.

And by sheer force of repetition and power of print, such sweeping statements become the truth. We believe. Tired by our daily tribulations, fatigued by the volume of attacks on our basic rights and fundamental faiths, rendered powerless by a system that is bogged down by poverty and corruption, we who make up the fabric of the nation, choose to accept what is easiest. That is our present culture. The culture of defeat. The culture that makes atrocities acceptable and converts lies to truth.

So if there is a national culture that dominates media reports and images, it would be a synthesis of aspirational Eurocentric dreams of stylish living on the one hand and the lack of accountability that leads to an irresponsible culture of contempt on the other. And both are about personality cults, lack of accountability and escapism.

But then, culture is not a static entity. It changes, it evolves—if ever so slightly—with every experience, every thought, every emotion of the individuals living in that system of values and symbols. Sooner or later, it will swing again and we shall pick up our wits, stand up for our rights as citizens, as individuals, as human beings, and rediscover our pluralistic, multicultural identity as Indians. Which is, finally, the permanent petri dish for our once and future national culture.

References and Notes

1. In a 1998 study, with a limited sample of four national newspapers in English (*TOI, HT, The Hindu* and *The Telegraph*), I had found that between December 1988 and December 1998 the space given in column centimetres to entertainment and lifestyle stories had gone up four times. Social awareness/development stories had gone down sharply in that decade, while the space taken up by general news remained the same.
2. Some of these arguments had been presented in my paper 'The Invisible Woman: How the Indian media spurn the problem ridden Indian woman to pursue the woman of dreams', delivered at the Reuter Foundation seminar, February 1999, Oxford University.
3. *Swami Vivekananda in Contemporary Indian News (1893–1902)*, Volume I, Ramakrishna Mission Institute of Culture, Calcutta.

SINGANAPALLI BALARAM is an educator, writer and principal designer at the National Institute of Design. He is presently chairperson of the Knowledge Management Centre as well as the head of Interdisciplinary Design Studies. He holds four patents for his innovations. He was the only designer to have been conferred the prestigious Helen Keller award for his work for disabled people, and the honorary fellowship of the Society of Industrial Designers of India for outstanding contributions to improve the quality of life. He has published more than 50 short stories in Telugu and several essays in English. His publications include the *Thinking Design* book and major chapters in *Britannica Encyclopedia Asia, Universal Design Hand Book, The Idea of Design* and *Universal Design: 17 ways of Thinking and Teaching*. He serves on the advisory board of *Design Issues*, MIT Press, USA, the Board of Governors of National Institute of Fashion Technology and the Centre for Environmental Planning & Technology.

UMA DAS GUPTA is a graduate of Presidency College, University of Calcutta, in history. She has a doctorate from the University of Oxford in history. Her doctoral research was on 'Indian Opinion and British Policy in India, 1870–1880', with her continuing post-doctoral research on 'A History of Santiniketan and Sriniketan 1901–1941'. She has held teaching positions in Jadavpur University, Visva-Bharati University, and is currently professor in the Social Sciences Division, Indian Statistical Institute, Calcutta. She has held fellowships in Columbia University in the City of New York and the University of Oxford. She is the author of *Rise of an Indian Public: British Policy in India 1870–1880, Santiniketan and Sriniketan, A Difficult Friendship: Letters of Edward Thompson and Rabindranath Tagore 1913–1940, Prasanta Chandra Mahalanobis O Rabindranath Thakur* (in Bengali).

LEELA SAMSON is among India's most dynamic and technically brilliant dancers, an outstanding representative of Kalakshetra, the famed institute for the classical arts founded by the late Rukmini Devi Arundale on the Chennai ocean front. Leela joined Kalakshetra as a young child and her formative years were spent in imbibing the nuances of bharata natyam and related arts at the feet of celebrated gurus.

Leela has choreographed a number of group and solo compositions in bharata natyam. One of her major choreographic productions, *Spanda*, was performed to high critical and audience acclaim and hailed as a seminal work. She has authored several articles as well as the book, *Rhythm in Joy*. Among many honours conferred on her, Leela Samson was awarded the prestigious Padmashri in recognition of her outstanding contribution as well as the Sangeet Natak Akademi Award.

MUSHIRUL HASAN teaches History at the Jamia Millia Islamia, New Delhi, and is Director, Academy of Third World Studies. He is the author of *Legacy of a Divided Nation: India's Muslims Since Independence* (1997); *Islam in the Subcontinent: Muslims in a Plural Society* (2002); and *Making Sense of History: Society, Culture and Politics* (2003). He has introduced and edited Mohamed Ali, *My Life: A Fragment* (1998) Halide Edib, *Inside India* (2002) and C.F. Andrews, *Zakaullah of Delhi* (with Margaret Pernau Reifeld), 2003.

KRISHNA KUMAR is Professor of Education at Delhi University where he has also served as Dean of Faculty. He is well known as a writer in Hindi and for his writing for children. Krishna Kumar was awarded the Jawaharlal Nehru Fellowship to make a comparative study of the representation of the freedom struggle in Indian and Pakistani school textbooks, to be published by Penguin. His books include *What is Worth Teaching, Learning from Conflict, Political Agenda of Education, Social Character of Learning, Raj, Samaj aur Shiksha,* and *Vichaar ka dar.*

NEERA CHANDHOKE is Professor of Political Science in Delhi University, and a recipient of the Jawaharlal Nehru Fellowship in 1997–98. She was a fellow of the Centre of Contemporary Studies, Nehru Memorial Museum and Library, Teen Murti 1989–92. She is the author of *State and Civil Society. Explorations in Political Theory* (Sage 1995) *Beyond Secularism. The Rights of Religious Minorities* (OUP 1999), and *The Conceits of Civil Society* (OUP 2003). She has edited numerous volumes.

ALOK RAI teaches English at the University of Delhi. He holds advanced degrees from Oxford and London. In addition to academic publications—the latest being *Hindi Nationalism* (Orient Longman)—he writes frequently on matters of wider social and cultural interest in the hope of promoting public reflection on our common, shared lives. In these dark times, he writes, the belief that such reflection is part of the essence of being human beings at all seems, variously, naïve, desperate, and ineluctable.

KAPILA VATSYAYAN, former President of IIC and former Academic Director of the Indira Gandhi Centre for the Arts, is internationally acknowledged for her inter-disciplinary work.. She was Secretary, Department of Arts in the Ministry of Education, Government of India. Her work moves from the deep understanding of primary textual sources of the east and west, and a direct experience of the arts as performer, and art historian. They focus attention on the inter-relationship of the concept, word and creative interpretation in architecture, sculpture, painting, music and dance. Through her writings, editing, multi-media exhibitions, seminars, documentary films and projects conceived, she has evolved new conceptual models for the study of cultures and artistic genres, particularly Asian and Indian. She has given a new orientation to the field of Indian studies by establishing many institutions of Sanskrit, Buddhist and Islamic Studies.

Dr. Vatsyayan is the author of fifteen volumes such as *The Square and the Circle of the Indian Arts and the Bundi Gita Govinda* and the *Jaur Gita—Govinda: a dated sixteenth century Gita-Govinda from Mewar*; and editor of as many books and more such as *Concepts of Space: Ancient and Modern*. She has lectured in universities in the USA, Europe and Australia, and is a fellow of the Russian Academy of Sciences, the French Academy of the Study of Asian Civilisation, the Sangeet Natak Akademi and Lalit Kala Akademi. She is the recipient of awards from the Asiatic Society, Bombay and Calcutta; the Sankaradeva Award for national integration, Women of the Year Award (1998), the Rajiv Gandhi Sadbhavana Award 2000, and the G. Shankar Pillai Award for theatre and the Arts (2003).

MAKARAND PARANJAPE is Professor of English at Jawaharlal Nehru University. A poet, novelist, critic, and columnist, he is the author of *The Serene Flame, Playing the Dark God,* and *Used Book* (poetry); *This Time I Promise It'll Be Different* and *The Narrator* (fiction); and *Mysticism in Indian English Poetry, Decolonization and Development,* and *Towards a Poetics of the Indian English Novel* (criticism). The books edited include *Indian Poetry in English, Sarojini Naidu: Selected Poetry and Prose, Nativism: Essays in Literary Criticism, The Best of Raja Rao, The Penguin Sri Aurobindo Reader,* and *In Diaspora: Theories, Histories, Texts.* He is also the founding editor of *Evam: Forum on Indian Representations.*

RUKMINI BHAYA NAIR is Professor of Linguistics and English at the Indian Institute of Technology, Delhi. She did her Ph.D. at the University of Cambridge, and her research interests are in the areas of cognitive linguistics, the philosophy of language and literary theory. Her books include *Technobrat: Culture in a Cybernetic Classroom* (Harper Collins, 1997); *Narrative Gravity: Conversation, Cognition, Culture* (Oxford University Press, 2002 and Routledge, 2003); *Lying on the Postcolonial Couch: the Idea of Indifference* (Minnesota University Press and Oxford University Press, 2002); as well as an edited volume, *Translation, Text and Theory: the Paradigm of India* (Sage, 2002). She is on the editorial boards of the *International Journal of Literary Semantics* (De

Gruyter: Berlin and New York) and *Biblio*. Also an award-winning poet, she has published two volumes of poetry: *The Hyoid Bone* and *The Ayodhya Cantos* (Viking Penguin, 1992 and 1999).

RAM RAHMAN is a photographer and designer. He studied at MIT and Yale Universities in the US, in an eclectic programme which included physics, astronomy, art and architecture history, cinema and photography. His graduation thesis at Yale was on the graphic design of the Russian Constructivist's of the 20's. Ram has been an active founding member of the Safdar Hashmi Memorial Trust, SAHMAT. He has exhibited his photographs around the world, with a recent one-man show at the Cleveland Museum of Art. *Dome Over India—The Rastrapati Bhavan*, published last year, is his most recent architectural photography publication. Known professionally for his architectural photographs, he has been associated with the Aga Khan Award for Architecture for many years. Ram has written on photography in India and curated a major exhibition of the work of Sunil Janah in New York in 1998.

GEETI SEN is a cultural historian, writer, and visiting lecturer at several institutes in India and abroad. She took her master's and doctoral degrees at the universities of Chicago and Calcutta, began her career in India as the assistant editor of MARG Mumbai, and was appointed art critic for the *Times of India*, Mumbai and *India Today*, Delhi. In 1982 she joined the India International Centre as the Editor, resuming this appointment in 1990.

Sen's books include *Paintings from the Akbar Nama* (1984) *Image and Imagination, Five Contemporary Artists in India* (1996), *Bindu: Space and Time in Raza's Vision* (1997), *Ganesh Pyne: Revelations* (2000) and *Feminine Fables: Imaging the Indian Woman in Painting, Photography and Cinema* (2002). Honours and awards include among them the Homi Bhabha Fellowship (1978–80) and the Jawaharlal Nehru Fellowship (1998–2000).

KAVITA SINGH is an art historian who is currently associate professor at the School of Arts and Aesthetics of Jawaharlal Nehru University. She is interested in the history of museums and their role in shaping our understanding of art. She is completing a book on the politics of display of Indian art in London from 1900–1950. Indian painting is another area of interest, and she has been guest curator with the San Diego Museum of Art's Edwin Binney III collection of Indian painting.

PATRICIA UBEROI has taught Sociology at the Delhi School of Economics and the Jawaharlal Nehru University, and is presently with the Institute of Economic Growth, Delhi. Co-editor of *Contributions to Indian*

Sociology, she has written widely on themes of gender, family and popular culture in both India and China.

RASHMI DORAISWAMY is Reader (Central Asia) at the Academy of Third World Studies, Jamia Millia Islamia, New Delhi. Her doctoral thesis was on Mikhail Bakhtin, the Russian philosopher. She was formerly Executive Editor, *Cinemaya*. She writes on films in prestigious Indian and foreign publications and was the recipient of the National Award for the Best Film Critic in 1995. She was awarded the MAJLIS research fellowship in 1999 for a project on Hindi commercial cinema. She has participated in national and international seminars on cultural issues and has served on several film festival juries in India and abroad. She has lectured extensively on cinema at film appreciation courses.

SHEBA CHHACHHI is an installation artist and photographer based in New Delhi. Her photographic work has been primarily focused on women. Since 1993 she has created a number of multimedia installations using photographs, text, sculpture and found objects. More recently her work also uses video, sound and light. She has exhibited widely in India and abroad and participated in several international art and photography shows in Europe, Japan, and the U.S.

ASHIS NANDY is a political psychologist, cultural critic and futurist. He has been Director, Center for the Study of Developing Societies, Delhi. He is the author of a number of pathbreaking and influential books, including *The Savage Freud* and *The Intimate Enemy*. Other notable books are *The Legitimacy of Nationalism, An Ambiguous Journey to the City*, and *Time Warps*.

SUDHANVA DESHPANDE is an actor, director and playwright, and has been a member of Jana Natya Manch, best known for its radical street theatre. He works as Editor in Left Word Books, New Delhi. He also teaches part time at the Mass Communication Research Centre, Jamia Millia Islamia.

BHASKAR ROY, a Special Correspondent of *The Times of India*, has written extensively on issues like the Dalit quest for a political identity and concerns of the minorities. He has sought to explore the interrelationship between social prejudices and the Dalit aspiration for space in post-Mandal politics. The causes of the Muslims' economic backwardness and its bearing on their political preferences have engaged him considerably. Alongside his journalistic writings Roy has produced two novels. *An Escape into Silence*, the latest one, is set in the backdrop of the Naxalite movement in 1970–71 and has addressed the problem of political violence and its impact on society. In 1989 he wrote about the increasing appeal of a group of leaders who, active only on the periphery of the political canvas, posed a serious threat to many mainstream politicians. The term 'fringe leaders' has been in vogue in political writing since then.

T.K. OOMMEN is an eminent social scientist and so far the only scholar from Asia and Africa to have been elected to the position of President (1990–94), International Sociological Association (ISA). He was also the secretary–general of the XI World Congress of Sociology, the quadrennial Congress of the ISA held in New Delhi in 1986 and President of the Indian Sociological Society (1998–99).

Author of ten books and over 80 research papers, Prof. Oommen has co-authored, edited or co-edited seven books. He has been given three prestigious awards: the V.K.R.V. Rao Prize in Sociology (1981); the G.S. Ghurye award in Sociology and Social Anthropology (1985) and the Swami Pranavananda Award for Sociology (1997) in recognition of his professional contributions. He has been a visiting professor/fellow at Berkeley, Paris, Berlin, Canberra, Sweden and Budapest. He retired from the Jawaharlal Nehru University in October 2002.

ANTARA DEV SEN is founding Editor of *The Little Magazine*, an independent journal of ideas and letters. A literary publication with an emphasis on social concerns and art, *TLM* is an attempt to bring into focus issues that do not get space in mainstream publications. Sen is also editor of TLM Books, the new line of titles from the *TLM* stable. She has been senior editor, *Hindustan Times*, and senior assistant editor, *Indian Express*, in Delhi. A media columnist for *Indian Express* and later *Hindustan Times*, she has researched trends in mainstream media as a Reuter Fellow at Oxford University (1998–99).